CATHOLIC THEOLOGICAL FORMATION SERIES

General Editor: Kevin Zilverberg

The Catholic Theological Formation Series is sponsored by The Saint Paul Seminary School of Divinity, the graduate school of theological formation for Roman Catholic seminarians and laity enrolled at the University of Saint Thomas in Saint Paul, Minnesota. As a premier institution of theological formation for the region and beyond, The Saint Paul Seminary School of Divinity seeks to form men and women for the task of fulfilling the specific call God has for them, a call grounded in their common baptismal vocation to serve one another in Christ.

The school is intentional in its commitment to priestly and diaconal formation; as an institution of graduate theological education, it also prepares the laity to make Christ known and loved in the world. Although the students prepare for diverse ministries, all enroll in a curriculum of theological formation within the context of holistic and integrated Catholic formation.

It is this challenge of theological formation—the challenge to faithfully inform one's understanding—that serves as the focus of this series, with special attention given to the task of preparing priests, deacons, teachers, and leaders within the Roman Catholic tradition. Although the series is academic in tenor, it aims beyond mere academics in its integrative intellectual approach. We seek to promote a form of discourse that is professional in its conduct and spiritual in its outcomes, for theological formation is more than an exercise in academic technique. It is rather about the perfecting of a spiritual capacity: the capacity on the part of the human person to discern what is true and good.

This series, then, aims to develop the habits of mind required of a sound intellect—a spiritual aptitude for the truth of God's living Word and his Church. Most often, it will draw from the more traditional specializations of historical, systematic, moral, and biblical scholarship. Homiletics and pastoral ministry are anticipated venues as well. There will be occasions, however, when a theme is examined across disciplines and periods, for the purposes of bringing to our common consideration a thesis yet undeveloped.

Despite the variety of methodologies and topics explored, the series' aim remains constant: to provide a sustained reflection upon the mission and ministry of Catholic theological formation of both clergy and laity alike.

The general editor of the Catholic Theological Formation Series, Fr. Kevin Zilverberg, serves as associate professor of Sacred Scripture and the founding director of Saint Paul Seminary Press at The Saint Paul Seminary School of Divinity.

CATHOLIC THEOLOGICAL FORMATION SERIES

Editor
Kevin Zilverberg

Editorial Board
Kelly Anderson
Matthew C. Briel
Paige Hochschild
Andrew Hofer, OP
Matthew Levering
Michael Monshau, OP
Christopher J. Thompson
Kevin Zilverberg

The Transcendent Mystery of God's Word

A Critical Synthesis of Antioch and Alexandria

Edited by
John W. Martens and Paul V. Niskanen

SAINT PAUL, MINNESOTA • 2024

Cover image: St. Jerome in His Study by Domenico Ghirlandaio, from Wikimedia Commons; license at https://creativecommons.org/licenses/by/3.0/
Cover design by Willem Mineur

© 2024 John W. Martens and Paul V. Niskanen
Saint Paul Seminary Press is a registered trademark of The Saint Paul Seminary.
All rights reserved

Published 2024 by
Saint Paul Seminary Press
2260 Summit Ave., Saint Paul, Minnesota 55105

Library of Congress Control Number: 2024936585
LC record available at https://lccn.loc.gov/2024936585

ISSN 2765-9283
ISBN 978-1-953936-10-3 (paperback)
ISBN 978-1-953936-60-8 (ebook)

spspress.com

To Ben F. Meyer (1926–1995)

*A biblical scholar who strived in all of his work
to bring together Antioch and Alexandria for the sake
of the proclamation of the Gospel*

Contents

Acknowledgments   ix
Abbreviations   xi

Introduction: The Transcendent Mystery of God's Word
John W. Martens and Paul V. Niskanen   1

1. Letter or Spirit? Toward a Testimonial Exegesis
   Luis Sánchez-Navarro, DCJM   13

2. Beyond Alexandria and Antioch: The Polyvalence of the Literal Sense in the Old Testament
   Paul V. Niskanen   24

3. Theological Riches from Sound Exegesis—Hearing the Full Range of Notes: Typology Valued
   Joseph Briody   38

4. Moses's Flight to Midian: Exodus 2:11–22 as a Case Study in Patristic Exegesis
   Hryhoriy Lozinskyy   54

5. The Book of Psalms: Challenges from the Past for Future Biblical Exegesis
   Maurizio Girolami   71

6. The Alexandrian and Antiochian Method of Exegesis of Psalm 75[74]: Toward a Rebalancing of Both Methods of Exegesis
   Juana L. Manzo   100

7. At the Jordan Christ Deposited for Us the Robe of Glory:
   Unjustified Hiatus between the Historical Event and the
   Theological Interpretation of the Baptism of Jesus
   Marcin Kowalski   114

8. Ancient and New: A Dialogue between Contemporary and Patristic
   Exegesis on the Scriptural Fulfillment Statements in the Johannine
   Farewell Discourse
   Isacco Pagani   144

Bibliography   167
Contributors   193
Index of Names and Subjects   197
Index of Scripture References   205

Acknowledgments

This volume would not be here today without the support, financial and academic, of the Institute for Catholic Theological Formation and the institute's Quinn Endowment for Biblical Studies, and Fr. Kevin Zilverberg, the institute's director at The Saint Paul Seminary School of Divinity. Kevin has been a patient guide, academic support, and wealth of knowledge, both practical and personal, as he helped us along the way with editing expertise and putting us in touch with all of the people who make such an enterprise possible. We also want to thank the Board of Directors for Saint Paul Seminary Press who supported the vision for the conference that allowed this group of scholars to meet together in Minnesota in June 2022 and then gave the go ahead for this volume to be published.

To the academic institutions which support our research and encourage us to engage in scholarship, we the editors thank the University of St. Thomas (Minnesota), and St. Mark's College, the affiliated Catholic college at the University of British Columbia.

I, Paul, am deeply grateful for the love and support of my wife Erin, and our children Adam, Noah, and Bianca. I wish to thank them as well as extended family and friends for all their help and support.

I, John, want to thank my family, especially the love of my life Tabitha, my children Jacob and Samuel, and all of my extended family who have supported me over the years.

Abbreviations

AASF	Annales Academiae Scientiarum Fennicae
ACCS	Ancient Christian Commentary on Scripture
ACCSOT	Ancient Christian Commentary on Scripture, Old Testament
ACNT	Augsburg Commentary on the New Testament
AGJU	Arbeiten zur Geschichte des antiken Judentums und des Urchristentums
AnBib	Analecta Biblica
AncB	Anchor Bible
ANRW	Aufstieg und Niedergang der römischen Welt
ATANT	*Abhandlungen zur Theologie des Alten und Neuen Testaments*
BECNT	Baker Exegetical Commentary on the New Testament
BAC	The Bible in Ancient Christianity
BDAG	Walter Bauer, Frederick W. Danker, William F. Arndt, and F. Wilbur Gingrich, *A Greek-English Lexicon of the New Testament and Other Early Christian Literature*, 3rd ed. (Chicago: University of Chicago Press, 2000)
BTCB	Brazos Theological Commentary on the Bible
BZNW	Beihefte zur Zeitschrift für die neutestametliche Wissenschaft
CBET	Contributions to Biblical Exegesis and Theology
CThFS	Catholic Theological Formation Series
CCC	*Catechism of the Catholic Church*, 2nd ed. (Washington, DC: United States Conference of Catholic Bishops, 2019)
CCSL	Corpus Christianorum, Series Latina
CM	Christianity in the Making
ConBOT	*Coniectanea biblica: Old Testament Series*
CSCO	Corpus Scriptorum Christianorum Orientalium
CSHB	Critical Studies in the Hebrew Bible
Dial.	Justin Martyr, *Dialogue with Trypho*
DtrN	"nomistic" Deuteronomist
ECCo	Eerdmans Critical Commentary

ABBREVIATIONS

EJL	Early Judaism and Its Literature
EKV	Essener Kulturwissenschaftliche Vorträge
FaCh	Fathers of the Church
FoFaNT	Foundation and Facets, New Testament
FOTL	Forms of the Old Testament Literature
FRLANT	Forschungen zur Religion und Literatur des Alten und Neuen Testaments
GCS	Griechischen christlichen Schriftsteller der ersten drei Jahrhunderte
HTKNT	*Herders theologischer Kommentar zum Neuen Testament*
ICC	International Critical Commentary on the Holy Scriptures
Int.	Interpretation: A Bible Commentary for Teaching and Preaching
JSNTSup	Journal for the Study of the New Testament Supplement Series
JSOTSup	Journal for the Study of the Old Testament Supplement Series
LBPT	I libri biblici, Primo Testamento
LCL	Loeb Classical Library
LEC	Library of Early Christianity
LiRo	Le livre et le rouleau
LSJ	*A Greek-English Lexicon*, ed. Henry G. Liddell and Robert Scott, 9th ed. (Oxford: Clarendon, 1940)
LXX	Septuagint
MBS	Message of Biblical Spirituality
MFC	Message of the Fathers of the Church
MoBi	Monde de la Bible (Paris)
MT	Masoretic Text
ML.B	Museum Lessianum, Section Biblique
MLT	Mowbrays Library of Theology
NICNT	New International Commentary on the New Testament
NIGTC	New International Greek Testament Commentary
NPNF 1	*A Select Library of the Nicene and Post-Nicene Fathers of the Christian Church,* First Series, ed. Philip Schaff (Buffalo, NY: Christian Literature, 1887–1894)
NSBT	New Studies in Biblical Theology
NTLi	New Testament Library
NTOA	Novum Testamentum et Orbis Antiquus
NTS	New Testament Studies
NTSI	New Testament and the Scriptures of Israel
OTL	Old Testament Library
OBT	Overtures to Biblical Theology
PaThSt	Paderborner Theologische Studien

PG	Patrologia Graeca, ed. Jacques-Paul Migne (Paris: J.-P. Migne, 1857–1866)
PilNTC	Pillar New Testament Commentary
PL	Patrologia Latina, ed. Jacques-Paul Migne (Paris: J.-P. Migne, 1841–1855)
Plant.	Philo of Alexandria, *De plantatione*
Praescr.	Tertullian, *De praescriptione haereticorum*
PTMS	Princeton Theological Monograph Series
QD	Quaestiones Disputatae
RSV	Revised Standard Version
SAE	Studien zur Adventistischen Ekklesiologie
SBAB	Stuttgarter Biblische Aufsatzbände
SBLDS	Society of Biblical Literature Dissertation Series
SBMat	Studia Bíblica Matritensia
SC	Sources Chrétiennes
SECT	Sources of Early Christian Thoughts
SHJ	Studying the Historical Jesus
SMWTUSK	Studia i Materiały Wydziału Teologicznego Uniwersytetu Śląskiego w Katowicach
SNTSMS	Society for New Testament Studies Monograph Series
SNTW	Studies of the New Testament and Its World
SP	Sacra Pagina
SPNT	Studies on Personalities of the New Testament
TB	Theologische Bücherei
TC	Traditio Christiana
TDNT	*Theological Dictionary of the New Testament*, ed. Gerhard Kittel and Gerhard Friedrich, trans. G. W. Bromiley (Grand Rapids: Eerdmans, 1964)
T.Jud.	*Testament of Judah*
TKNT	Theologischer Kommentar zum Neuen Testament
T.Levi	*Testament of Levi*
TU	Texte und Untersuchungen zur Geschichte der altchristlichen Literatur
VD	Verbum Domini (series)
WBC	Word Biblical Commentary
WGRWSup	Writings from the Greco-Roman World Supplement Series
WMANT	Wissenschaftliche Monographien zum Alten und Neuen Testament
WUNT	Wissenschaftliche Untersuchungen zum Neuen Testament

Introduction

The Transcendent Mystery of God's Word

John W. Martens and Paul V. Niskanen

Introduction

In June 2022, a small number of biblical scholars who teach in Roman and Byzantine Catholic seminaries and universities throughout North America, Africa, and Europe met at the Alverna Center in Winona, Minnesota, sponsored by the Monsignor Jerome D. Quinn Endowment for Biblical Studies at The Saint Paul Seminary School of Divinity and the University of St. Thomas (St. Paul, Minnesota), and its director Fr. Kevin Zilverberg. The Quinn Endowment allowed us to bring scholars to Minnesota to consider the question of how to express the transcendent mystery of God's Word in current seminary teaching of biblical studies. The late professor Ben F. Meyer believed that the "most pressing exigence in biblical hermeneutics today is for a critical synthesis of Antioch and Alexandria," which for him represented not precisely the schools of the ancient Church, but two stances toward the Bible.[1] Today's biblical studies is sensitive to historical consciousness, but so often closed to the presence of the divine that suffuses the Bible. This stance Meyer labeled "Antioch," without intending to dismiss the value of historical study of the Bible or the value of the ancient school. But Meyer knew that for biblical studies to do its proper work it needed to be theological and for it to be theological it needed to be attentive to "the transcendent mystery of salvation" that permeates God's Word, not

---

1. Ben F. Meyer, *Critical Realism and the New Testament*, PTMS 17 (San Jose, CA: Pickwick, 1989), 33.

just attentive to historical context or development.² Such openness to the mystery of the saving function of Scripture Meyer designated "Alexandria," which represents not precisely the allegorical methods of the ancient school but that school's openness to the mysterious depth of Scripture that transcends historical time and place.

The articles which appear in this book were prepared for and presented at the conference in June 2022. Each scholar who presented at the conference was asked to consider how biblical studies might in its current context attend to both Antioch and Alexandria, for the benefit of seminarians and other university students and for the benefit of the Church and the world, by examining a biblical passage or passages in light of these two orientations to Scripture. Before appearing in this book, each article went through a rigorous process of double-blind peer review in order to meet the highest academic standards, and not every paper presented at the conference appears in this volume. Prior to summarizing each of these papers, it is necessary to offer a bit more background on Ben F. Meyer's project and accomplishments and why he was chosen as a means by which we would consider ways to invigorate the biblical text for students, preachers, and other students of the Bible today.

A Sketch of Meyer's Project

In a series of books and articles, written from 1979 to his death in 1995, especially *The Aims of Jesus, Critical Realism and the New Testament, Reality and Illusion in New Testament Scholarship*, and his entry on "Jesus Christ" in the *Anchor Bible Dictionary*, Ben F. Meyer undertook a project through which he intended to make clear for biblical scholars the philosophical underpinnings of historical research on the Bible and biblical interpretation.³ Though a Roman Catholic biblical scholar, influenced deeply by the work of Bernard Lonergan, SJ, Meyer's work was ecumenical and intended for all scholars of goodwill. At the heart of his project was his understanding that history, valuable in itself as a tool for understanding the literal sense of the Bible and reconstructing the contexts in which the biblical texts emerged, was not up to the task of grappling with the depth of the mystery of God's Word and the questions of faith. For that

---

2. Meyer, *Critical Realism and the New Testament*, 33.
3. Ben F. Meyer, *The Aims of Jesus* (London: SCM Press, 1979), reprinted in 2002 with an Introduction by N. T. Wright, PTMS 48 (Eugene, OR: Pickwick, 2002); *Reality and Illusion in New Testament Scholarship* (Collegeville, MN: Michael Glazier, 1994), reprinted in 2016 (Eugene, OR: Pickwick, 2016); "Jesus Christ," 773–96 in *The Anchor Bible Dictionary*, vol. 3, ed. David Noel Freedman et al. (New York: Doubleday, 1992).

Antioch was not sufficient, and Alexandria would need to be brought into the equation. But how to balance Antioch and Alexandria?

The first step was understanding the process and nature of interpretation. As Meyer conceived it, interpretation has limits, for it "does not do everything. . . . It does not try to do all theology, but limits itself to the single question: what is the intended sense of the text?"[4] For Meyer, seeking the intended sense of the biblical text was an ongoing and complex process that took seriously advances in textual criticism, philology, historical criticism, and new methods of analysis. Meyer's interpretive program of interpretation rejected all forms of fideism, whether religious or secular, that attempt to reduce the Bible's meaning to one single thing or nothing at all. It takes seriously all the concerns of the text, which, with respect to the Bible, includes spiritual and religious meanings that are often difficult to determine.

Theology is always at the heart of the continuing exegetical task because this is what the biblical texts demand. The attempts of religious fideists to read the Bible "in the plain sense" (and by this Meyer did not mean the fuller sense of literal that Thomas Aquinas and other medieval scholars envisioned[5]), and postmodern attempts to jettison the theological realities of the Bible and its ultimate meaning, both fail in Meyer's eyes as either "a flight from interpretation" or "a flight from the intended sense of the text."[6] What Meyer sought was the transcendent mystery of God's Word, utilizing all the tools of the scholar's toolbox in order to open up Scripture for its divine purpose: to make the name of Jesus known and loved. This takes us, however, beyond technique and into the heart not of interpretation but of the interpreter.

Goodwill Comes First

How does one approach the Bible? With goodwill, said Meyer. With openness. With a willingness to hear. Yet, Meyer did not feel that approaching the text with goodwill was the end of the story, as he ended the phrase "goodwill comes first" with an interesting corollary, "but suspicion has its uses."[7] The text was not the end of the story, but a part of the story: the interpreter, whose questions are raised in conjunction with the text, is the necessary completion of the story. And this is where we begin, with the subject asking questions of the object.

The question of the relation of the subject to the object has been at the

---

4. Meyer, *Critical Realism and the New Testament*, 49.
5. On this comparison, consult Paul Niskanen's article in this volume.
6. Meyer, *Reality and Illusion in New Testament Scholarship*, 94–101; *Critical Realism and the New Testament*, 28–29.
7. Meyer, *Critical Realism and the New Testament*, 78–96.

heart of a shift in interpretation ascendant since the Enlightenment in biblical studies, and other areas of study dependent upon interpretation of texts. At the heart of the Enlightenment project was an attempt to free texts from their ecclesial, dogmatic, and doctrinal constraints, imposed on the New Testament—said these newly freed interpreters—by the Church and its interpreters. Thus liberated, the text would be available to a study unencumbered by the presuppositions of the Church. The New Testament would be available in its original, pristine form for the practitioners of *religionswissenschaft* or *religionsgeschichte*. These scientific experts would guide the interpretation of the New Testament, and would allow modern interpreters access, in an objective manner, to the meaning of the text.

Such a scientific method, with the objectivity construed as inherent in the interpreter, was bound to fail. The most searching critique is that such objective interpreters failed to see themselves as bringing their own presuppositions and biases to the Bible, that their scientific method was often dependent upon their subjective stance that rejected the truth of the Bible a priori. The next stage was a series of postmodern thinkers arguing that the issue was not one of objectively reading the Bible but of placing the biases, interests, and tendencies of the interpreting subject front and center. Now the newly freed subject could read the Bible with new questions and new methods, guided by the different presuppositions and biases inherent in every interpreter. The subjectivity of the interpreter became not something to avoid, but something to explore, embrace, and unleash. Objectivity was passé, subjectivity the new vanguard. In practice, then, the Bible means what any interpreter wants it to mean, which has led to questions currently about why should we even focus on the Church's canon as Scripture, that is, why should this collection of texts take precedence over other ancient Jewish and Christian texts? Lost in these developments was often the sense and meaning of the Bible as God's Word for humanity.

Meyer's Response

Meyer's response to the issue of objectivity and subjectivity in interpretation steered a middle course. He placed the subject, the interpreter, front and center but insisted that the subject was moored by the biblical text. The text was the necessary limit on the interpreter, for Meyer believed that the text demanded to be interpreted in light of its intended sense. Not every interpretation was valid, for the Bible offered the necessary checks and balances on flights of fancy, or, more significant for him, on flights from the intended sense of the text. Objectivity resided in the text, not the interpreter. But there was an additional condition for biblical interpretation that can extract the salvific mystery of the Bible, which is as important as establishing the objectivity of the text itself: the stance of the subject, the interpreter, toward the biblical texts.

Every act of interpretation is a meeting between object and subject, and subjectivity was all to the good, but subjectivity needs to meet the demands of the Bible. There are two ways to determine, in general, the interpreter's worthiness for the task: one, was the interpreter willing to manage *all* of the *data* found in the text, not just Antioch or not just Alexandria, or did the interpreter reject or ignore passages or meanings which were not amenable to their personal understanding or beliefs; and two, was the interpreter approaching the text from a stance of *goodwill*, that is, a willingness to hear and be formed by the religious and spiritual content of the Bible. Interpreters today often see *suspicion* as the controlling dynamic for reading biblical texts, not *goodwill*.

In Meyer's interpretive understanding, the role of every interpreter was balanced by the objective nature of the biblical texts, while still allowing free rein to subjectivity formed by the teaching of the Church and the Bible, which today must include careful use of modern methods of interpretation. Key to this balancing act for Meyer were cognitional processes, derived from Bernard Lonergan's study of human operations, which each person, so every interpreter, ought to bring to their tasks: attentiveness, reasonableness, intelligence, and responsibility.[8] Was the interpreter willing to use these cognitional operations to grasp the "thing" of the text, the referent, or *die Sache*? When the interpreter meets and knows *die Sache*, the intended meaning, the intended sense of a text heaves into view.[9]

In the case of the Bible, the "thing" of the text is God's saving acts in history culminating in Jesus Christ. What if the interpreter does not know *die Sache*? What if the interpreter is not aware of "the thing of the text," whether it represents Antioch or, more likely, Alexandria? This, Meyer argued, was at the heart of many problems in biblical studies. The result of this inability to meet with the thing of the Bible was the subsequent attempt to jettison the data which the interpreter did not find sympathetic. What this has meant in practice, Meyer claimed, was that many interpreters today, though in tune with themselves as subjects, share one thing in common with interpreters from

---

8. See, for examples, Bernard Lonergan, *Method in Theology* (New York: Herder and Herder, 1972) 3–25, 153–73; *Insight: A Study of Human Understanding* (New York: Philosophical Library, 1970), 173–44, 271–316, 319–47.

9. Meyer, *The Aims of Jesus*, 96–104; *Reality and Illusion in New Testament Scholarship*, 91–92, 178. This does not mean that someone with such a vital relationship to the "thing" understands all texts or that the process does not demand intensive work. It is not a magic trick to understanding but demands ongoing and sustained work.

INTRODUCTION

the Enlightenment, who saw themselves functioning with a transcendent sort of objectivity: both groups are unable or unwilling to deal with data dealing with, for instance, the miracles, exorcisms, healings, and the resurrection.[10] For scholars of the Enlightenment this all could be cast off as an ancient relic, unable to be synthesized with a new science, ancient primitivism that had crept into the heart of modernity; for postmodern thinkers, these data are generally ignored—probably laboring more than they think under these same Enlightenment presuppositions that reject the work of God in the world—and other questions are asked, which often have nothing to do with the religious questions and answers the text is asking and offering. Often, Meyer felt, analysis took the place of interpretation as a "flight" from interpretation.[11]

The reason for such flight was due to the interpreter's "alienation" from the Bible, and analysis could allow one to sidestep interpretive issues instead of handling them head-on.[12] Meyer's most controversial stance on interpretation is his position that what might be required for the interpreter is conversion. By conversion, Meyer argued for the need for an interpreter to be "in tune" with the world of the text.[13] As it does not help a musician to come to a piece of music without any sense of melody or rhythm, and as it does not help a painter to have no stance one way or another toward the use of color and shade, so it does not help an interpreter to come to a theological text without any sense of the theological concerns at stake in the Bible or without a sense of goodwill toward the "thing" of the text.[14] This stance marks, in our words, a "great divide" in biblical studies, and gets to the heart of interpretive fault lines and the inability to speak to one another in many cases: it is not precisely a matter of methods, but whether one accepts the Bible as the Word of God.

If conversion to *die Sache*, the "thing" of the Bible, is needed, then the great divide is a philosophical and theological issue, not one of historical methods and scholarly tools. What it does imply is that someone who is "in tune" with the Bible takes seriously the theology of the Bible, and takes seriously all of the biblical data and the historical doctrines of the Church that developed with and from the earliest Church's documents.[15] Theology must be in view at all times, because that is the concern of the Bible. What also guides the interpreter, then, is the tradition of the Church, doctrinally and more broadly in terms of the

10. Meyer, *The Aims of Jesus*, 95–110.
11. Meyer, *Critical Realism and the New Testament*, 28–29.
12. Meyer, *Reality and Illusion in New Testament Scholarship*, 177–78.
13. Meyer, *Critical Realism and the New Testament*, 57–75.
14. Meyer, *Critical Realism and the New Testament*, 77–96.
15. Meyer, *The Aims of Jesus*, 93–110.

history of interpretation, from the New Testament to the Church Fathers, to the medieval period, and beyond.

If an interpreter's horizons are limited, unable to grasp *die Sache* with which the Bible is concerned, they will be unable to grasp the biblical text or interpret it fully. It is worth citing Meyer at length on this matter:

> It may be that the problem of the interpreter is not met by resources such as encyclopedias, handbooks, Oxford Dictionaries of one kind or another, and that what is needed is neither information nor the solution of a problem, but the cure of a blind spot, which might be massive. The cure might lie (it often does lie) only in a conversion—religious, moral, or intellectual. The inadequate interpreter probably will be unaware of the need of conversion; so the conversion may never be forthcoming. A Ph.D. might be a union card of sorts, but it does not guarantee that its holders are able to measure up to the texts of the New Testament in the sense that they are able to figure out what such texts mean and how they mean it, or (if others have figured it out) to catch on to what others say such texts mean.[16]

Conversion, as Meyer sees it, in debt to Lonergan, is

> a revolutionary transition from one horizon to another. Intellectual conversion is a transition from the horizon of cognitional myth (knowing is something like seeing) to that of transcendental method made fully thematic and affirmed. Moral conversion is a transition from the horizons of satisfactions to the existential primacy of values. Religious conversion is a transition from the horizon of this-worldly commitments to the primacy in one's life of the love of God.[17]

Meyer states simply: "The theologian lacking in religious and moral conversion cannot function."[18] This is the key to Alexandria.

Meyer's claim that "conversion" was necessary for the interpreter did not rule out historical questions, nor the methods and tools of historical-critical and other modern methods, as the role of Antioch in interpretation can never be ignored, but he was insistent that such methods and tools were not the end of the process. The end of the process was to interpret biblical texts, singly, and so come to an overarching sense of the spiritual meaning of the Bible and its salvific concerns as a whole. Meyer felt that there was always room for more questions, there was always a place for new insights, there were always contours and trajectories to any given text of the Bible not before considered. But

---

16. Meyer, *Reality and Illusion in New Testament Scholarship*, 93.
17. Meyer, *Reality and Illusion in New Testament Scholarship*, 69–70.
18. Meyer, *Reality and Illusion in New Testament Scholarship*, 70.

INTRODUCTION

all of this was in the service of determining the theological import of the individual biblical texts and the Bible as a whole. Our goal in this volume is to bring some of his insights to bear in the papers you find here.

Summary of Papers

In the first chapter, "Letter or Spirit? Toward a Testimonial Exegesis," Luis Sánchez-Navarro begins by noting that Alexandria and Antioch are sometimes presented as a false dichotomy. Neither is a pure model, and the two are not mutually exclusive. In fact, Scripture presents us with "sacred letters" and is (in the words of Joseph Ratzinger) "the essential witness of revelation." Sánchez-Navarro answers the question in his title by asserting that neither letter nor spirit exists without the other. But even more than this, he argues that a truly critical exegesis must also take into account a third reality: the believing community that has experienced the revelation of God. Scripture is not only a human word and a divine word, it is essentially an ecclesial word.

In chapter 2, Paul Niskanen also considers the sometimes overly simplistic opposition between Alexandria and Antioch. The lines between literal and allegorical readings are not as sharp as some would imagine. Working with Meyer's "intended sense" of Scripture, which in itself is closely related to Aquinas's literal sense, Niskanen argues that this literal sense of Scripture is itself frequently polyvalent. He illustrates this point with examples of theologically weighty texts that defy a simple or straightforward "literal" reading. The very language and imagery of biblical texts invite an encounter with the transcendent that cannot always be neatly bound or classified according to our exegetical categories.

Joseph Briody, in chapter 3, turns to a closer examination of typology. He argues that typology can serve as a model for Catholic biblical exegesis. As an extension of the literal sense that grounds allegory, typology can respect the Old Testament in itself as well as in relation to the New. Using the Deuteronomistic History as an example, Briody shows how a sound exegesis of the historical-literal sense can lead to a rich theological interpretation.

In chapter 4, Hryhoriy Lozinskyy gives a close examination of a particular text, Moses's flight to Midian in Exodus 2:11–22, in order to analyze the different interpretive techniques of Alexandria and Antioch. In this case study, he looks at Moses's flight into Midian within the context of the book of Exodus as well as from the perspectives of Alexandrian and Antiochene exegetes. Finally, he also considers its use in the Byzantine liturgical tradition. Each in their own ways, allegory, *theoria* and liturgy all strive to read this text in the light of Christ.

Chapters 5 and 6 take us to the book of Psalms. First, Maurizio Girolami examines how ancient interpretive techniques that were applied to the book of Psalms (especially the prosopological method) are still very much relevant for contemporary and future biblical exegesis. While ancient exegetical techniques can sometimes appear dated or irrelevant to us, their questions and concerns regarding the meaning of texts are very much our own. Next, Juana L. Manzo compares Alexandrian and Antiochian exegesis of a single text, Psalm 75. While noting a certain overlap in themes and theological content, Manzo also perceives that a critical piece may be missing from both schools, pointing toward the need for a greater synthesis.

In chapter 7, Marcin Kowalski also weighs the merits and shortcomings of both Antioch and Alexandria while examining the baptism of Jesus. While contemporary exegesis might separate the historical-critical and theological approaches that these cities represent (privileging the former), Kowalski argues that the latter is not a dubious addition. The union of Antioch and Alexandria is essential to discerning the full meaning of the biblical narrative.

Finally, Isacco Pagani reckons with Meyer's claim that much biblical scholarship lacks "the responsiveness to the note of definitive fulfillment" that Scripture offers. Pagani's analysis of "fulfilment" statements in John 13–17 is based on a careful reading of the Gospel texts and is illumined by narrative theory. Pagani's paper is a fitting conclusion to this study, as he asks, like Meyer, that we continue to work toward "a more in-depth exploration" of the relationship between Antioch and Alexandria, "following different paths" of examining personal and collective memory, narrative memory, and the memory of the Scripture of Israel.

Conclusion

These papers respond to, engage with, and build on Meyer's insights from the late twentieth century. Meyer stood against what he saw as the positivistic debris of the Enlightenment that saw history in its narrowest form, as simply facts available to the five senses. This sort of historical stance decided in advance that such things as prophecy, miracles, healings, and such could not have taken place, and so the historian could exclude these from the data a priori. He called this "an undiscriminating ideological stance" that has "had a deeply negative impact on the exegetical and historical appropriation of the New Testament."[19] Again, on this matter he needs to be cited at length:

19. Meyer, *Critical Realism and the New Testament*, 92.

INTRODUCTION

> If the historian of religions cannot entertain the meaningfulness of "saving acts in history," then he cannot envisage miracle as a concrete possibility. There follows this dilemma. It is his business to give an account of data en route to answering questions about matters of fact. Now, in fact, he has no basis on which to exclude miracle *a priori* from either the data or the answer. On the other hand, he has pledged himself as historian not to envisage the possibility of miracles. He accordingly finds himself in a situation which does not allow him as historian to come to grips with history, for he cannot know whether or not the possibility he dutifully omits to consider offers the best account of a given constellation of data.[20]

If this residue of the Enlightenment still exists among biblical interpreters in their attacks on Christian tradition and the biblical texts and the meaning found in them by the Church and its interpreters, it is not to be found in this volume. Meyer bemoaned biblical interpretation that

> trails off into the capricious, thwarted by absorption in pretentious or unpretentious trivia. This includes, on the part of literary scholars who for whatever reason find themselves with nothing very compelling, or even definite, to do, a misplaced hankering to break out into creativity and inventiveness. There follow declarations of independence from the tyrannies of philology and history, from the merely intended sense of the text, and finally from the text itself. But faddism, and particularly the faddism that hinges on forms of alienation, is notoriously ineffective occupational therapy.[21]

Yet Meyer traced this alienation back to the beginnings of biblical scholarship:

> Modern biblical studies took shape as twin streams, one of continuity, the other of discontinuity, with biblical religion.... Both streams or wings have made tangible contributions to technical progress. The differences between them have always been hermeneutical. The strong point of the tradition of discontinuity (dogma-free scholarship) has been its resolutely critical stance. Its weakness has lain in the sometimes latent, sometimes patent, alienation pervading its critical distance from the biblical text. Conversely, the strong point of continuity (religious and theological conservatism) has been its connaturality with the text; its weakness, a propensity to harmonize divergences and to underestimate the discontinuities between past and present. The ideal is somehow to comprehend these extremes and occupy

---

20. Meyer, *The Aims of Jesus*, 102.
21. Meyer, *Critical Realism and the New Testament*, 87.

the space between them, to temper the warmth of connaturality with the coolness of critical distance.[22]

Our goal at our conference in Winona and in this volume of papers collected from that conference was and is to "occupy the space between" extremes, by bringing "dialectic" to bear on the judgment of biblical interpretation and theology, that is, by occupying both Antioch and Alexandria. Meyer felt that biblical scholarship was often

> a flood of monographs and articles that divide into two streams, with plentiful dry land between them. The one stream is the mass of positivist-tinctured works—sober, cautious, timid—sometimes meant to shore up religious assurance; the other stream, reminiscent of the "chatter and contradictions of what is falsely called knowledge" (1 Tim. 6), is up-to-the-minute, indulgent toward bright ideas, original and hungry for acknowledgment as such, tempted to be all-explanatory. The large middle ground between these streams ought to be flooded with the work of an international, interconfessional community of scholars, products with a plausible claim on being acknowledged as intelligent, reasonable, and responsible. The ascertainment that this is far from true should prompt our best efforts to bring about improvement and progress.[23]

It is our hope that in our work at our conference and in this volume, we have helped to bring about some improvement and progress by occupying a large part of that middle ground, by drawing inspiration from the theological truth of God's Word, intended for our salvation, and by demonstrating how to draw on both Antioch, with its careful attention to historical detail and modes of interpretation, and Alexandria, which highlights the depth of God's Word. It is our hope that this volume will encourage others to produce scholarship for our students, our colleagues, and our parishes that helps make the transcendent mystery of God's Word come alive.

---

22. Meyer, *Critical Realism and the New Testament*, 196–97.
23. Meyer, *Reality and Illusion in New Testament Scholarship*, 126.

CHAPTER 1

Letter or Spirit? Toward a Testimonial Exegesis

Luis Sánchez-Navarro, DCJM

The age of two millennia that biblical exegesis (still young) has reached poses this question for us today: in order to be faithful to the revealed Word, especially with regard to the Old Testament, must we be subject to the letter (i.e., the historical dimension) or, on the contrary, does Christian faith oblige us to read *something else* ("allegory")? Should we choose between Antioch and Alexandria? Should we move our spiritual abode to Syrian soil, or to the fertile Nile delta? In the pages that follow we immerse ourselves in the well-known contrast between "Alexandria" and "Antioch" in order to address, in light of this contrast, more recent issues found within the comparison of historical and spiritual exegesis.

Alexandria and Antioch, Two Pure Models?

Studies on the exegetical schools of Alexandria ("allegory") and Antioch ("theory," literalism) are innumerable; although the "Alexandrian school" flourished from the third century onward and the Antiochene school since the fourth century, in a certain way these two schools function as catalysts of all patristic exegesis, even since the second century.[1] If the reference par excellence of allegory is Origen, "the first systematic theoretician of Christian allegorism,"[2]

---

1. Cf. Manlio Simonetti, "Exegesis, Patristic," 897–903 in *Encyclopedia of Ancient Christianity*, Vol. 1, ed. Angelo Di Berardino (Downers Grove, IL: IVP Academic, 2014).

2. Charles Kannengiesser, *Handbook of Patristic Exegesis*, BAC 1 (Leiden: Brill, 2006), 251.

in Antiochene exegesis, Diodorus of Tarsus and Theodore of Mopsuestia stand out above all, although its best known representative is John Chrysostom. But even for the latter, it is pointed out that allegory and history coexist in him: "Chrysostom favors a literal reading... but also often used a typological understanding and at times even allegory."[3] It is in fact a commonplace that, except in extraordinary cases, the authors themselves show a certain fluidity between allegorism and literalism; even when, as in the case of St. Jerome, stages can be identified (allegorical at the beginning, more literalist later), none of them dispenses with the other element. The biblical writings are so varied in their nature (homiletic, catechetical, didactic, exegetical) that it is not uncommon for an author who applies allegory at one moment to adhere to a more or less strict literalism in another context.

Gnosticism, with its overvaluation of the New Testament to the detriment of the Old, contributed *a contrario* to the development of this double possibility, for all of the interpretive possibilities are already present in the New Testament writings.[4] For it was an occasion that induced the ecclesiastical writers to show the goodness of the Old Testament; to this end some of them developed literal exegesis, which presented the Scripture of Israel as the place of divine pedagogy and *praeparatio evangelii* (thus Irenaeus),[5] and for others, allegory revealed hidden in that ancient letter the mysteries of the New Covenant. Among the latter, it was Origen who made explicit the raison d'être of this technique: "Beyond the distinction into two, three or even four senses, [allegory] finds unity and maximum density in the conviction that the word of God has an inexhaustible fecundity that no interpretation can circumscribe or exhaust: continual study allows us to know it ever better in its inexhaustible plurality of meanings."[6] But at the root of both trends is a shared conviction:

> The biblical littera was for patristic interpreters pregnant of an equally divine message. In their unanimous conviction, God's message could not be better registered than in the very "letter" of the Bible. Even when the most learned among them applied the rules and principles of a philological analysis to the

---

3. Bernard McGinn and Susan E. Schreiner, "According to the Scriptures: Biblical Interpretation Prior to 1600," 1891–1922 in *The Jerome Biblical Commentary for the Twenty-First Century*, ed. John J. Collins et al. (London: T&T Clark, 2022).

4. The literal interpretation of the Old Testament can be seen, for instance, in the fulfillment quotations in Matthew. For typology, see Rom 5:14; 1 Cor 10:6; Heb 9:24; 1 Pet 3:21. For allegory, Gal 4:24. See for example John W. Martens, "Catholic Hermeneutics of the New Testament," *St. Vladimir's Theological Quarterly* 63, no. 2 (2019): 215–21.

5. Cf. Simonetti, "Exegesis, Patristic," 898.

6. Simonetti, "Exegesis, Patristic," 899.

sacred text, their first instinct was to approach the literality of the biblical text as gifted in itself with supernatural power. "The meaning deserves to be explored because divine scripture says nothing that would be useless or out of consideration.".... Thus a constant and universal canon of patristic interpretation is the insistence on the intimate connection between the littera and any "spiritual" comments generated by it.[7]

The "Sacred Letters"

This sheds light on the question that we have set out to examine, and which we now critically address: letter and/or spirit? The second letter to Timothy helps us to do so: "*All Scripture is inspired by God and useful*" (2 Tim 3:16).[8] That "Scripture" which is "inspired by God" has been designated in the previous verse as "the sacred letters." There is therefore a real coincidence between "inspired Scripture" and "(sacred) letters." Let us look at this passage in its entirety:

> 2 Tim 3:14–17: You however, Timothy, persevere in the things you learned and became sure of. You are well aware of the people you learned from and that from your tenderest years you have known the sacred letters ([τὰ] ἱερὰ γράμματα) which have the power to make you astute in attaining salvation (τὰ δυνάμενα σε σοφίσαι εἰς σωτηρίαν) through faith which comes from union with Christ Jesus. All the Scripture is inspired by God and useful (πᾶσα γραφὴ θεόπνευστος καὶ ὠφέλιμος)—for instruction, for censuring, for straightening people out, for giving training in upright conduct, so that the man of God may be complete, that is, completely equipped for every excellent deed.[9]

These words reveal the vision that the biblical authors have of the "letters" of Scripture: they are not reduced to a bare materiality, but are impregnated with the Spirit (that is why they are *sacred* letters) and therefore transmit a divine force:

> Here the letters are signs that contain and conduct a power that is quite beyond them *qua* visible marks with ink or audible human words. There is a *dynamis* with which they are charged (cf. the *dynamis* of 2 Tim 1:7–8

---

7. Kannengiesser, *Handbook*, 174–75. The quotation is from Ambrosiaster, *Quaestiones* 10.1.

8. Scripture citations in this chapter are from the Revised Standard Version: Catholic Edition.

9. Translation: Jerome D. Quinn and William C. Wacker, *The First and Second Letters to Timothy*, ECCo (Grand Rapids, MI: Eerdmans, 2000), 746–47.

and 3:5), the divine *dynamis*, the *Spirit* (cf. *theopneustos* in v. 16 *infra*) which "empowers" the Scriptures to make a man wise "for salvation."[10]

A biblical letter can certainly be stripped of the spirit, and thus made the slave of a literalism that prevents us from perceiving its depth; Paul speaks of it when he opposes it to the Spirit (cf. Rom 2:27-29; 7:6; 2 Cor 3:6-7). But two things must be said. First, that such a crudely nominalistic conception of the word does not take into account the density of the human word, which the philosophy of language has made apparent. All true human speech *is* spirit. Secondly, this vision, rightly criticized by the Apostle of the Gentiles, is a distortion of the biblical message; in fact, the Bible understands the word as a living reality and as a source of life, to the point of being the means by which God worked creation (Gen 1). The Bible does not conceive of the letter except as imbued with the Spirit. The book of Revelation describes God the Father (Rev 1:8; 21:6) and the risen Christ (22:13) as "the Alpha and the Omega"— letters which, by embracing the entire alphabet as *arkhe* and *telos*, symbolically contain all words and so recapitulate the whole of reality and all its meaning. It is not surprising, then, that the second letter to Timothy labels as "sacred" those "Letters" that so effectively instruct Paul's young disciple in virtue, for they enjoy the presence of the divine Spirit.[11] By this presence, moreover, these Letters are capable of moving those who accept them in faith along the path of life. This was also the point of view of the Church Fathers: "For the exegetes of the early church the correct interpretation of the *littera* was in itself a *spiritual* exercise, because for them the materiality of the written text itself was filled with divine mysteries."[12]

This allows us to understand that, in fact, all the Bible's insistence on the *letter* is *spiritual*—that is, symbolic. We discover this in Jesus's insistence on the materiality of the Law: "For truly, I say to you, till heaven and earth pass away, not an iota, not a dot, will pass from the law until all is accomplished" (Matt 5:18.) It is he who came precisely to "fulfill it," that is, to accomplish, to give it fullness. Revelation manifests this same idea in a serious final warning:

> Rev 22:18-19: I warn every one who hears the words of the prophecy of this book: if any one adds to them, God will add to him the plagues described in this book, and if any one takes away from the words of the book of this

---

10. Quinn and Wacker, *1&2 Timothy*, 759.
11. "Here that *hiera* is being further explained by a neologism" [*theopneustos*]: Quinn and Wacker, *1&2 Timothy*, 761.
12. Kannengiesser, *Handbook*, 168 (italics in the original).

prophecy, God will take away his share in the tree of life and in the holy city, which are described in this book.

The literal interpretation of these words would have condemned to the most severe penalties, and deprived of the greatest goods, all the scribes who have transmitted this book to us, omitting, correcting or adding words.[13] But this is not what the author intends: in the alteration of the words is symbolized the alteration of *the sense* of these words; therefore, whoever alters this sense, even if formally he does not modify the terms (this is how the heretics of yesterday and today try to proceed), will receive the indicated punishments. Heresy does not consist in altering the letter, but the meaning of that letter—its spirit.[14]

But how do these material signs (written word), or these *flatus vocis* (spoken word), enjoy a presence that constitutes them in living reality?

Scripture Inspired by God

Recently, I have had the opportunity to review the doctrine of biblical inspiration.[15] The "Neo-Bonaventurian" proposal of Joseph Ratzinger, which discovered the divine origin of Scripture in the circular interaction of three subjects (God, the believing community, and the hagiographer, i.e. the inspired author), was a particular object of comment. Let us recall it:

> One could say that the books of Scripture involve three interacting subjects. First of all, there is the individual author or group of authors to whom we owe a particular scriptural text. But these authors are not autonomous writers in the modern sense; they form part of a collective subject, the "People of God", from within whose heart and to whom they speak. Hence, this subject is actually the deeper "author" of the Scriptures. And yet likewise, this people does not exist alone; rather, it knows that it is led, and spoken to,

---

13. The key reference work on the textual criticism of Revelation is by Josef Schmid, *Studien zur Geschichte des griechischen Apokalypse-Textes* (München: Karl Zink, 1955–1956).

14. Concerning the distortion of the meaning of biblical passages by heretics, the Arian controversy offers numerous examples. Suffice it to quote John 14:10, "I am in the Father and the Father in me." The Arians ridiculed this saying of the Lord, "How can the greatest be in the smallest?," and saw it as proof of the non-divinity of the Son, since in another place it is said of all men that "in him we live and move and have our being." But this, Athanasius affirms, shows their error because they understand God in a corporal way, and not according to his personal spiritual being; on the contrary, this saying of the Lord manifests his consubstantiality with the Father (cf. *Against Arians*, 3.3–5).

15. Luis Sánchez-Navarro, "The Inspiration and Truth of Scripture: Do They Still Matter?," 7–21 in *The Word of Truth, Sealed by the Spirit*, ed. Matthew C. Genung and Kevin Zilverberg (CThFS; Saint Paul, MN: St. Paul Seminary Press, 2022).

by God himself, who—through men and their humanity—is at the deepest level the one speaking.[16]

This "corporate dimension of biblical authorship"[17] has been ignored by the exegesis of recent centuries, since modern man conceives its corporate dimension only, at best, as something proper to an infantile stage that must be left behind. But this dimension is constitutive of personal identity;[18] therefore, it is necessary to integrate into the theological explanation of the charism of inspiration the communitarian, that is, ecclesial dimension.[19] The hagiographer, the recipient of such a charism, can accept it only to the extent that he remains integrated into the ecclesial body;[20] thus, on different and complementary levels, God, as the ultimate origin, is the author of 100% of the biblical text, as are the human authors on their own level, as is the ecclesial community in communion with the Great Church. Without the Church there is no inspiration; therefore, without the Church there can be no interpretation. The New Testament itself clearly states: "No prophecy of scripture is a matter of one's own interpretation [*idías epilýseōs*], because no prophecy ever came by the impulse of man, but men moved by the Holy Spirit spoke from God" (2 Pet 1:20–21).

Scripture, then, can only be understood in the Church; in fact, the Church—partner of revelation—belongs to the concept of Holy Scripture: the bare materiality of Scripture ("*sola littera*") can serve as an instrument of revelation, but "Holy Scripture comprises an ensemble of text-plus-believing-subjects. Revelation thus exists only *in act*."[21] Hence, "the Word of God is structured somewhat like a set of Russian dolls: the text is enfolded by the

---

16. Joseph Ratzinger / Pope Benedict XVI, *Jesus of Nazareth*, vol. 2, *From the Baptism in the Jordan to the Transfiguration* (New York: Doubleday, 2007), xx–xxi. See Aaron Pidel, *The Inspiration and Truth of Scripture. Testing the Ratzinger Paradigm*, VD 4 (Washington, DC: Catholic University of America Press, 2023).

17. Aaron Pidel, "*Christi Opera Proficiunt:* Ratzinger's Neo-Bonaventurian Model of Social Inspiration," *Nova et Vetera English Edition* 13 (2015): 693–711, at 694.

18. Two classical studies: Henry Wheeler Robinson, *Corporate Personality in Ancient Israel*, 2nd ed. (Edinburgh: T. & T. Clark, 1981 [original publication: 1936]); Jean de Fraine, *Adam et son lignage: Études sur la notion de "personnalité corporative" dans la Bible*, ML.B 2 (Bruges: Desclée de Brouwer, 1959).

19. Cf. Luis Sánchez-Navarro, *Un cuerpo pleno: Cristo y la personalidad corporativa en la Escritura*, SBMat 4 (Madrid: Universidad San Dámaso, 2021), 146–47.

20. On the interdependence of individual and communal religion, of "man's conversation with God and men's conversation with one another," see Josef Ratzinger, *Introduction to Christianity*, trans. J. R. Foster, 2nd ed. (San Francisco: Ignatius, 2004), 94–95. See also Ben F. Meyer, *The Aims of Jesus* (London: SCM Press, 1979), 93–110.

21. Pidel, "Neo-Bonaventurian Model," 697.

reader, who is enfolded by the faith of the Church, which is enfolded by God."[22] Therefore, the broad understanding of the charism of inspiration (involving also the reader), something that has so often been viewed with suspicion as a door to the free interpretation of Scripture (and therefore rejected, or at least admitted only silently), imposes itself radically: for without a reader there is no true inspiration. But it requires specifying who the reading subject is: not the individual as such, but *the Church in each of its members*. To the extent that the individual places himself on the margins of ecclesial communion, he ceases to be a reader of Scripture and becomes a mere "user" of Scripture at the service of his own vision; only he who reads Sacred Scripture *in* the Church and *from the faith* of the Church can claim to have a full understanding of it.

This brings us back to a fundamental reality: the testimonial dimension of Sacred Scripture.

Sacred Scripture, Testimony of Revelation

In his autobiography, Joseph Ratzinger spoke of Scripture as "the essential witness of revelation."[23] This description manifests, at the same time, its greatness and its limits. First of all, its greatness: "the essential witness" speaks to us of an irreplaceable function; the Christian religion, which is not a religion of the Book,[24] is necessarily a religion *with a Book*. First, because—uniquely in the history of religions—it found a Book in its cradle (the Old Testament); and secondly, because, as I have written elsewhere, "the presence of the apostolic testimony consigned to [New Testament] Scripture is so deep and essential that the Church could not be understood in herself without this great Book of books."[25] The Church is a "textual community."[26]

But at the same time, the fundamental limit of Sacred Scripture comes to light: it is a witness to revelation, it does not stop at itself, but goes beyond. Its inspired character directs us with certainty toward revelation, but revelation

---

22. Pidel, "Neo-Bonaventurian Model," 698.

23. Joseph Ratzinger, *Milestones: Memoirs 1927–1977*, trans. Erasmo Leiva-Merikakis (San Francisco: Ignatius, 1998), 127.

24. *CCC*, §108.

25. Luis Sánchez-Navarro, "The Ecclesial Reading of Scripture," in Carlos Granados and Luis Sánchez-Navarro, *In the School of the Word: Biblical Interpretation from the New to the Old Testament*, trans. Kristin Towle, with an introduction to the English edition by Kevin Zilverberg, CThFS (Saint Paul, MN: Saint Paul Seminary Press, 2021), 72–86, at 85.

26. Juan Chapa, "La materialidad de la Palabra: manuscritos que hablan," *Estudios Bíblicos* 69 (2011): 9–37, at 11.

transcends Scripture, because "revelation is something alive."[27] The Letter is not enough if it does not enter into the "dialogue of revelation"; it is then that, deprived of the Spirit, it remains a dead letter. Sacred Scripture manifests its vitality, then, when it brings us into communion with the living God revealed in his Son, Jesus Christ. It attains its greatness by referring to the reality to which it bears witness: in it, the Hebrew or Greek language is no longer necessary, textual or literary criticism is no longer relevant; the *res* overflows the *testimonium*.

Thus understood, Sacred Scripture appears as a permanent witness to revelation, and at its service. On the one hand, it bears witness to the truth of the revelation that culminates in Jesus Christ, in both the historical and the confessional dimensions of that truth.[28] From this point of view, Scripture needs to preserve the marks of its history (language, literary genre, etc.);[29] because of its written character, it is a permanent and objective reference for ecclesial life. On the other hand, and as a consequence of the above, Sacred Scripture allows the renewal of the experience of revelation—we could say, the renewal of Pentecost—in every believer who, by means of this written testimony, approaches in the Church the living God. They are thus an eminent instance of ecclesial witness:

> Incorporated into the Church's authoritative office of witness, which derives its rights and power from the presence of the Spirit, from Christ's contemporaneity with all our days, in which he is ever the Christ today, the office of witness that belongs to the unique word of Scripture set down once and for all will have to be restored to rights and power; that office of witness of the Scriptural word derives its enduring validity from the uniqueness of the historical act of salvation of Jesus Christ, who once gave up his crucified body.[30]

---

27. Ratzinger, *Milestones*, 127.

28. Cf. Luis Sánchez-Navarro, "The Testimonial Character of Sacred Scripture," in Carlos Granados and Luis Sánchez-Navarro, *In the School of the Word*, 17–31.

29. "The once-only aspect of the Incarnation naturally privileges those writings emanating from the authority of the apostolic eyewitnesses. Dogmatic writings serve and preserve this one, originary witness for all time." Pidel, "Neo-Bonaventurian Model," 709.

30. Joseph Ratzinger, "The Question of the Concept of Tradition: A Provisional Response," 41–89 in *God's Word: Scripture, Tradition, Office*, ed. Peter Hünermann and Thomas Söding, trans. Henry Taylor (San Francisco: Ignatius, 2008), 67.

Two Understandings of Revelation, Two Models of Exegesis

We have recalled the concept of divine revelation. The concept advocated by Ratzinger (then, only a brilliant young theologian) was accepted by the Second Vatican Council;[31] it is not objective but relational, according to the *Wort/Antwort* model: without a response (*Antwort*) of faith there is no revelation (*Wort*, "word").[32] It is interesting to consider this model's implications for exegesis in comparison with the previous one.

The bipartite model of inspiration, preferred by modernity (God → hagiographer), implies a whole conception of the way of relating to God;[33] according to it, revelation is constituted by the fact of inspiration. It is a matter, we might say, of *revelation as content* that, inspired by God, is put in writing and transmitted. To this model of inspiration corresponds an analogous model of exegesis, which consists in unraveling the content of the sacred book; this is the task of the exegete as a scholar, who in most cases will be a person of the Church, but who works in his own name and tends to avoid external "interference" in his work. In this way, biblical exegesis would govern the faith and the Magisterium of the Church. Of course, this does not mean that every exegete lets himself be carried to the ultimate consequences; but the interesting thing is to understand where this structure of biblical inspiration points. The scheme would be:

God → hagiographer → *sacred book* → exegete
→ content of the book (revelation)

The tripartite model includes a new subject: the believing people (Israel, the Church). Revelation does not appear as a consequence of inspiration, but as its source: only after God's encounter with his people can the sacred author become the spokesman, at the same time, of God and of the community of faith, within which he receives from God the charism of inspiration. It is therefore *revelation as an event*; the hagiographer is not understood as an isolated individual, but as a member of a body, who, inspired by God, writes with all his personal ability and skill, yes, but *as a member of that body*. And he writes what, coming from God, has been transmitted to him in that body. The content of his

---

31. Cf. Peter Seewald, *Benedict XVI: A Life*, vol. 1, *Youth in Nazi Germany to the Second Vatican Council 1927–1965*, trans. Dinah Livingstone (London: Bloomsbury, 2020), 412–13, and ch. 29: "The Genoa Speech."

32. Joseph Ratzinger, "Die Bedeutung der Väter für die Gegenwärtige Theologie," *Tübinger Theologische Quartalschrift* 148 (1968): 257–82.

33. "The program of the early Augustine, 'God and the soul—nothing else', is impracticable; and it is also unchristian." Ratzinger, *Introduction to Christianity*, 95.

writing, therefore, does not spring from his own inventiveness, but from what he has received in the community (cf. Luke 1:1–4). The model of exegesis that corresponds to this vision is very different from the previous one. For, although the exegete must share the same spiritual, literary, historical, and philological competence, he nevertheless understands himself as a member of the community of faith, who from within it interprets the sacred text as a witness to that lived faith. The scheme would therefore be as follows:

> Revelation of God → believing people → hagiographer → *sacred book* → exegete in the community → witness of the book to God's Revelation

The exegete no longer acts as an individual subject, but as a member of the community that has experienced God's revelation in its history; this community is not unstructured but has certain persons, appointed by God himself, who are responsible for the tradition of faith.[34] It is therefore unthinkable that such an exegesis should lead to any conclusion that is incompatible with that communitarian experience of the apostolic faith. Consequently, this exegesis will result in a testimonial exposition of the content of the writing, which, while elucidating its historical and literary aspects, affirms its historical and salvific truth at the same time. It is obvious that, in this model, the witness of the ecclesial faith governs exegesis: not as an external imposition, but as an internal requirement of rationality. For the spirit with which the "Sacred Letters" are imbued is an eminently ecclesial spirit.

Conclusion: Spiritus in Littera

We thus return to the initial dilemma; our journey now allows us to refocus it and thus overcome it. It is not a question of choosing between Antioch and Alexandria, between the letter and the Spirit, but of the shared conviction that lies at the root of both trends. Because the letter does not exist without the Spirit, and vice versa: it would be like saying that a man can exist without a soul, confusing realities as different as the human body and the corpse; or that the soul is equivalent to the whole man and can therefore do without the body. Without spirit there are only inarticulate sounds: the meaning of the letter

---

34. Richard Bauckham, in dialogue with Kenneth Bailey, speaks of a "formal controlled model" of tradition, according to which "the 'clearly identified' teachers would be, in the first place, eyewitnesses, and their 'clearly identified' students would be community teachers authorized as tradents because they had learned the tradition from the eyewitnesses": *Jesus and the Eyewitnesses: The Gospels as Eyewitness Testimony*, 2nd ed. (Grand Rapids, MI: Eerdmans, 2017), 293.

comes from its spirit. And without letter there is no spirit, without sign there is no meaning.

But this inspired letter is intrinsically ecclesial, since it springs from a charismatic personality who writes from within the community of faith constituted by the encounter with the living God. This was also a fundamental conviction shared by Antioch and Alexandria. For this reason, exegesis, in order to be truly critical, must be ecclesial; and its form will be testimonial.

CHAPTER 2

Beyond Alexandria and Antioch:
The Polyvalence of the Literal Sense in the Old Testament

Paul V. Niskanen

Introduction: The Intended Sense of Scripture

Ben Meyer proposed a synthesis of the schools of Alexandria and Antioch by arguing for the primacy of what he referred to as "the intended sense" of Scripture.[1] By this he appears to understand "the intention of the author as intrinsic to, or encoded in, or expressed by the text."[2] This strikes me as a rather sensible balance between critics who would ignore or deny any interpretive role to authorial intention and others for whom "authorial will" would override considerations from the actual text, being extrinsic to it. What he proposes sounds very similar to what Aquinas referred to as the literal sense: "The literal sense is that which is primarily intended by the words, whether they are used properly or figuratively."[3] So the authorial intention is key, but it is found precisely in the words of the text and not outside them.

These words of the text may be used, in the language of Aquinas, either properly or figuratively. By "properly" Aquinas refers to what many today would call "literally" or according to the plain meaning of the words. This also is close to the center of what constitutes Antiochene exegesis with its literalistic and historicist tendencies. "Figuratively" refers to the fact that sometimes words are not intended to be understood literally even according to the literal sense. When employing metaphor or writing poetry, the literal sense is

---

1. Ben F. Meyer, *Critical Realism and the New Testament*, PTMS 17 (San Jose, CA: Pickwick, 1989), ch. 2, "The Primacy of the Intended Sense of Texts," 17–55.
2. Meyer, *Critical Realism and the New Testament*, 36.
3. Thomas Aquinas, *The Literal Exposition on Job*, trans. Anthony Damico (Atlanta: Scholars Press, 1989), 1.6.

figurative. In other words, to read an allegory as allegory (for example Judg 9:7–15, Jotham's allegory of the trees) is not by Aquinas's reckoning allegorical interpretation, but still very much literal.[4]

This rather commonsensical approach of Aquinas is sometimes attested in the earlier exegetes of both Alexandria and Antioch. But at other times they appear more preoccupied with their opposed methods of either *allegoria* or *historia* to see that there may be room for both in biblical exegesis and that the lines between them may be somewhat blurred when texts themselves employ figurative, ambiguous, and symbolic language. The false dichotomies of the past have surfaced again in our times as the post-Reformation and post-Enlightenment push for the singular, literal, and critical meaning of Scripture clashes once more with the spiritual, typological, and theological reaction. The literal sense of Aquinas and the intended sense of Meyer point to a synthesis beyond this false dichotomy. I propose that one key aspect of Aquinas needs to be further highlighted along this trajectory. That is the polyvalence of the literal sense. Aquinas recognized that a text may have multiple meanings even on the literal level before having recourse to spiritual interpretations. We would be well served to recall this principle, which seems lost in many of the exegetical disputes of our day.

Alexandria and Allegory

The initial turn to allegory as a method of biblical interpretation can be seen in Philo of Alexandria in the early first century AD. Operating within the Greek and Jewish worlds of his time and place, he sought a way to reconcile the Jewish Scriptures with Greek philosophy. The use of allegory was absolutely necessary to Philo whenever the Scriptures appeared to assert anything unworthy of God. Theological considerations thus guided his exegesis, and I would add rightly so. He did not, however, automatically employ allegory at every

---

4. Thomas's understanding of the literal sense is broader not only than that of Antioch, but also of most modern exegetes. This flows from his understanding of God as the author of Scripture. So if God intends something in the Old Testament as a figure or type of Christ, then that too pertains to the literal sense according to Aquinas. See Franklin T. Harkins, "Christ and the Eternal Extent of Divine Providence in the *Expositio Super Iob ad Litteram* of Thomas Aquinas," *Viator* 47 (2015): 123–52. When Meyer speaks of the intended sense, it seems that he has in mind more the intention of the human author through the language and literary forms that are employed in their historical context (see esp. his Summary of Part One on p. 34). Note that his desire is to unite this intended sense with "the transcendent intelligibility and unity of the mystery of salvation."

opportunity. The text itself suggested whether or not allegory must be used. He writes:

> So we must turn to allegory, the method dear to men with their eyes opened. Indeed the sacred oracles most evidently afford us the clues for the use of this method. For they say that in the garden there are trees in no way resembling those with which we are familiar, but trees of Life, of Immortality, of Knowledge, of Apprehension, of Understanding, of the conception of good and evil.[5]

I am not sure how many trees he is envisioning here, but what is clear is that he knows that Genesis cannot be interpreted literally since there do not exist such trees as those of Life and Knowledge. Would that many a contemporary biblical literalist were so wise.

I find this example intriguing because I wholeheartedly agree with Philo's non-literalist reading of Genesis; however, I would classify my own reading of Genesis not as allegorical but rather closer to literal. That is to say that I consider the literal sense of Genesis not to be an attempt at a historical narrative involving actual trees, but rather a symbolic narrative with an instructional purpose. Is the story of the Garden of Eden an allegory? I suppose the answer depends upon whom you ask and how the term is defined. J. R. R. Tolkien once famously asserted, "I cordially dislike allegory in all of its manifestations," yet others have argued that his magnum opus, *The Lord of the Rings*, is precisely that. Whether we call the narrative in Genesis 2-3 allegory, myth, parable, or symbolic narrative, the point is that it was never intended to be read and understood as a literal or historical sequence of events. So to read it as what it is, rather than as what it is not (science or history) is the proper way to read the text. Should such a reading be called allegorical or perhaps literal? The discerning reader is not generating any allegorical interpretation but has been supplied a symbolic meaning by the author. Such an interpretation falls under Aquinas's literal sense or Meyer's intended sense.

As we move to the early Christian exegetes of Alexandria, we find them continuing in the allegorical method of Philo. Origen is the most prominent and prolific practitioner of the allegorical method. If the Antiochenes attacked him and his fellow Alexandrians for dismissing the literal or historical meaning of the text in favor of allegory, modern critics are likely to question his method more for its seeming arbitrariness and raw eisegesis. To return to the question

---

5. *Plant.* 36; trans. F. H. Colson, G. H. Whitaker (LCL 247; Cambridge, MA: Harvard University Press, 1930), 231.

of Eden, most moderns would agree that this text should be read symbolically rather than literally or historically. Origen writes in *De principiis*:

> And who is so foolish as to suppose that *God*, after the manner of a human farmer, *planted a paradise in Eden towards the east*, and placed in it a visible and perceptible *tree of life*, so that one tasting of the fruit by bodily teeth would obtain life, and again that one could partake of *good and evil* by chewing what was received from the tree there?[6]

What historical-critical scholar today would not agree with Origen here? The passage is clearly meant to be read figuratively, not as history per Antiochene exegesis.

On the other hand, the precise manner in which an Alexandrian might allegorically interpret a passage could raise some eyebrows. It does seem at times that the allegorists simply find whatever they want in a text by what Harnack would deride as "biblical alchemy." One of Origen's most famous allegorical interpretations is found in his treatment of Jesus's parable of the Good Samaritan. Although this passage is already a parable—that is, not to be taken literally as the description of a historical event, but rather a story with a deeper underlying message—Origen proceeds to thoroughly allegorize it beyond its "literal" sense. The man overtaken by thieves is Adam, the Samaritan is Christ, the donkey is Christ's body, etc. While such an interpretation may be theologically "correct" and the story may provide a nice analogy to the story of salvation history, I would argue that none of this is what the text is actually saying. This is raw eisegesis that is far removed from the point of Jesus's parable, which is a further explication of the commandment to love your neighbor as yourself (Luke 10:27–29).

Allegorical interpretation can be used to make texts that seem rather irrelevant to us more meaningful by providing a contemporary application. Such was the method of the *pesharim* at Qumran. Pesher Nahum (4Q169), for example, takes the words of the seventh-century prophet and applies them to events of the first century BC. A portion of the text reads:

> Whither the lion goes, there is the lion's cub, [with none to disturb it] [Nah 2:11b].

> [Interpreted, this concerns Deme]trius king of Greece who sought, on the counsel of those who seek smooth things, to enter Jerusalem. [But God did not permit the city to be delivered] into the hands of the kings of Greece,

---

6. Origen, *De principiis*, ed. and trans. John Behr, *On First Principles: A Reader's Edition* (Oxford: Oxford University Press, 2019), 4.3.1.

from the time of Antiochus until the coming of the rulers of the Kittim. But then she shall be trampled under their feet.... (fragments 3-4, col. I, 1-4)[7]

In Nahum's prophecy, the lion was a poetic reference to the king of Assyria who once did as he pleased but whose preying on others is about to end. The author of the *pesher* is little concerned with such ancient history and so applies the text by means of allegory to more contemporary figures. The figures referenced are probably the Seleucid King Demetrius III (95-88 BC) who attacked Jerusalem, Antiochus IV (175-164 BC) who plundered and profaned the Jerusalem Temple, and the Romans (Kittim) who first appeared in Judea under Pompey and his lieutenants in 64 BC.

As with Origen's allegorical interpretation of the Good Samaritan, few would argue that Pesher Nahum's interpretation lies within the literal sense of the book of the Prophet Nahum. It is in keeping with the spirit of the text, however. Nahum's oracle against the arrogant and predatory king of Assyria can rightly be applied to similar tyrants and colonizing powers of any age. The Seleucids and the Romans are guilty of actions quite similar to those for which Nahum condemns Assyria. Should we call such an interpretation an example of the spiritual sense? Perhaps more precisely we might even specify it as the tropological or moral sense. Or might it even be seen as the literal sense or intended sense, inasmuch as Nahum's use of imagery (lion and cub) by its very literary nature is open to more than one referent?

When Scripture uses symbolism to communicate its message—as the mythic, poetic, and prophetic genres of Scripture all especially do—does not that very fact give to the literal sense of Scripture an open-ended quality? The author may intend a very particular identification for a specific image; nevertheless, the presentation by means of symbolic imagery gives an openness to the interpretation of a text that a straightforward "literal" account would not have. I will return to some specific examples of this phenomenon later, but first let us turn to the school of Antioch.

Antioch, Historia and Theoria

The Antiochenes reacted quite vehemently against the allegorical excesses of Alexandria. Many moderns, including myself, would see this reaction as justified inasmuch as unrestrained allegorical exegesis quickly devolves into pure eisegesis. If a given interpreter can find whatever he wishes in a particular text,

---

7. Geza Vermes, *The Dead Sea Scrolls in English*, 4th ed. (Sheffield: Sheffield Academic, 1995), 337.

to what extent is this an act of interpretation at all? If a text can mean anything, it in fact means nothing. But the literal or historical exegesis of Antioch was not entirely free of its own blind spots and limitations, many of which are imitated by contemporary interpreters of Scripture.

I once thought that the popular reductionistic tendency to equate truth with what has happened historically was a post-Enlightenment phenomenon.[8] Yet this tendency may be observed in many of the exegetes of the Antiochene school. At times they seem at pains to argue and insist that everything recounted in the Bible must be historical (as opposed to allegorical) or else it has no validity or significance. Theodore of Mopsuestia, perhaps the most prominent of the exegetes of Antioch, excluded the wisdom books from the Bible precisely because they were neither prophecy nor history. He considered anything that was not historical to be "pagan fables" and "fictions."[9] For Theodore it was important to maintain that Scripture was a true history of events. Therefore, when he cannot demonstrate such history, he is liable to dismiss the text as non-scriptural. Conversely, like many a conservative scholar today, he and his fellow Antiochenes have a tendency to argue for the historicity of a text even when the historical nature of the text is dubious at best.

The Antiochenes insist that Scripture is a true history of events. This insistence on the historical reality of biblical revelation extends even to passages of Scripture that no critical scholar today would regard as historical. A good

---

8. Much of it does seem to be a reaction to modern historical criticism in the post-Enlightenment world. The overemphasis on truth as historical truth can be found in some of the reactionary claims of the Pontifical Biblical Commission in its early years, as it sought to refute the attacks of a historical criticism that was still very much attached to Rationalist presuppositions at odds with orthodox Christian faith. Tendentious or exaggerated claims about what is historical in the Bible (especially in Genesis) continue to be found in many conservative Catholic commentators of more recent years, especially in more popular works (e.g. Scott Hahn, Curtis Mitch, and Dennis Walters, *Genesis: with Introduction, Commentary, and Notes*, rev. standard version, 2nd Catholic ed. [San Francisco: Ignatius, 2010]; John Bergsma and Brant Pitre, *A Catholic Introduction to the Bible*, vol. 1, *The Old Testament* [San Francisco: Ignatius, 2018]). This seems to be something of a reaction against historical-minimalist scholars who question and downplay what is historical in Scripture (e.g. the Jesus Seminar) by going to the other extreme of historical maximalism. It may also be due to the importation of a tendency toward biblical literalism by converts from Evangelical Christianity to Catholicism. History certainly is important for a historical religion like Christianity, but that admission should not warrant an excessive zeal to attempt to find history even where it is not present in Scripture. One might contrast the balanced and measured approach of *Sancta Mater Ecclesia* (1964) with the extreme polemical positions of the early Pontifical Biblical Commission on questions of historical truth in Scripture.

9. Theodore of Mopsuestia, *In Jobum* (PG 66:697–98). The book of Job is dismissed as full of "*paganis fabulis*" and "*figmenta*."

example may be seen in the polemic against Alexandrian "spiritual interpretations" of Genesis. In his commentary on Galatians, Theodore of Mopsuestia writes of his opponents: "They claim that Adam is not Adam, paradise is not paradise, the serpent not the serpent. I should like to tell them this: If they make history serve their own ends, they will have no history left."[10] This is typical of the Antiochene response to Alexandria. When Origen and his followers interpret allegorically, they are claiming that a "thing" in Scripture is not what is plainly stated but something else. In so doing, they deny the historical existence of these allegorized things. What Theodore says is correct. For Origen, as for Philo and other allegorists, there is (as we have seen) no garden and no tree, and it would be absurd to attempt to read this literally. For Theodore and the Antiochenes, the historical reality of what is narrated in Scripture is non-negotiable.

Just as an Alexandrian could give a literal interpretation when warranted, so too the Antiochenes venture beyond mere history in their own interpretations. But they distinguish their own spiritual interpretations from those of Alexandria by referring to them as *theoria* (better translated into English as "contemplation" instead of "theory") rather than *allegoria*. While the Alexandrians used *theoria* synonymously with *allegoria*, the Antiochenes used it for a meaning beyond the literal yet grounded in and not denying the literal sense. The relationship between *historia* and *theoria* at Antioch is somewhat similar to the distinction between the literal and allegorical senses of Scripture at Alexandria. However, the connection of *theoria* to the literal sense is much tighter than Alexandrian allegory. It insists that the literal sense is real and not just a symbol for something else (so there was a tree and a garden). It further insists that the deeper meaning (*theoria*) is also intended by the author, so that there is something of a double meaning on the level that Meyer refers to as the intended sense of Scripture.

Although modern historical-critical scholarship has much more affinity with the school of Antioch than with that of Alexandria, there are exceptions to this rule. As we saw in Origen's interpretation of the story of Eden, his exegesis is more in line with contemporary scholarship than that of an Antiochene like Theodore who insists on the literal historicity of the narrative of Adam and Eve in the garden of Eden.[11] Among the areas where modern scholarship differs

---

10. Theodore of Mopsuestia, Commentary on Galatians 4:22-31, cited in in Karlfried Froehlich, *Biblical Interpretation in the Early Church*, SECT (Philadelphia: Fortress, 1984), 97.

11. There are of course modern outliers of a fundamentalist bent who insist on a literal and historical reading of all biblical narrative. Theodore and the Antiochenes might be excused on

from both Alexandria and Antioch is in its discernment between what is historical, and ought to be read as such, and what is figurative and therefore open to a more allegorical, or otherwise nonliteral, approach. It must be noted that this is not a new concept. As we saw at the very dawn of allegorical interpretation of Scripture, Philo argued that it is the specific text of Scripture that suggests to us whether allegory is appropriate or not. Origen himself, the master of allegory, often insisted on the literal meaning of biblical passages. He writes that "the passages that are true on the level of the narrative are much more numerous than those which are woven with a purely spiritual meaning."[12] Nevertheless, by the sober standards of modernity, the frequent flights of allegorical fancy found in Alexandria seem both excessive and arbitrary. On the other hand, the Antiochene insistence on historicity goes far beyond what is tenable today.

Toward a New Appraisal of What is Literal

The close connection between *historia* and *theoria* at Antioch can help us to appreciate that a text can have more than one meaning on the level of the intended sense, or what I would even dare to call the literal level. Biblical narrative and biblical poetry both frequently employ ambiguity or multiple meanings. Perhaps we err in too quickly characterizing one or more of these meanings as allegorical or spiritual. The prevalence of ambiguity and polyvalence in biblical Hebrew is attested both by the wide range of translational choices that are made on certain biblical texts and by the theological debates that texts often generate. One translation will capture one dimension of what is present in the literal sense of the text, while another translation will pick up on another aspect. One interpretation might catch a glimpse of some truth the text wishes to communicate, while another perceives a different but equally present truth. A few examples of rather famous texts will help to illustrate this point.

The Imago Dei in Genesis 1:27

While writing an article on Genesis 1:27 and the meaning of "the image of God" in this passage, I was struck by the volume of literature that had already been written on this question and by the wide variety of responses that the question

---

this point, given the limitations of their historical knowledge. Modern biblical literalism, however, is an indefensible and untenable position given the state of our historical knowledge today. As *The Interpretation of the Bible in the Church* so aptly put it, fundamentalist interpretation is an invitation to "intellectual suicide."

12. *De principiis* 4.3.4 (trans. Behr, 268).

had generated.[13] Some argued that this phrase referred to the relational nature of human beings.[14] Others argued that "there is no answer to be found" to the question of the phrase's meaning.[15] Others confidently asserted that it refers only to the function of ruling.[16] Although it rarely comes up in contemporary exegetical debates, one could also include Aquinas's assertion that the image of God's principal signification is our intellectual nature.[17] For the most part every interpretation that has been made has been theologically and anthropologically correct in itself. The only real question is whether the text is actually asserting this or not. It is my contention that a close reading of the biblical text justifies more than one interpretation. Indeed, a careful analysis of the text reveals that it has a quite deliberate double meaning.

Without attempting to summarize all of the arguments made in the aforementioned article on Genesis 1:27, I would like to highlight two very significant points. First of all, the very poetry of the verse (a rather typical Hebrew tricolon) points to more than one meaning of the phrase "image of God" as applied to human beings, by the way the Hebrew *adam* is differentiated with first a singular and then a plural pronoun in the second and third lines. Secondly, the broader literary structure of the Priestly account of creation gives a very strong indication of a doubly intended sense to the verse. Human beings, created in God's image, are called in Genesis 1:28 to 1) "be fruitful and multiply, and fill the earth" as well as to 2) "subdue it; and have dominion." This parallels exactly the divine activity in the six days of creation by which God exercises dominion on days 1–3 and brings forth life on days 4–6.[18] To argue for one meaning as the literal (or historical-critical) sense of the text over and against the other is to miss the polyvalent sense that the text quite literally has.[19]

---

13. Paul Niskanen, "The Poetics of Adam: The Creation of *Adam* in the Image of *Elohim*," *Journal of Biblical Literature* 128 (Fall 2009): 417–36. Much of the varied and contradictory history of interpretation is summed up in Gunnlauger A. Jónsson, *The Image of God: Genesis 1:26–28 in a Century of Old Testament Research*, trans. Lorraine Svendsen, ConBOT 26 (Lund: Almqvist & Wiksell International, 1988).

14. Karl Barth, *Church Dogmatics*, vol. III/1, trans. Harold Knight et al. (Edinburgh: T&T Clark, 1960), 183–84.

15. James Barr, "The Image of God in the Book of Genesis: A Study of Terminology," *Bulletin of the John Rylands Library* 51 (1968): 11–26, at 13.

16. Phyllis Bird, "'Male and Female He Created Them': Gen 1:27b in the Context of the Priestly Account of Creation," *Harvard Theological Review* 74 (1981): 129–59.

17. *Summa Theologiae* I, q. 93, a. 4.

18. Michael D. Guinan, *The Pentateuch*, MBS 1 (Collegeville, MN: Liturgical Press, 1990), 25.

19. This is what Bird explicitly does in her article, arguing for the exercise of dominion to the exclusion of any creative/procreative capacity.

When Scripture introduces terminology that it does not directly define, or metaphors or imagery that it does not explicitly explain, it may be noted that the very language and literary modes of expression found in Scripture actually invite an interpretive dialogue with the reader. Note that this does not mean that the text means whatever the reader wishes it to mean, nor does it suggest that all interpretations are equally valid or even valid at all. The intended sense governs meaning, but it does not necessarily limit meaning to one precise literal signification.

The Name of God in Exodus 3:14

Another intriguing and theologically dense passage is the revelation of God's name as "I am who I am" (*ehyeh asher ehyeh*) in Exodus 3:14. The difficulties of translation/interpretation and the variety of opinions as to the meaning conveyed by the revelation of this name are many. A brief summary of this variety might note the following. Aquinas understood by this verse that the existence of God is his very essence.[20] Many contemporary biblical scholars argue for a causative sense of the Hebrew that would identify God as the Creator.[21] Others point to the tenseless nature of Hebrew verbs and suggest that the imperfect aspect of *ehyeh* in this context points to a promise of God's continued presence in the future (compare also with God's response to Moses in Exodus 3:12).[22] Finally, the enigmatic nature of God's tautological response is "a Semitic idiom . . . employed where either the means, or the desire, to be more explicit does not exist."[23] So in effect, God's response could be translated with a Brooklyn accent as "Who wants to know?"

It appears once more that there are a number of possible understandings of the verse. Each is theologically correct in itself. Namely, with reference to the four interpretations briefly sketched above, God is Absolute Being, Creator, with us, and mystery. Once more, being theologically correct does not mean that this interpretation is either supported or intended by the text. Without

---

20. *Summa Theologiae* I, q. 13, a. 11.

21. So the footnote on Exod 3:14 in the *New Oxford Annotated Bible with the Apocryphal/Deuterocanonical Books*, ed. Bruce Metzger and Roland Murphy (New York: Oxford University Press, 1991): "YHWH is a third person form and may mean 'He causes to be.'"

22. R. W. L. Moberly, *The God of the Old Testament* (Grand Rapids: Baker, 2020), 71. Moberly writes: "The nonuse of the verb 'to be' in present-tense statements of identity, together with the straightforward use of *'ehyeh* as 'I will be' in Exodus 3:12, leads many to conclude that the sense of the repeated *'ehyeh* in 3:14a should be in the future tense."

23. S. R. Driver, *Notes on the Hebrew Text and the Topography of the Books of Samuel* (Oxford: Clarendon, 1913), 185–86.

attempting an evaluation or judgment of each of these interpretations, I would simply note that the text is rather ambiguous and open-ended. It lends itself to more than one understanding, and not all of the proposed interpretations are mutually exclusive. R. W. L. Moberly, commenting on the ambiguity in the Hebrew verb, concludes that "translating *'ehyeh 'asher 'ehyeh* either with the future-tense 'I WILL BE WHO/WHAT/AS I WILL BE' or with the present-tense 'I AM WHO/WHAT/AS I AM' seems possible, as the philology is open-ended."[24]

Exodus 3:14, therefore, gives a good example of the inherent ambiguities that often reside in the Hebrew text of the Old Testament. We are often forced to make a choice in meaning when translating, but it would be a mistake to argue that this choice represents the actual literal sense over and against any options that we have not chosen. Rather the literal sense of the text is open-ended and our translations betray the fuller meaning of the original text by restricting possible meanings. For a final example, we now turn to a text employing prophetic symbolism.

The Servant of YHWH in Second Isaiah

Another theologically heavy and hotly contested text is the series of passages in Second Isaiah that refer to the Servant of YHWH.[25] As with the previous theologically significant yet exegetically obscure passages discussed, the amount of literature on the Servant of YHWH passages is tremendous.[26] Rather than attempting a detailed analysis of the many proposed identifications of the Servant of YHWH, I would like to point to two conclusions drawn by Paul Hanson. First of all he notes: "Although dozens of candidates have been advanced as the person or group designated as the Servant, the matter is as confused as ever."[27] Far from despairing over this gloomy state of affairs, Hanson goes on to describe what he terms "a pleasant discovery: The meaning of the Servant passages, far from being withheld from the reader by the opacity of symbolism, unfolds precisely within the multivalence of that symbolism."[28]

---

24. Moberly, *The God of the Old Testament*, 71.

25. References to YHWH's servant show up as early as Isa 41:8, where YHWH refers to Israel as "my servant." The figure is most prominent, however, in the four extended "songs" of Isa 42:1-4; 49:1-7; 50:4-11; and 52:13-53:12.

26. H. H. Rowley (*The Servant of the Lord: and Other Essays on the Old Testament*, 2nd ed., rev. [Oxford: Blackwell, 1965]) provides a brief overview of some of the many proposals, which include the nation of Israel, the prophet himself, an unknown martyr, Zerubbabel, Jehoiachin, Moses, etc.

27. Paul D. Hanson, *Isaiah 40-66*, Int. (Louisville: John Knox, 1995), 41.

28. Hanson, *Isaiah 40-66*, 41.

Just as the Hebrew language often lends itself to multiple interpretations of a text through its many ambiguities and nuances, so too many biblical literary genres (such as poetry, prophecy, and apocalyptic) lend themselves to a variety of meanings by their use of symbolic imagery. It is worth emphasizing that such meanings are not (or at least not entirely) extrinsic to the text. They are not allegorical impositions or eisegetical intrusions as was the case with Origen's interpretation of the parable of the Good Samaritan. This is not to say that the intended sense necessarily foresees every possible identification of the Servant in the imaginations of future readers. Rather, it is the claim that the author, through the use of symbolism and imagery, is inviting a reflective response from both the original audience and all future audiences of the text. In other words, the open-ended nature of the symbolism is the intended sense of the text, or we might even call it the literal sense.[29]

Father Kevin Zilverberg, in his 2022 Ireland Lecture, nicely highlighted the fact that when a text's genre involves symbolic imagery the multivalence that results is at the level of literal interpretation. Speaking on the reinterpretation of Jeremiah's "seventy years" in Daniel 9 as "seventy weeks of years," he says:

> The human author's cryptic language of his genre opens the possibility of multiple fulfillments of the text's literal sense throughout history. As I often remind my students, the Catholic terminology of the "literal sense" of the text takes into account the genre employed, already at this basic level of interpretation before pursuing spiritual senses. Daniel's literal sense already lends itself to metahistorical interpretations, which, in turn, provide a strong basis for spiritual interpretations in the patristic spirit.[30]

With regard to the Servant of YHWH, it is indisputable that the author intends more than one meaning according to the literal sense of the text. This can be seen most clearly in the second of the so-called Servant Songs in Isaiah 49:1–7. In v. 3 the Servant is clearly identified as Israel: "You are my servant, Israel, in whom I will be glorified." Yet a mere two verses later in v. 5 the servant is distinct from Israel, for the Lord has formed his servant "to bring Jacob back to him, and that Israel might be gathered to him." The imagery shifts back and forth between referring explicitly to Israel and referring to an individual

---

29. This is keeping with Aquinas's definition of the literal sense as that sense intended by the author.

30. Fr. Kevin Zilverberg, "Daniel Reinterprets Jeremiah's 'Seventy Years': A Biblical Interpretive Trajectory up to the Present Day," Archbishop Ireland Memorial Library Lecture, University of St. Thomas, St. Paul, MN, April 25, 2022.

prophetic figure. Clearly the author has more than one thought as to the "identity" of the Servant of YHWH.

In the subsequent use and interpretation of the Servant of YHWH passages in the New Testament, one notes a polyvalent understanding there as well. While each of the four main passages is quoted or alluded to in the Gospels as being fulfilled or realized in the person and mission of Christ (Matt 12:17–21; Luke 2:32; Matt 26:67; Matt 8:17), the Servant of YHWH is also invoked in the New Testament as referring to the Christian disciple when Paul applies Isaiah 49:6 to himself and Barnabas (Acts 13:47). The multivalent interpretation of the Servant of YHWH in the New Testament is further highlighted when one considers how a unified literary work (Luke-Acts) can apply the same Servant of YHWH text (Isa 49:6) to both Jesus (Luke 2:32) and to his followers (Acts 13:47).[31]

Conclusion

From these three brief examples, it can be seen that the interpretation of Old Testament texts is frequently not a simple and straightforward task. The ambiguities and multiple meanings that can be found, both at the level of language (vocabulary, grammar, and syntax) and at the level of genre (especially those that employ symbolism, such as myth, poetry, prophecy, and apocalyptic), generate complex and polyvalent meanings in the text. Since the patristic era, multiple meanings of the text have often been sorted into the categories of historical and allegorical, or literal and spiritual (with the further subdivisions of the latter). But if such meanings are in fact intended by the author through the text, they pertain to what Meyer terms the intended sense. Furthermore, these multiple intended meanings fit what Aquinas and the Catholic tradition refer to by the literal sense.

There is no denying that Alexandrian allegory has a track record of eisegetical excesses. Nevertheless, when approaching a text that is densely symbolic, Origen and his fellow Alexandrians could give a far more accurate, and one might claim a far more "literal," interpretation than their Antiochene counterparts. Antioch provided a great corrective to Alexandria by grounding the senses of Scripture in the literal. Yet, in their overinsistence on the historical nature of the Old Testament texts, they could stray into a naïve literalism and

---

31. I do not intend to weigh in on scholarly debates over the authorship of Luke and Acts. I would simply note that the two books clearly present themselves as a two-volume work by their respective prefaces (Luke 1:1–4; Acts 1:1–20).

historicism that would rival that of many a fundamentalist today. Both ancient and contemporary literalists, who insist on such things as a 6,000-year-old universe based upon a "literal" reading of Scripture, are actually missing the literal sense of Scripture. The interpretive task is to discern what the intended meaning of a text is. Applying but one framework, be it history or allegory, to the multiple and varied Old Testament texts might be a simpler approach, but it is inadequate. One must allow oneself to be guided by the text itself. And one must be open to the possibility that the literal sense of Scripture may in fact be polyvalent.

CHAPTER 3

Theological Riches from Sound Exegesis—Hearing the Full Range of Notes:[1] Typology Valued

Joseph Briody

Introduction

Easter 2022 saw an opinion piece in the *New York Times* recommending God be "passed over" because of his slaying of the Egyptian firstborn on that first Passover.[2] Blame for a violent world was levelled against the scriptural presentation of a violent God. It was a reminder that Scripture is never merely an academic pursuit, nor is it ever out of season. What texts originally meant—and mean for us—matters greatly. This is the concern of this paper. How best do we move from what texts originally meant to what they mean for us?

Understanding the past is not enough for a text that purports to speak with the voice of God. The Old Testament text has what Brueggemann calls a "generative power" that lies beyond its basic scope of intention: "The text refuses

---

1. The title is a centonization of phrases used by Brevard Childs where he describes typology as an "extension of the literary sense" and hearing "the full range of notes." It also paraphrases the suggestion of Pope Pius XII that sound exegesis pays rich theological dividends. See Brevard S. Childs, "Psalm 8 in the Context of the Christian Canon," *Interpretation* 23 (1969): 20–31, at 31; Brevard S. Childs, *Biblical Theology of the Old and New Testaments: Theological Reflection on the Christian Bible* (Minneapolis: Fortress, 1993), 13; Pope Pius XII, Encyclical On Promoting Biblical Studies *Divino afflante Spiritu* (September 30, 1943) (Washington, DC: National Catholic Welfare Conference, 1943), §27.

2. Shalom Auslander, "In This Time of War, I Propose We Give Up God," *New York Times*, April 15, 2022, https://www.nytimes.com/2022/04/15/opinion/passover-giving-up-god.html. A meaningful response was given by Jeffrey Salkin, "Hey, New York Times—Leave My God Alone!," religionnews.com, Religion News Service, April 18, 2022, https://religionnews.com/2022/04/18/times-auslander-god/.

to stay past."³ The Word of God still speaks. The emergent theological-spiritual understanding may be even more urgent and important in shaping lives than an academic knowledge of the historical-literal sense. Restoration of the past to the Bible through critical scholarship should not relegate the Bible to the past.⁴ However, it is also true that the spiritual sense builds on the literal-historical sense. Important here is the need for an authentic biblical theology, that is, an openness in our time to these texts saying something about God and his relationship with us. Unless the reach of exegesis extends to theology, Scripture remains a text like any other—an important text, but not "the soul of theology."⁵ The Alexandrians and the Antiochenes appreciated that the text was not just from the past. It continued to speak and in it God continues to speak. There is a movement from letter to spirit.

Continuity, movement, and direction can be shown between the emergence of texts in the biblical period and the interpretation or re-actualization of these texts in later times. This can be traced in the Bible itself and in the Church's ongoing reflection on biblical texts in the living tradition, especially in the Fathers of the Church and the liturgy. Typology emerges as a model for such interpretation.

In this paper I make the case that typology is a model for Catholic biblical theology. The Bible was assembled as theology and is best read as such. I argue that the Deuteronomistic History provides a model of continued theological reflection. From the Deuteronomistic History, the theme of kingship and its reconceptualization is chosen to illustrate the theological depth of the biblical text itself. We see this in the decline of Saul and rise of David, with the failure of kingship in general, and with the gradual idealization of the figure of David who becomes a type of a future, perfect, king. Hundreds of years before the New Testament was written, the Deuteronomistic theologians had already idealized the figure of David and established him as much more than the mere mortal who sinned. Already in the Deuteronomistic History, the inner direction of the text is opened to fulfilment in a future Son of David. Preserving the integrity of the Old Testament through typology, Jesus Christ emerges as the measure

---

3. Walter Brueggemann, *Theology of the Old Testament* (Minneapolis: Fortress, 1997), 732–33.

4. Paraphrasing Jon Douglas Levenson, *The Hebrew Bible, the Old Testament, and Historical Criticism: Jews and Christians in Biblical Studies*, 1st ed. (Louisville: Westminster John Knox, 1993), 98 and 123.

5. Benedict XVI, Post-Synodal Apostolic Exhortation On the Word of God in the Life and Mission of the Church *Verbum Domini* (September 30, 2010) (Rome: Libreria Editrice Vaticana), §35.

of Scripture. Old Testament meaning is extended in a direction sympathetic to and present in it. In this way, the sacred text gives up its inner direction or thrust. The ancient reality is opened up to the fuller truth. God speaks through what the text means. With typology, Old Testament integrity is preserved, yet a pathway is opened up for continuity and newness.

Using the Deuteronomistic example of kingship, I will argue that typology preserves the significance of personages, events, and texts, while broadening their application and range of fulfilment. First, however, it will be helpful to sketch the bare bones of allegory and typology.

Allegory, Typology, *Sensus Plenior*

Philo of Alexandria, writing in the first half of the first century AD, interpreted Scripture using allegory, a method well known in Alexandria.[6] Philo stressed "the literality of scripture, whose meaning is to be teased out through allegorical exegesis." This involved the search for "a deeper meaning that transcends the literal sense."[7] It is important to note that for Philo and his allegorical exegesis the starting point for deeper reflection on the meaning of the text was "the external, literal meaning of words."[8] This implies that the text could not just mean anything at all or have an arbitrary sense imposed on it. In Philo, we glimpse remotely the later exegetical principle that the spiritual should somehow flow from the literal. Indeed, Philo of Alexandria "must be seen as the true father of the genre of philological commentary on the books of the Bible.... In this way he laid the groundwork for the form of textual exegesis that would be taken up and further developed by Origen."[9] For Origen of Alexandria (AD 185–253), Scripture interpretation moved from letter to spirit, from narrative meaning to allegorical meaning.[10] Origen, then, "epitomizes spiritual interpretation and the methodology that sees theology as wisdom gained through meditation on Scripture."[11]

---

6. The writings of Philo were transmitted only by Christians: otherwise, they would have been lost. Konrad Schmid and Jens Schröter, *The Making of the Bible: From the First Fragments to Sacred Scripture*, trans. Peter Lewis (Cambridge, MA: Belknap Press of Harvard University Press, 2021), 226.
7. Schmid and Schröter, *The Making of the Bible*, 177.
8. Schmid and Schröter, *The Making of the Bible*, 177.
9. Schmid and Schröter, *The Making of the Bible*, 181.
10. Rowan A. Greer, "The Christian Bible and Its Interpretation," 107–203 in James L. Kugel and Rowan A. Greer, *Early Biblical Interpretation* (Philadelphia: Westminster, 1986), 179.
11. For a good summary see Peter S. Williamson, *Catholic Principles for Interpreting Scripture: A Study of the Pontifical Biblical Commission's* The Interpretation of the Bible in the Church (Rome: Pontifical Biblical Institute, 2001), 196.

Origen was criticized by the Antiochenes, concerned that his allegory would abolish the significance of events recorded in Scripture. The Antiochenes proposed typology instead.[12] Typology sees an anticipation of aspects of the mystery of Christ in Old Testament people, events, practices, accounts, texts, e.g., the great flood is a type of baptism; Adam is a type of Christ; David is a type of Christ, etc. What the Old Testament describes is seen as fulfilled fully in Christ. The connection involved in typology clings to the Old Testament description and language, while expanding or deepening it and so, with typology, the concern of this paper, "one can speak of a meaning that is truly scriptural."[13] There is continuity and newness or fulfilment.

With the Enlightenment, there was a downplaying of allegory, often seen as arbitrary, alien, subjective, and deprecating the role of history. This downplaying had some value. While Philo took philology seriously and allegory was used to spiritual advantage in Alexandria, Brevard Childs pointed out, "The problem with traditional Christian allegory was its refusal to hear the Old Testament's witness, and to change its semantic level in order to bring it into conformity with the New Testament."[14]

With the Enlightenment, there was also a downplaying of typology. Typology, however, respects the integrity of the Old Testament and its literal sense. Brevard Childs noted that typology, in contrast to allegory, was viewed as "an extension of the literal sense of historical events . . . and served to signal the correspondence between redemptive events in a single history of salvation."[15] Childs's definition is valuable. Typology is an unforced way of preserving the inner unity, continuity, and coherence of both Old and New Testaments, while respecting the witness and integrity of both.[16] It is valuable in Christian usage. Typology does not entirely crush allegory. It grounds allegory. Antioch grounds Alexandria. The connection with the literal sense grounds the spiritual sense.

---

12. Greer, "The Christian Bible and Its Interpretation," 181.

13. Pontifical Biblical Commission, *The Interpretation of the Bible in the Church* (Rome: Libreria Editrice Vaticana, 1993), §II.B.2. The document gives the example of the voice of Abel crying out (Gen 4:10; Heb 11:4; 12:24).

14. Childs, *Biblical Theology*, 78

15. Childs, *Biblical Theology*, 13.

16. Childs cautions that while in the Christian Bible Old and New Testaments have been joined, this does not mean that the integrity of each has been destroyed. The Old Testament still remains distinct from the New Testament: "It is promise, not fulfillment, yet its voice continues to sound and it has not been stilled by the fulfillment of the promise." It has its own integrity. "It must be heard on its own terms." Childs, *Biblical Theology*, 77–78.

The *sensus plenior* fits well with typology. It is the perception of a fuller or wider sense to the text that may not, at the time of writing, have been fully appreciated by the human author. It, too, is a legitimate extension of the meaning as a sense not merely imposed on the text, but later perceived, drawn out from the literal sense, and seen by Christians as intended by God in light of the mystery of Christ (e.g., Isa 7:14 and Matt 1:23). Allegory, typology, and the *sensus plenior* are various stages or levels of insight along the interpretative spectrum. The more these are rooted in the literal sense, the closer they are to the authentic meaning. They attest that Scripture has a message for us, that God continues to speak, and that the Bible offers not just a foundational history but also a theology.

Biblical Theology

Pope Pius XII proposed a synthesis, "a happy and fruitful union" between the ancient authors with their "spiritual sweetness" (the Fathers) and "the great erudition and mature knowledge of the modern," and this is with a view to "new progress in the never fully explored and inexhaustible field of the Divine Letters."[17] He proposed "a deeper and more accurate interpretation of Sacred Scripture."[18] For Pius XII, St. Jerome's efforts to bring out the literal sense of the psalms furnished a fine example of the search for the full meaning of a text—literal and theological—and how, as the pope noted, the text provides its own theological richness.[19] The Word of God does not need "artificial devices." It is already "rich in original meaning" and "endowed with a divine power."[20] With sound exegesis, the theological riches emerge unforced from the inspired text. This is hardly surprising since the Bible was assembled for theological motives.[21] Jewish and Christian scholars generally agree that the Hebrew Bible was written for *theological* ends.

---

17. Pope Pius XII, *Divino afflante Spiritu*, §30.
18. Pope Pius XII, *Divino afflante Spiritu*, §31.
19. Pope Pius XII, *Divino afflante Spiritu*, §31. He gives the example of Fathers of the Church struggling to interpret the first chapters of Genesis, without, presumably, comparative accounts of creation from surrounding cultures. Pius XII also refers to Jerome's attempt to translate the Psalms so that the literal sense—what is clearly expressed by the words themselves—might emerge.
20. Pope Pius XII, *Divino afflante Spiritu*, §27.
21. Some scholars like Bernhard Duhm (1847–1928) pointed out that the canon of the Hebrew Bible was assembled by theologians. Konrad Schmid, *Is There Theology in the Hebrew Bible?*, CSHB 4, trans. Peter Altmann (Winona Lake, IN: Eisenbrauns, 2015), 71.

The Biblical Theology movement of the 1940s sought to articulate not just what biblical texts meant originally (the historical or literal sense), but also what they mean theologically. This Biblical Theology approach had promise: the Bible was written as theology and is read most profoundly as such. In the mid-twentieth century, historical-critical work was carried out with a view to theological gains, holding together critical practice and theological interest. Such work was a uniting factor among scholars of different approaches. John Collins notes that "historical criticism remains the most satisfactory context for biblical theology," providing a "broad framework for scholarly dialogue."[22] He notes that historical criticism sets limits to the range of what a text may mean in a particular context. This does not mean that a text can have only one valid meaning. "Historical criticism, properly understood, does not . . . claim that the original historical context exhausts the meaning of a text." It "tries to set limits to the meaning of a text, so that it cannot mean just anything at all."[23] Collins cites Bultmann's belief that historical reconstruction presumes Scripture has something to say to us today.[24] "There are limits to the range of valid interpretations, but there is also a legitimate diversity of ways in which the Bible can be read."[25] Jon D. Levenson explains how Jewish and Christian scholars can work together in pursuit of the historical and literary sense of Scripture.[26] They can agree on the literal or historical meaning of textual units; however, when it comes to the broader literary setting or canon, the traditions part company.[27]

Put simply, on the one hand, the literal-historical sense does not exhaust the meaning, significance, or wealth of a text. On the other hand, the spiritual/theological sense should emerge from the literal sense. The biblical text refuses to stay in the past and has a generative quality enabling it to speak anew. Brevard Childs sums this up well in a profound statement that could well be axiomatic:

---

22. John J. Collins, *Encounters with Biblical Theology* (Minneapolis: Fortress, 2005), 22.
23. Collins, *Encounters*, 2.
24. Collins, *Encounters*, 3.
25. Collins, *Encounters*, 77.
26. Levenson, *Hebrew Bible*, 80.
27. For the Christian, Levenson observes, Romans and Galatians could be viewed as part of the wider canonical context of the Abraham story, but not for the Jewish scholar (Levenson, *Hebrew Bible*, 80–81). For the Jewish and Christian scholar, the study of the Hebrew Bible takes place in the context of a broader oral tradition. See Leo G. Perdue, *Reconstructing Old Testament Theology: After the Collapse of History*, Overtures to Biblical Theology (Minneapolis: Fortress, 2005), 199. An example would be the Catholic understanding of Sacred Tradition.

The challenge of the Christian interpreter in our day is to hear the full range of notes within all of Scripture, to wrestle with the theological implication of this biblical witness, and above all, to come to grips with the agony of our age before a living God who still speaks.[28]

That God continued to speak, even as history unfolded and circumstances changed, was the firm conviction of deuternomistic theologians.

The Deuteronomistic History: Biblical Theology Unfolding

From Pius XII's assertion that the text itself is rich in theological meaning, I would like to illustrate more concretely the link between the literal-historical and the spiritual-theological, especially with the interpretive value of typology. Interpretation includes allowing the "salvific power of Scripture" to shine forth brightly in our time.[29] To paraphrase Pius XII, the text is already disposed to theological interpretation and calls for it. I will take the example of the Deuteronomistic History, indicating its theological depth. This famous history has its own connection with the pontificate of Pius XII.

The year 1943 was important for biblical studies. Two publications bore significantly on biblical interpretation in the academic and ecclesial communities.[30] The 1943 document of Pius XII (*Divino afflante Spiritu*) gave new impetus to biblical studies in the ecclesial context, mentioning both literary and historical criticism and highlighting the "art of criticism."[31]

It was also in 1943 that Martin Noth first published his *Überlieferungsgeschichtliche Studien*, arguably the most influential work in Old Testament studies in the twentieth century.[32] In it, Noth proposed what is now called the "Deuteronomistic History." The Deuteronomistic History is viewed as a distinctive and unified literary narrative stretching from Joshua to 2 Kings. It

---

28. Childs, "Psalm 8," 31.

29. Adapted from Ben F. Meyer, *Critical Realism and the New Testament*, PTMS 17 (Allison Park, PA: Pickwick, 1989), 33.

30. I make this point in Joseph Briody, "The Rejection of Saul in First Samuel 13:7b-15 and 15:1–35: Synchrony, Diachrony, Theology" (STD diss., Boston College, 2020), ProQuest Dissertations and Theses, 1.

31. Pope Pius XII, *Divino afflante Spiritu*, especially §§16, 24, 23–25.

32. Martin Noth, *Überlieferungsgeschichtliche Studien*, vol. 1, *Die sammelnden und bearbeitenden Geschichtswerke im Alten Testament*, 2. unveränderte Auflage (Tübingen: M. Niemeyer, 1957). First published in German in 1943. The section on the "Deuteronomistic History" was translated into English as Martin Noth, *The Deuteronomistic History*, 2nd ed., trans. Jane Doull et al., JSOTSup 15 (Sheffield: JSOT Press, 1991).

was compiled and composed in the light of how the law of the Lord given to Moses in the book of Deuteronomy was lived out (or not) in the lives of the people, especially in the lives of their kings. The novelty of Noth's work lay, not so much in seeking redactional layers, as in discovering the literary plan behind the redaction.[33] A literary plan suggests a rationale. The intentional collection, preservation, transmission, expansion, shaping, and coherence of this history—an immense undertaking completed in the sixth century BC—implies purpose. That purpose was to teach about God and life lived before God.

For Noth, this history offers a "clearly defined and strongly emphasized theological interpretation of history."[34] The Deuteronomistic History traces how the relationship between the Lord (YHWH) and Israel was interpreted over an extended time. That history was colored by the exile of 587 BC, with an eye to how present and future life might be lived and built anew in the light of the deuteronomic covenant. It is a history whose overriding concerns are theological. Much of the Deuteronomistic History is "about the role of God in the events of Israel's past," describing "how God was acting or not acting in our midst."[35] Yairah Amit notes that the texts were developed "to educate the readers or listeners and to persuade them to cling to the covenant and obey God's precepts."[36] The deuteronomistic view of history was "governed by the conviction that God had acted in the history of Israel in a visible way" in deeds and words.[37] Awareness of such intentionality on the part of the deuteronomistic editors is important for interpretation. They compiled a purposeful, theological history, seeing it as a "sacred task"— "the act of interpreting God's 'speech' in the events of the past" with lessons to be drawn from it.[38] It is a "theologically motivated" history,[39] "a kind of theological historiography that submits

---

33. Thomas Römer and Albert de Pury, "Deuteronomistic Historiography: History of Research and Related Issues," 24–139 in *Israel Constructs Its History: Deuteronomistic Historiography in Recent Research*, English Language ed., JSOTSup 306, ed. Albert de Pury, Thomas Römer, and Jean-Daniel Macchi (Sheffield: Sheffield Academic, 2000), 47.

34. Noth, *Deuteronomistic History*, 4.

35. Antony F. Campbell, *1 Samuel*, FOTL 7 (Grand Rapids, MI: Eerdmans, 2003), 27.

36. Yairah Amit, *Reading Biblical Narratives* (Minneapolis: Fortress, 2001), 3.

37. Timo Veijola, *Das Königtum in der Beurteilung der deuteronomistischen Historiographie: eine redaktionsgeschichtliche Untersuchung*, AASF B 198 (Helsinki: Suomalainen Tiedeakatemia, 1977), 104. Veijola is summarizing Noth here. The Word of God was the central power of the history, especially clear in prophecy and its sure fulfillment (Veijola, *Das Königtum*, 110).

38. Kugel and Greer, *Early Biblical Interpretation*, 23.

39. Alison L. Joseph, *Portrait of the Kings: The Davidic Prototype in Deuteronomistic Poetics* (Minneapolis: Fortress, 2015), 20.

to religious axioms."[40] Soggin notes the dominance of the "theological" over other concerns in the Deuteronomistic History.[41] It is a *theological* history with a theological message.

In general, biblical authors were not so much interested in reconstructing exactly what had happened as in interpreting and expressing the meaning of events—how "history itself held a sacred message, the unfolding of God's will" and how that meaning gives direction to life.[42] This view of historiography captures well the approach of the Deuteronomistic History, the focus of which is not just the past but also the present and future. It is about God and his action in history, his will expressed in the Torah, and the human response in obedience. The Deuteronomistic History moves effortlessly from its historical-literal concerns to the theological message it seeks to convey. In the history, prophets speak and prophecies are unfailingly realized. It is, after all, also called the Former Prophets. Often, the narrator provides explicit theological reflections, of which 2 Kings 17:7–41 is a fine example. The Deuteronomistic History seeks not only to describe the past but also to give hope of future restoration because it provides the "foundations for faith and life."[43] It is primarily a religious work that seeks to impart a religious message or theology. Even more, a "*covenantal* vision underlies these interests and covenantal ends are served."[44] In compiling their texts, the deuteronomistic historians were purveyors of theological plenty. To overlook the theological in the Deuteronomistic History would be to read it "without attending to the main thing it is about."[45] Much the same could be said, *mutatis mutandis*, of other Scripture texts.

Deuteronomistic Theological Riches

For some, the Deuteronomistic History would have been the last resort in the quest for theological largesse. For a time, Deuteronomistic "Theology" fell

---

40. Walter Dietrich, "The Layer Model of the Deuteronomistic History and the Book of Samuel," 39–65 in *Is Samuel among the Deuteronomists?: Current Views on the Place of Samuel in a Deuteronomistic History*, ed. Cynthia Edenburg and Juha Pakkala (Atlanta: SBL Press, 2013), 59.

41. J. Alberto Soggin, *Introduction to the Old Testament: From Its Origins to the Closing of the Alexandrian Canon*, OTL, rev. ed., trans. John Bowden (Philadelphia: Westminster, 1980), 163.

42. Kugel and Greer, *Early Biblical Interpretation*, 201–2.

43. Noth, *Deuteronomistic History*, 13. He refers especially to the Pentateuchal traditions here.

44. Robert Alter, "How Convention Helps Us Read: The Case of the Bible's Annunciation Type-Scene," *Prooftexts* 3, no. 2 (1983): 115–30, at 116.

45. I borrow the phrase from C. S. Lewis, *Reflections on the Psalms* (Boston: Mariner, 1958, 2012), 3.

out of favor, misunderstood as a stultifying, stifling, overly legalistic ideology. Scholars went, rather, to the earlier writing prophets or to Job for what they imagined were more original, pure, pristine, unfettered, theological insights uncluttered by later layers of legal or cultic baggage. Berhard Duhm, who acknowledged that the canon of the Hebrew Bible was formed by theologians, had little esteem for the deuteronomists. He thought they were "clumsy scribes whose sole obsession was for Mosaic Law."[46] An incomplete and unjust characterization! Rather, the deuteronomists were both faithful and creative—ever-responsive to developing situations, while guarding the YHWH–Israel covenantal relationship expressed in the Law given at Horeb. Rather than being promoters of the systematization or fossilization of earlier vibrant traditions, deuteronomistic editors preserved, reinterpreted, and went beyond the inherited traditions. They responded to new crises by delving deeply into their cherished, God-given tradition, faithfully recalibrating it for later times. Many examples could be taken from Deuteronomistic Theology. One, in particular, stands out. That is kingship. This theme will be used as a specific example of the dynamic theological depth of the biblical text, the continuity between literal and spiritual senses, between Old Testament and New, and between type and antitype.

Here, I would like to show that the "Son of David" typology, realized in Jesus Christ, is already present and developing in the Deuteronomistic History and tending toward deepening and fulfillment.

Reconceptualization of Kingship: Decline of Saul and Idealization of David

Scholars identify several strata of deuteronomistic editing of the biblical text, including the "nomistic" Deuteronomist (abbreviated as DtrN), identified as a later editorial layer of deuteronomistic revision with a particular interest in the observance of the law. For DtrN, renewed fidelity to the law of the Lord was the best and perhaps only response to the exile and its suffering. Ironically, while kingship occupies much of the history, this later DtrN, the focus of which was the law, was the first to draw the remarkable theological conclusion that *"there

---

46. See Römer's summary of Duhm's view in Thomas Römer, *The So-called Deuteronomistic History: A Sociological, Historical, and Literary Introduction* (London: T&T Clark, 2007), 21. See also an account of Duhm's view in Schmid, *Is There Theology In the Hebrew Bible?*, 18. Texts like Job were treasured over other texts by Duhm and others since, in their view, these depicted a *living* relationship with God hidden beneath the overlaid theology of the Hebrew Bible.

should be no human king at all."[47] This insight, "among the most valuable in the theology of DtrN," was neglected in research because of the perceived legal focus of DtrN.[48] This insight of DtrN was, in fact, a dramatic breakthrough, a liberating overturning of monarchical ideology, a purification of theological outlook to which future theology is indebted. The absolutist, royal background of the ancient Near East—especially Assyria, Babylon, and even Israel and Judah—is the context out of which the DtrN view developed.[49] Reflection on this royal model, on the disaster that was kingship, on the exile itself, and greater appreciation of the kingship of the Lord, led deuteronomistic thought to this dramatic conclusion.

This remarkable insight found expression in the accounts of the fall of Saul, the rise of David, and then in the later development of Davidic aspiration, idealization, and theology. What was worst in kingship is present in Saul, though he is not its worst expression (compare with Jeroboam or Manasseh).[50] What was most longed for would be found in an idealized vision of David, projected into the future, and expressive of deuteronomistic obedience and hope, giving rise to a Davidic theology that continued right down to St. Luke's Annunciation scene and much of the New Testament (e.g., Luke 1:69; Acts 13:22-23; cf. Ps 89).

Deuteronomists as Good Theologians

The Deuteronomistic History provides a model of continued theological reflection. An earlier Josianic version of the history (c. 640-609 BC) expressed confidence and hope founded on the unconditional promises of 2 Samuel 7.[51] In its final exilic form, however, the history explains the devastation of 587 BC caused by disobedience. The emphasis shifts to an appeal for repentance and a new obedience. Various redactional levels suggest developing deuteronomistic

---

47. Veijola, *Das Königtum*, 122: "*dass es gar kein menschliches Königtum geben dürfte*" (author's italics). The translation of Veijola's work in these passages is mine.

48. Veijola, *Das Königtum*, 122: "Wenn ich recht sehe, gehört diese Einsicht zu dem Wertvollsten in der Theologie des DtrN, der in der bisherigen Forschung wegen seiner monotonen Betonung der Gesetzestreue etwas stiefmütterlich behandelt worden ist."

49. Veijola, *Das Königtum*, 122.

50. This conclusion inspired DtrN to reuse ancient prophetic material at his disposal, inserting the accounts of Saul's rejection as we know them in 1 Sam 13:7b-15 and 15:1-35. I argue this in Briody, "The Rejection of Saul in First Samuel 13:7b-15 and 15:1-35."

51. Joseph, *Portrait*, 97. Joseph argues that the promises of 2 Sam 7 are "mostly unconditional," against Weinfeld, who sees them as conditional on obedience. Moshe Weinfeld, *Deuteronomy and the Deuteronomic School* (Winona Lake, IN: Eisenbrauns, 1992), 5.

reflection as the life of the nation spiraled toward destruction and exile as monarchy declined and collapsed. Martin Rose praises the "up-to-date nature of the theological concepts of the deuteronomists in their time."[52] Like good theologians, they displayed sensitivity to contemporary issues as they attempted to "give a *response* to the questions of the time."[53] As authors and editors, they used the traditional material available, giving it shape, unity, and finality. They moved from tradition to interpretation as evolving events demanded new responses.[54]

This reconceptualization of kingship is expressive of a living movement, a theology that is vital and robust. The deuteronomistic movement went beyond explaining the past, as Martin Noth had thought, to providing a meaningful theology, an invitation and challenge to live well in the present crisis with an eye on the future. There was hope in repentance and in renewed obedience and fidelity. There was also hope in the unconditional promise of 2 Samuel 7, a hope glimpsed by some at the end of the history (2 Kgs 25:27–30) where "a scion of David . . . is yet alive and well."[55]

Idealized Davidic Type Points to "Son of David" Antitype

In the end, with the rejection of Saul and kingship as experienced, it is not the monarchy but David who becomes a type of fidelity to the Lord. Kings like Hezekiah and Josiah are good kings only because of David-like fidelity. The Lord permits the monarchy, though the reason for this seems to be more for the sake of David than for the sake of the monarchy (1 Sam 8:7–9; 13:14; 15:28; 16:1, 7, 12–13). In the Deuteronomistic History, the figure of David develops and becomes more important than the institution of the monarchy. David is the faithful king imagined in Deuteronomy 17:14–20. Josiah, the best king after David, "out-davids" David in being the *only* one to fulfill perfectly the command of Deuteronomy 6:5, loving the Lord with all three dimensions, heart, soul, and might.[56] All Judean kings are measured against David (1 Kgs 9:4;

---

52. Martin Rose, "Deuteronomistic Ideology and Theology of the Old Testament," 424–55 in *Israel Constructs Its History: Deuteronomistic Historiography in Recent Research*, JSOTSup 306, ed. Albert De Pury, Thomas Römer, and Jean-Daniel Macchi (Sheffield: Sheffield Academic, 2000), 452.

53. Rose, "Deuteronomistic Ideology," 450.

54. Rose, "Deuteronomistic Ideology," 451, 453.

55. Jon D. Levenson, "The Last Four Verses in Kings," *Journal of Biblical Literature* 103, no. 3 (1984): 353–61, at 357–58, 361.

56. Joseph, *Portrait*, 164: "Only Josiah (not even David) completely fulfills the injunction of Deut 6:5."

11:4, 6, 38; 14:8). The deuteronomistic writers had an image of "the perfect anointed" against which the entire history of the monarchy would be measured and found wanting.[57] This idealized image of David, very different from that of the so-called succession narrative (2 Sam 6–20; 1 Kgs 1–2), became a type of one whose heart is entirely attuned to the Lord and perfectly obedient to his law. The image of this Davidic, kingly figure is rooted in 2 Samuel 7, preserving what the deuteronomistic writers took to be the "real meaning of the Nathan prophecy."[58] The promise of 2 Samuel 7 is viewed as an eternal, unconditional covenant (Pss 89:34–38; 132:11–12). For Childs, the idealization of David led to a vision of David as "the ideal ruler of Israel, even as a type of the righteous rule of God," "a symbol of the rule of God."[59] This explains why DtrN, so negative about the monarchy, includes a positive view of David.[60]

What this glimpse of the Deuteronomistic History, and in particular the idealization of David, shows is the inherently theological thrust of the biblical text itself. The text is, as Pius XII observed, already theologically richly weighted. This is due to the original intention and purposefulness of the inspired writers behind this masterful composition. Such theological openness allows themes to be carried through and developed right into the New Testament. The Deuteronomistic History, more traditionally called the Former Prophets, is also prophecy. It facilitates the emergence of a future, faithful, perfect, royal, Davidic figure—the Messiah, *the* Son of David (2 Sam 7:11–17, 26–29; Luke 1:32–33). This theological thrust allows Christians to see, in the light of the Glorified Christ, the literal sense of the promise of 2 Samuel 7 and of the Royal Psalms. This literal sense lies not merely in their original historical context, but even more, in their future, definitive, *literal* fulfilment in Christ who is truly enthroned at the right hand of God (Ps 110:1) and whose kingdom will indeed have no end (2 Sam 7:13–16). *The Interpretation of the Bible in the Church* observes that these Davidic prophecies, once thought to be hyperbole, "must now be taken literally."[61] Long before the New Testament was written, the deuteronomistic theologians had *already* idealized the figure of David. The foundation or inner direction was *already* there, open, sympathetic, and in place, when Christ came as the true Son of David. David was a type of Christ.

---

57. Gerhard Von Rad, *Old Testament Theology*, vol. 1, *The Theology of Israel's Historical Traditions*, trans. D. M. G. Stalker (New York: Harper and Row, 1962), 345. Von Rad lists references to David as model of perfect kingship. Alison Joseph makes a similar point (*Portrait*, 5, 226–27).
58. Von Rad, *Old Testament Theology*, 345–46.
59. Childs, *Biblical Theology*, 154–55.
60. Veijola, *Das Königtum*, 120.
61. Pontifical Biblical Commission, *The Interpretation of the Bible in the Church*, §II.B.2.

Typology does not crush the historical David but extends his meaning and significance from the inside out, with continuity and surpassing newness.

Typology Valued: Openness to Theological Reading

The Saul-David narrative of the Deuteronomistic History offers a textbook example of how the biblical text itself requires a theological and spiritual reading. These Scripture texts offer a *religious* vision of great depth and subtlety.[62] The deuteronomists were great theologians, and their history gives us a theology and a spirituality. The covenant with David (1 Sam 13:14; 15:28; 16:1) is "a divine answer to human failure,"[63] the failure of Saul and kingship, but also to the wider, deeper human failure that is sin in general. Out of their concern with the disobedience of kings, embodied in Saul, there emerged in an organic and inspired way an image of the future and faithful "Son of David." Jesus Christ assumes the full sense of this title. The David of the Deuteronomistic History (1 and 2 Samuel) was real, but Christ inhabits the fullness of what was intended by "Son of David." Christ, "the true Messiah and Son of David," reveals and fulfills all the Davidic expectations and promises.[64] Paul's address in the synagogue of Antioch in Pisidia clearly illustrates the theological trajectory from King Saul to King David and finally to the Savior, Jesus (Acts 13:21–23). This biblical "extension of the literal sense" respects the integrity of the Old Testament type yet permits continuity in the one history of salvation.[65] The inner direction of the text is drawn out, showing continuity and newness. Ancient narrative speaks to how we are to live. The historical account also makes an existential appeal.[66]

This view of typology, summarized by Childs and illustrated here with the example of David from the Deuteronomistic History, is also shared by the Church. The *Catechism of the Catholic Church* presents typology as a focused

---

62. I borrow the phrases "religious vision" and "depth and subtlety" from Robert Alter, emphasis added. Robert Alter, *The Art of Biblical Narrative*, rev. ed. (New York: Basic, 2011), 23. Alter is describing how Scripture in general serves its message by deploying the resources of narrative.

63. Jean-Pierre Sonnet, "God's Repentance and 'False Starts' in Biblical History (Genesis 6–9; Exodus 32–34; 1 Samuel 15 and 2 Samuel 70)," *Vetus Testamentum Supplements* 133 (2010): 469–94, at 471–72, 493.

64. Here I am adapting the language of *CCC* §2579, describing the Psalms of David and their fulfilment in the prayer of Christ.

65. Childs, *Biblical Theology*, 13.

66. "The biblical account... contains an existential appeal addressed to the reader" (Pontifical Biblical Commission, *The Interpretation of the Bible in the Church*, §I.B.2). The document deals here with theological reflection.

instance or subset of the broader, allegorical, spiritual sense, one which reflects a "more profound understanding" of events or persons described in the Old Testament text.[67] Typology sees a prefiguration in the Old Testament of an element of the mystery of Christ. In this light, the Old Testament discloses its "inexhaustible content."[68] Yet the Old Testament retains its own integrity. Just because elements of the Old Testament, like the patriarchs and the exodus, are intermediate stages, this does not mean that they lose their value in God's plan. "Typology indicates the *dynamic movement* toward the fulfilment of the divine plan."[69]

Pope Pius XII observed that Scripture is *already* "rich in original meaning" and "endowed with a divine power." Scripture has its own value, beauty, and splendor, provided it is "fully and accurately explained" so that all its treasures are brought to light.[70] Attempting to hear that "full range of notes"[71] helps avoid an interpretation that is lopsided. Sound exegesis takes account of the literal-historical and leads to the theological-spiritual and ultimately to holiness.

Conclusion

Reading the Old Testament *theologically* permits its inner direction to be recognized. The typological model is especially valuable, since, as Childs opined, typology is really an extension of the literal sense within the one history of salvation.[72] The theological-spiritual sense should flow naturally from the historical-literal sense. Consequently, the "Son of David" of the New Testament can be understood fully only in the light of the historical David of the Old Testament and his good qualities (obedience, trust, surrender, a man after the Lord's own heart [1 Sam 13:14]), the promises made him, the longing for that future Davidic scion, and the idealization of his person. A future Son of David is longed for. The historical David, son of Jesse the Bethlehemite of Judah, is the basis for this type of Christ the Lord. With typology, we might say, in words borrowed from Benedict XVI, the Old Testament is not confined to the past, rather "passageways" open up "to the present and the future."[73]

---

67. *CCC*, §117 places "type" under allegorical sense.
68. *CCC*, §129.
69. *CCC*, §130, emphasis added.
70. Pius XII, *Divino afflante Spiritu*, §27.
71. Childs, "Psalm 8," 31.
72. Childs, *Biblical Theology*, 13.
73. Benedict XVI, *What Is Christianity?: The Last Writings*, ed. Elio Guerriero and Georg Gänswein, trans. Michael J. Miller (San Francisco: Ignatius, 2023), 168.

Theological Riches from Sound Exegesis

With typology, the later, fuller truth is intimately related to the original, historical, literal truth expressed in the Old Testament. In this way, Christ is recognized as the measure of Scripture, while, at the same time, the integrity of the Old Testament is preserved. The inspired Old Testament author was "in touch with that very same reality in which the fuller truth is rooted."[74] C. S. Lewis, a contemporary of Pius XII and Martin Noth (and to some extent, Brevard Childs), aptly summarizes:

> Reading [the Old Testament author's] words in the light of that fuller truth and hearing it in them as an overtone or second meaning, we are not foisting on them something alien to his mind, an arbitrary addition. We are prolonging his meaning in a direction congenial to it. The basic reality behind his words and behind the full truth is one and the same.[75]

The better we come to know Holy Scripture, the more we give a foothold to the Holy Spirit to speak. The more we wrestle with the Word—attempting to discover what the author intended to say through what is actually expressed—the better we discover what God desires to say to us. Respecting the important link between the literal and spiritual senses, we allow what God wants us to hear to flow from what the text means and contains. In a privileged way, this helps us, like the ancient Fathers of the Church, to live *from* the Bible, in communion with our brothers and sisters.[76] The authentic drawing out of the spiritual sense of Scripture, especially through typology, benefits exegesis in terms of depth and direction. Most importantly, it nourishes and inspires the people of God.[77]

---

74. C. S. Lewis, *Psalms*, 102–3.
75. C. S. Lewis, *Psalms*, 102–3.
76. Pontifical Biblical Commission, *The Interpretation of the Bible in the Church*, §III.B.2.
77. Williamson, *Catholic Principles for Interpreting Scripture*, 203.

CHAPTER 4

Moses's Flight to Midian: Exodus 2:11–22 as a Case Study in Patristic Exegesis

Hryhoriy Lozinskyy

In the introduction to the volume on Exodus, Leviticus, Numbers, and Deuteronomy in the Ancient Christian Commentary on Scripture series, Joseph Lienhard expressed the approach of patristic exegesis of the Old Testament in the following terms: "The point of departure for much of patristic exegesis of the Old Testament is the Fathers' belief that the Old Testament is wholly a prophecy of Christ; or, inversely, that Christ is the key to understanding the Old Testament."[1] It is a classic statement that summarizes how a great number of Fathers looked at the Old Testament, yet it may present some difficulties, especially when it comes to the interpretation of several Pentateuchal texts in the early Church.

Ancient Christian interpretation of Scripture is commonly related to two exegetical schools, Alexandria and Antioch, and the approaches of their representatives to the Pentateuchal texts can raise the following questions:[2] How far can one apply the allegorical interpretation traditionally associated with the school of Alexandria to certain texts within the five books of Moses? What is the spiritual sense of the many legal texts that permeate the books from Exodus

---

1. Joseph T. Lienhard, ed., *Exodus, Leviticus, Numbers, Deuteronomy*, ACCSOT 9 (Downers Grove, IL: InterVarsity Press, 2001), xxviii.

2. The present paper offers a study in the context of these schools since it reflects the general theme of the Quinn Biblical Conference, "The Transcendent Mystery of God's Word: A Critical Synthesis of Antioch and Alexandria," held at the Alverna Center, in Winona, MN, June 2022, where this paper was presented.

through Deuteronomy? Ultimately, if "the Old Testament is wholly a prophecy of Christ,"[3] do *all* the Pentateuchal texts point to Christ? When it comes to the school of Antioch, the following questions can be asked: To what degree can many Pentateuchal texts be interpreted only within their literal meaning and how open are they to the spiritual sense? Should typological interpretation be applied to only some texts in the Pentateuch, mostly narrative passages, such as patriarchal stories, exodus accounts, and some narrative texts in the book of Numbers? Without typological and allegorical interpretations,[4] some pages of the Pentateuch would be almost "dry"; for example, the abundance of the patristic interpretation of Exodus 12 or Origen's interpretation of the forty-two stopping places in Numbers 33. To sum up, how should we read and interpret the Pentateuch keeping in mind the interpretative tradition of the early Church?

There are countless studies on the question of the relationship between the schools of Alexandria and Antioch. That is why the limits of this study will be clarified here. This is not more research on this large and well-studied question. Yet, what is offered here is a case study on one passage: the intent is to show how one specific Pentateuchal text can be studied first within its context, then by authors from two ancient exegetical schools, and finally how it is interpreted in the liturgical tradition. Through this analysis some considerations will be given on how to read the Pentateuchal passages from the perspective of the critical synthesis between the two ancient schools.

Introductory Remarks

Ben Meyer presents the advantages and weaknesses of both Alexandria and Antioch and focuses on some methodological guidelines for the critical synthesis between the two schools, instead of highlighting the traditional distinction between them.[5] He talks about "theologically responsible biblical hermeneutics,"[6] and this is how he would describe the synthesis between the two schools. The present study will analyze one pericope in the light of Meyer's insights:

---

3. Lienhard, *Exodus, Leviticus, Numbers, Deuteronomy*, xxviii.

4. For the difference between typology and allegory, so as not to confuse these two terms, see Christopher A. Hall, *Reading Scripture with the Church Fathers* (Downers Grove, IL: InterVarsity Press, 1998), 133; Peter W. Martens, "Revisiting the Allegory/Typology Distinction: The Case of Origen," *Journal of Early Christian Studies* 16 (2008): 283–317.

5. Ben F. Meyer, *Critical Realism and the New Testament*, PTMS 17 (Allison Park, PA: Pickwick, 1989), 45–49.

6. Meyer, *Critical Realism and the New Testament*, 46.

Moses's fleeing to Midian in Exodus 2:11–22. This choice is due to the fact that Exodus 2:11–22 is dealt with by at least two representatives of each school: John Chrysostom and Theodoret of Cyrus from the Antiochene school, and Clement and Cyril from the Alexandrian school; moreover, this text is also used in the living liturgical tradition.[7] Even if this passage is not dealt with by the other Fathers to the same extent (at times through brief homiletical remarks and sometimes in more extensive commentaries), these factors make this passage a better case study than many other Pentateuchal passages. To our knowledge, it is a rare find that one Pentateuchal passage is treated by more than one author from each school and then is also found in the living liturgical tradition.[8] Such an approach will show how each school interpreted the text as a case study for identifying implications for further research of other Pentateuchal texts.

Meyer outlines three elements for this hermeneutics:

> So there will be at least three elements in a theologically responsible biblical hermeneutics: first, the claims of the biblical text, i.e., the primacy of its intended sense; second, the claims of human authenticity, i.e., Antiochene rejection of premature and artificial interpretative solutions; third, the claims of Christian authenticity, i.e., Alexandrine insistence on the intelligibility and cohesiveness of salvation and of the scriptures that attest it in hope and in celebration.[9]

Based on these elements, the study will unfold in four stages. First, the biblical text will be presented in its context. Second, the exegesis of some representatives of the Antiochene school will be outlined. Further attention will be drawn to the Alexandrian school via a brief text of St. Clement of Alexandria and an extensive portion of St. Cyril of Alexandria's *Glaphyra* on the Pentateuch. Finally, it will be shown how this pericope is proclaimed in the liturgy: it is another interpretative context, and is related to the patristic exegesis. The study will conclude with some perspectives and challenges for the use of Pentateuchal texts as interpreted by each of the two schools (in the context of the exegesis of the two schools). Although a case study on one passage clearly cannot do justice to the many aspects of Pentateuchal exegesis, it will still have the advantage of presenting differences as well as similarities in approach to the same pericope.

When it comes to the term "synthesis," a clarification should be made. If it represents one of the goals of research, what does it mean when it describes

---

7. For more on this point and its relevance, see below, "Exodus 2:11–22 in the Byzantine Liturgical Tradition."

8. Among other examples, see also Exod 15:22–27; 33:11–23.

9. Meyer, *Critical Realism and the New Testament*, 46.

the relationship between the two schools? Understanding this relationship in terms of opposition should be avoided. The sharp distinction between Antioch and Alexandria has been challenged by a number of scholars.[10] Indeed, the Antiochene Fathers do not deal only with the literal sense. On the other hand, although Origen says the literal sense is not enough,[11] it is still where exegesis should start.[12] At the same time, these two schools maintain their differences, and thus each has its own specificity.[13] In sum, the term "synthesis" avoids highlighting "opposition" while still acknowledging the distinction between the two schools.

Analysis of the Text

Exodus 2:11–22 in Its Context

The analysis will start from the biblical text, as suggested by the first step of theologically responsible biblical hermeneutics outlined by Meyer.[14]

Before the well-known prophetic calling of Moses in Exodus 3:1–12, there is a series of episodes that prepare the setting for the rise of the great leader

---

10. Karlfried Froehlich, *Biblical Interpretation in the Early Church*, SECT (Philadelphia: Fortress, 1984), 20. For a more recent contribution, see Miriam DeCock, *Interpreting the Gospel of John in Antioch and Alexandria*, WGRWSup 17 (Atlanta: SBL Press, 2020), 1: "As is well known, scholars of early Christian exegesis have recently challenged the traditional distinction between the two opposing schools of exegesis, the allegorically inclined Alexandrians and the historical-literal Antiochenes."

11. Origen, *De principiis*, trans. G. W. Butterworth (Notre Dame, IN: Ave Maria Press, 2013), 1.2.1.

12. Origen, *Homilies on Genesis and Exodus*, trans. Ronald E. Heine, FaCh 71 (Washington, DC: Catholic University of America Press, 1982), 2.6. For similarities and differences between the two schools, see Darren M. Slade, "Patristic Exegesis: The Myth of the Alexandrian-Antiochene Schools of Interpretation," *Socio-Historical Examination of Religion and Ministry* 1, no. 2 (2019): 155–76, at 161–69.

13. This is one of the concise ways to highlight the identity of each school, and it is given as an example: "Unlike their Alexandrian adversaries who employed allegorical exegesis to find deeper meanings in the Bible, the mystical meanings of the Antiochene exegetes were said to have been based upon and congruent with the literal sense of the text," Bradley Nassif, "Antiochene Θεορια in John Chrysostom's Exegesis," 51–66 in *Exegesis and Hermeneutics in the Churches of the East*, ed. Vahan S. Hovhanessian (New York: Peter Lang, 2009), 51. For a good synthesis of the exegesis in both the schools and their specific accents, see Hall, *Reading Scripture with the Church Fathers*, 132–76. See also a brief statement of DeCock: "In response to this scholarship, I argue that despite much important research to demonstrate the overlap between the two schools of Alexandria and Antioch, the traditional scholarly distinction remains helpful," *Interpreting the Gospel of John in Antioch and Alexandria*, 2.

14. Meyer, *Critical Realism and the New Testament*, 46.

of the Israelites. The context that necessitates his appearance is the oppression of the Israelites, highlighted by a series of unfavorable circumstances and measures, which is also the main topic of Exodus 1–2: the ascent of the new Pharaoh, the hard labor imposed on the Israelites, and the command that the midwives kill the Hebrews' male children. The summary of 2:23–25 marks a significant change in this situation, since after a long time, the cry of the Israelites finally has been heard by the Lord.

Exodus 2:11–22 focuses on what happens in the meantime.[15] The Qal וַיִּגְדַּל, "had grown up," makes a transition from an infant Moses whose life was endangered (vv. 2–10) to an adult who is now able to protect from harm. The passage unfolds in two scenes:[16] first Moses's flight from Pharaoh (2:11–15), and then his arrival in Midian and creation of a new family (2:16–22). In the first scene Moses's fight for justice is highlighted. Indeed, the adult Moses notices the toils of his people (2:11) and shows himself not indifferent to what happens to them. The use of the term רָשָׁע, "wicked/wrongdoer" (v. 13), points to the fact that not only is his outburst an impromptu one, but that the issue he stands for is justice. Ancient and modern commentators focused on Moses's killing of the Egyptian and its moral evaluation, justifying Moses on one hand and pointing to the sinfulness of this act on the other.[17] In addition, Pharaoh's hostility toward Moses in 2:15 anticipates the continuous confrontation between the two characters in Exodus 7–14.

The second scene (vv. 16–22) starts with the episode at the well, the traditional place of meeting a future wife in patriarchal stories (Gen 24:11–27; 29:1–14). For Moses too, this encounter at the well leads to a wedding and the birth of a son.[18] The latter forms an *inclusio* with the first birth announced at

---

15. Compared to the MT, the LXX contains some modifications. First, the LXX specifies that the brothers of Moses are sons of Israel in 2:11. Moreover, it adds the name Jethro in 2:16, probably to harmonize the text with the same name found in Exod 3:1. Finally, the LXX also adds the pronouns where they are missing in the MT. Yet, overall, the LXX does not have any significant difference as compared to the MT.

16. This is how the commentators usually divide this passage, see for instance Brevard Childs, *The Book of Exodus: A Critical, Theological Commentary* (Philadelphia: Westminster, 1974), 30–33; Victor P. Hamilton, *Exodus: An Exegetical Commentary* (Grand Rapids, MI: Baker Academic, 2011), 27–39; Michelangelo Priotto, *Esodo: nuova versione, introduzione e commento*, LBPT 2 (Milan: Paoline, 2014), 70.

17. For the summary of the positions on Moses's killing of the Egyptian, see Thomas Joseph White, *Exodus*, BTCB (Grand Rapids, MI: Brazos, 2016), 33–34.

18. Exod 2:22 mentions the birth of *one* son, Gershom. Moreover, one son is circumcised in 4:24–26. Yet, in 4:20 one learns about בָּנָיו, Moses's *sons* in plural. Also, in 18:4, during Jethro's visit, the second son is mentioned, Eliezer.

the beginning of the chapter, where the same phraseology is also used (וַתֵּלֶד בֵּן, "[the woman] bore a son" in 2:2a and 2:22a), thus making Exodus 2:1–22 an account of the birth of two sons. One should notice the meaning of the name Gershom, "I have been a sojourner" (Exod 2:22 RSV): even if Moses apparently did not share much with his people (raised in Pharaoh's house until he fled to Midian), he recognizes that he belongs to them.[19] The next episode, 3:1–12, will completely reverse Moses's situation.

If on the one hand these episodes keep Moses distant from Egypt, his people, and Pharaoh, on the other they serve as the preface for his prophetic vocation when he will be engaged more than anyone else in the history of his people. Moses thus spends some time in the desert of Midian before being called for a unique mission. God has already initiated the deliverance of his people that will be carried out by Moses.

Two Examples from the School of Antioch

The second element Meyer suggests in theologically responsible biblical hermeneutics is "the claims of human authenticity, i.e., Antiochene rejection of premature and artificial interpretative solutions,"[20] and this is where the analysis will focus now. Hence the comments of two Fathers will be taken into consideration. First, St. John Chrysostom has brief observations on Exodus 2:11–22 in his homilies on 2 Corinthians and Hebrews. Here Chrysostom focuses mostly on the literal sense. Second, St. Theodoret of Cyrus has a brief comment on Moses's marriage to a foreign wife (Exod 2:21–22). This case provides an example of a typological interpretation by an Antiochene author.[21]

St John Chrysostom and His Homiletical Remarks
The "golden-mouthed" pastor (†407) did not leave any commentary on the book of Exodus, yet his New Testament homilies also have insights for Old

---

19. Childs, *Exodus*, 32.
20. Meyer, *Critical Realism and the New Testament*, 46.
21. Here the works of two interpreters are mentioned, John Chrysostom and Theodoret of Cyrus, yet, to have a complete picture of the Antiochene exegesis on the book of Exodus, one should also consult the work of a lesser known representative of the same school, namely Eusebius of Emesa (†360) and his *Commentary on the Octateuch*. It is mostly his commentary on Genesis that has been studied, not the other biblical books whose commentaries exist in Armenian. For an analysis on the work of this author, see R. B. ter Haar Romeny, "Early Antiochene Commentaries on Exodus," 114–19 in *Studia Patristica* 30, ed. Elizabeth A. Livingstone (Peeters: Leuven, 1997).

Testament exegesis. Hebrews 11 defines faith (11:1) and lists ancestors who exemplified it (cf. Heb 11:4–38). Out of eleven individual characters named in this chapter, Moses received more extensive treatment than anyone except Abraham. Chrysostom focuses on two aspects: first he deals with Moses's fear, and then he presents his faith.

While commenting on the prophet's fright, he refers to two passages: first, he quotes Hebrews 11:27 where it is stated Moses was not afraid, and then he alludes to Exodus 2:14 when saying "and yet the Scripture says that when he heard, he 'was afraid.'"[22] By doing this, he lets Scripture comment on Scripture: he questions the statement of Hebrews 11:27 by making an appeal to the passage in Exodus. Moreover, Chrysostom further connects Hebrews with another passage in Exodus, namely 5:1, where Moses presents himself again before Pharaoh. In sum, when dealing with the fear of Moses, Chrysostom looks at other places in Scripture. In these remarks, he also connects both Old Testament and New Testament passages. The interior unity of both testaments was one of the principles of Antiochene θεωρία.[23] Although these homiletical remarks do not seem to be, strictly speaking, the example of the application of this principle of θεωρία, they still show how Scripture comments on Scripture, how, in this case, an Old Testament passage illumines a New Testament pericope. To interpret one passage, John Chrysostom has recourse to other places in the Scriptures.

Related to the question of fear, one can also notice the meticulousness with which Chrysostom reads the biblical text. He examines the question of Moses's fear in detail, referring to it three times in such a brief homily. First, he mentions that Moses was afraid, then he adds an adverb, "he was *exceedingly* afraid," and finally he refers to the absence of fear when Moses presents himself to Pharaoh. This "exceeding fear" is especially worthy of notice here since in Exodus 2:11–22 it is not evident where such a fear is found. Most likely, Chrysostom

---

22. John Chrysostom, *Homilies on Hebrews*, 26.5 (trans. NPNF 1/14:484).

23. Nassif, "Antiochene Θεορία in John Chrysostom's Exegesis," 56–59. Yet, this concept of the unity of the two Testaments was present in the authors of the Alexandrian school as well; see for instance Clement of Alexandria, *Stromateis*, trans. John Ferguson, FaCh 85 (Washington, DC: Catholic University of America Press, 1991), 2.6.29. The notion of Antiochene θεωρία has been attracting the attention of more scholars recently, and several contributions have been written on it. See Bertrand de Margerie, *Introduction a l'histoire de l'exégèse*, vol. 1 (Paris: Cerf, 1980), 188–213; Bradley Nassif, "Antiochene Theoria and Theological Interpretation of Scripture," 347–62 in *The Oxford Handbook of the Bible in Orthodox Christianity*, ed. Eugen J. Pentiuc (Oxford: Oxford University Press, 2022); Richard J. Perhai, *Antiochene Theōria in the Writings of Theodore of Mopsuestia and Theodoret of Cyrus* (Minneapolis: Fortress, 2015).

refers to Exodus 2:15a: "When Pharaoh heard of it, he sought to kill Moses. But Moses fled from Pharaoh" (RSV). The act of flight is considered to be done out of exceeding fear, whereas the first fear refers to Moses's reaction to the words of the Hebrew man (2:14).

When it comes to the faith of Moses, Chrysostom draws a parallel with Christ: "And this the devil said to Christ, 'Cast yourself down.'"[24] Yet, this cannot be considered an example of typological reading: Chrysostom simply uses the episode from the Synoptic Gospels to shed light on Moses's action. It is another example in this homily of how Scripture is used to comment on Scripture, on how to read the two Testaments together.

Related to the literal interpretation of the text, another example from the homilies on 2 Corinthians can be quoted.[25] Chrysostom comments on the question addressed by the Hebrew man, "Who made you a prince and judge over us?" (Exod 2:14 RSV). He explains Moses's act of leadership by an example: it is foolish to ask the physician why he uses the knife and to ask Moses why he acts as ruler. Here as well Chrysostom focuses exclusively on the literal meaning of the text.

At least in these homiletical remarks, while referring to the flight to Midian, Chrysostom combines passages from both Testaments. He does not apply an allegorical or a typological interpretation but rather asks about the possible issues the text raises, such as presence or absence of fear, returning to Pharaoh, or tempting God. What is interesting is that already the author of the letter to the Hebrews interprets the conduct of Moses in a Christological key (cf. Heb 11:26). Chrysostom, while dealing with both texts (Heb 11 and Exod 2), in his turn, focuses on the literal meaning of the passage. Although he makes a parallel with the temptation of Christ, it is not a Christological interpretation in this text.

Theodoret of Cyrus and His Remarks on Exodus 2:21

A later representative of the same school, Theodoret of Cyrus (†457), composed *Questions on the Octateuch*, written in form of questions and answers, and this work contains plenty of exegetical material on the books from Genesis through Ruth. Its special value consists in the fact that it is one of few commentaries (not homilies) on the Pentateuch preserved from the early Church.[26] In the pericope in question, Theodoret addresses only Moses's marriage to

---

24. John Chrysostom, *Homilies on Hebrews*, 26.5 (trans. NPNF 1/14:484).
25. John Chrysostom, *Homilies on 2 Corinthians*, 15.4 (NPNF 1/12:352).
26. Lienhard, *Exodus, Leviticus, Numbers, Deuteronomy*, xxi.

Zipporah (Exod 2:21): "Why did Moses marry a foreign wife? He was a type of Christ the Lord, who, though a Jew by bodily descent, called the Gentile Church his 'bride.'"[27] This very concise answer is an example of the typological reading, used by both Antioch and Alexandria. Moses thus becomes the type of Christ, and his marriage to a foreign woman points to Christ calling Gentiles to the Church. Such a reading is scripturally based, and the spousal image comes from the Old Testament. Typological reading of Old Testament texts is indeed found in the New Testament; for instance, Hebrews 7:15–25 presents Christ as the new Melchizedek, and thus reads Genesis 14:17–24 in a Christian light. In addition, the Old Testament typically uses spousal imagery to express the relationship between God and his people. Although brief, Theodoret's comment on the same pericope is important: it shows how this Antiochene author employed *typological* interpretation and thus did not focus exclusively on the literal meaning of the text.

Two Examples from the Alexandrian School

Two Fathers will be considered here as well in the following paragraphs. First, an earlier member of the Alexandrian school, St. Clement of Alexandria (died between 211 and 215), who comments on Moses in his *Stromateis* where he provides brief remarks on Moses's birth and life. Second, a considerably lengthy commentary on Exodus 2:11–22 of much later representative, St. Cyril of Alexandria (†444), who deals with a variety of issues found in Exodus 2:11–22.[28]

Clement of Alexandria's Commentary on Moses

Chapters 23–28 in Clement's *Stromateis* book 1 are dedicated to a variety of issues related to Moses. Chapter 23 is especially grounded in the biblical text and here, Clement paraphrases the biblical passages with his particular comments here and there, often depending on Philo's *Life of Moses* or the pseudepigraphical *Assumption of Moses*. Two elements refer to Exodus 2:11–22: Moses's slaying of the Egyptian and his tending of the sheep of his father-in-law. Clement interprets the first as zeal for the ancestral traditions: "When he [Moses]

---

27. Theodoret of Cyrus, *The Questions on the Octateuch*, trans. Robert C. Hill, LEC 1 (Washington, DC: Catholic University of America Press, 2007), 2.4.
28. When it comes to another giant of the Alexandrian school, namely Origen, among the preserved texts he does have a series of homilies on the book of Exodus, yet he does not comment on Exod 2:11–22: in Homily 2 he focuses on the midwives and Moses's birth (cf. Exod 1:15–2:10), and then in Homily 3 he starts dealing with Moses's speech (cf. Exodus 4–5), see Origen, *Homilies on Genesis and Exodus*, 2.2–3.

Exodus 2:11–22 as a Case Study in Patristic Exegesis

reached the age of manhood he developed his practical wisdom, being zealous for his national, ancestral educational traditions, to the point of striking down and killing an Egyptian who was unjustly attacking a Hebrew."[29] The second point especially captures our attention: shepherding flocks is seen by Clement as preparation for leading the "tamest of all flocks, the human."[30] Clement sees in this the hand of God who was leading Moses from there to the leadership over Hebrews.[31] This sheds light on the above-mentioned question of the Hebrew man, "Who made you a ruler?" (Exod 2:14 RSV). God had assigned Moses this preeminent position; God's hand is evident in Moses's life. At least in these two elements of Exodus 2:11–22, Clement focuses only on the literal meaning; indeed, for this Alexandrian Father the meaning is also in the letter (yet not exclusively in the literal sense).[32] Yet elsewhere in chapter 23, Clement applies an allegorical interpretation, as for example where he lists several characters' names: Moses, Joachim, and Melchi. The literal sense remains a sort of beginning point, that which is accessible to the majority, but readers need to seek what is hidden in the Scriptures. Thus, Clement of Alexandria evidently does not stop at the level of the literal sense and invites us toward the richness that is concealed in the Scriptures.[33]

Cyril of Alexandria and His Glaphyra on the Pentateuch[34]

Cyril's interpretative key for the book of Exodus is given at the beginning of book 8 of his *Glaphyra on the Pentateuch*, where he starts to present the passages related to Moses. This prophet indeed shows the "mystery of Christ," and it is in the light of Christ that the subsequent portions of Exodus are interpreted.[35] Although this fact does not surprise, it is noteworthy that he

---

29. Clement of Alexandria, *Stromateis*, trans. John Ferguson, FaCh 85 (Washington D.C.: Catholic University of America Press, 1991), 1.23.

30. Clement of Alexandria, *Stromateis*, 1.23.

31. Clement of Alexandria, *Stromateis*, 1.23.

32. Guido I. Gargano, *Clemente e Origene nella Chiesa cristiana alessandrina: Estraneità, dialogo o inculturazione* (Cinisello Balsamo [MI]: Edizioni San Paolo, 2011), 51–52.

33. See esp. Clement of Alexandria, *Stromateis*, 6.15, where Clement deals with theoretical considerations concerning the interpretation of the Scriptures.

34. Cyril of Alexandria's works have been appreciated by the scholarly world only recently, and thus they represent a true discovery for the history of exegesis of the early Church. See for instance Robert L. Wilken, "Cyril of Alexandria as Interpreter of the Old Testament," 1–21 in *Theology of Cyril of Alexandria: A Critical Appreciation*, ed. Thomas G. Weinandy and Daniel A. Keating (London: T&T Clark, 2003).

35. Cyril of Alexandria, *Glaphyra on the Pentateuch*, trans. Nicholas P. Lunn, FaCh 138 (Washington, DC: Catholic University of America Press, 2019), 8.1.

sets the exegetical premise of his interpretation at the very beginning. In this way, Moses is also interpreted as a type of Christ, and this is how Cyril begins his treatment of Exodus 2:11–22: "But now let us also explore another way in which Emmanuel is given form in Moses. For Christ is the end of the law and the prophets."[36]

Cyril offers a detailed commentary on Exodus 2:11–22, and he focuses on a variety of matters: Moses's going out to his kinsmen, his killing and hiding of the Egyptian, the fight between the two Hebrews, Moses's departure for Midian, Jethro/Reuel, the number of his daughters, and the marriage to Zipporah. We will deal here with those issues that have already been presented by the Antiochene Fathers: Moses's role as ruler, his flight to Midian, and his marrying a foreign wife. These will show the difference of approach to the same passages by the representatives of the two schools.

When dealing with 2:11–15, and thus with the question "Who made you a prince and a judge over us?" (Exod 2:14 RSV), Cyril points to parallels between this passage in Exodus and Christ's salvific work. The following chart will illustrate the similarities that are drawn between Moses and Christ in such a short passage:

Moses hides the Egyptian	Christ hides Satan
Moses is ruler and judge	Christ is the "arbitrator of righteousness"
Moses gives peace to two Hebrews	Christ gives peace to the disciples
Refusal of Moses by Hebrew man	Refusal of Christ by people of Israel
Reproach of Moses	Reproach of Christ

As the text of *Glaphyra* shows, Cyril focuses briefly on the picture of Moses but then deals much more in detail with seeing Christ in this episode. Such a disproportion between Moses and Christ points already to the author's interest and the way he interprets this passage. What is striking is how Cyril reads the episode in the light of Christ's work of salvation on Holy Saturday: Christ places Satan, who oppresses man, in Hades. "This, I say, is the meaning of hiding the dead Egyptian in the sand. That the mass of unclean and God-hating demons were driven together into Hades by the ineffable power of our Savior."[37]

Two remaining issues have similar implications. First, the flight from Midian also receives a Christological interpretation: "Moses, then, removed himself from the land of the Egyptians to go to Midian in the same way that Christ

---

36. Cyril of Alexandria, *Glaphyra on the Pentateuch*, 8.6.
37. Cyril of Alexandria, *Glaphyra on the Pentateuch*, 8.7.

Exodus 2:11–22 as a Case Study in Patristic Exegesis

went from Judea into Galilee."[38] Chrysostom, in his turn, looks at the flight as an act of faith, and he does not interpret it in the light of Christ. Moses remains the main character with whom the Antiochene pastor deals. It is interesting also that Cyril does not call it flight, nor does he use the term "fear," yet it is presented as a deliberate act without negative connotation. Second, his treatment of the foreign wife has similarities with Theodoret of Cyrus's interpretation: just as Moses marries Reuel's daughter, so Christ joins himself to the Gentiles. Yet, contrary to Theodoret, Cyril comments extensively on Moses's marrying a foreign woman, and he focuses especially on two names, Zipporah and Gershom, that give him incentive for further commentary. What especially catches attention is that this part of the commentary is Trinitarian and ecclesiological. Since Zipporah means also "free gift of breath,"[39] Cyril talks about the Holy Spirit given by Christ to the Gentile church.[40] When it comes to Gershom, Cyril focuses on the members of the Gentile Church and calls them "heavenly citizens." Although he does not make any verbatim quotation, the idea is very similar to the Johannine language of being in the world but not belonging to it (cf. John 17:14; 1 John 2:15). In brief, it is a Christian reading of this Old Testament passage that embraces the salvific work of the Trinity with implications for the life of the Church.

Overall, one can notice that Cyril does more than read this Exodus passage in the light of Christ. There is almost a sort of revealing of Christ through Moses as Cyril states "the way in which Emmanuel is given form in Moses."[41] As regards allegorical interpretation, one also finds its use in his commentary, but it is not abundant compared to the rest of the text, and in this case it is limited to the moment when Cyril talks about Jethro representing the world, the significance of his name, and his seven daughters representing all the nations. Common to everything Cyril treats in Exodus 2:11–22 is that he applies Christological interpretation, which for him represents the "inner meaning" of the Scriptures.[42] Moses does have a Christological reference in Cyril's view, and this is how he reads the passages related to him.[43]

---

38. Cyril of Alexandria, *Glaphyra on the Pentateuch*, 8.8.
39. Cyril of Alexandria, *Glaphyra on the Pentateuch*, 8.8.
40. God the Father is also mentioned, later in the commentary where Cyril quotes Hebrews: "For he looked forward to the city that has foundations, whose architect and builder is God" (Heb 11:10 RSV).
41. Cyril of Alexandria, *Glaphyra on the Pentateuch*, 8.6.
42. Cyril of Alexandria, *Glaphyra on the Pentateuch*, 8.6.
43. John A. McGuckin, "Moses and the 'Mystery of Christ' in St. Cyril of Alexandria's Exegesis—Part 1," *Coptic Church Review* 21, no. 1 (2000): 24–32, at 25.

In addition to the extensive commentary on the Pentateuch, there is another merit of Cyril's works for the synthesis between Antioch and Alexandria. He writes *after* he learns about the critics from the Antiochene school. So, although he remains faithful to the exegesis of the Alexandrian school, he takes into account indications from Antioch that highlight the importance of the literal sense.

There is another question: what prompts Cyril to see Christ behind all the issues of Exodus 2:11–22? Such a stark accent on the Christological interpretation may be due to the theological debates still present in Alexandria, the city of which Arius was a presbyter. Alternatively, McGuckin notes Cyril's desire to have converts from Judaism in the context of the rivalry between Jews and Christians in Alexandria of the first half of the fifth century.[44] These are possible reasons behind such an interpretation. What is also important is the very fact that for Cyril, failing to see Christ there means failing to delve into the inner meaning of Scripture.[45]

Exodus 2:11–22 in the Byzantine Liturgical Tradition[46]

When presenting "theologically responsible biblical hermeneutics," Meyer points to its three elements and concludes by mentioning "celebration": "Third, the claims of Christian authenticity, i.e., Alexandrine insistence on the intelligibility and cohesiveness of salvation and of the scriptures that attest it in hope and in celebration."[47] Although he does not explicitly refer to *liturgical* celebration in this statement, it is still meaningful to look at how the same passage is interpreted in the context of the liturgy since it is related to patristic interpretation.

In the Byzantine liturgical tradition, the Pentateuch is read in a disproportionate way. Genesis is read almost in its entirety, Exodus is the second most frequently read book, but Leviticus through Deuteronomy receive little attention. Exodus 2:11–22 is one of two Old Testament readings at the Liturgy of the Presanctified Gifts on Wednesday of Holy Week. What is especially important

---

44. McGuckin, "Moses and the 'Mystery of Christ'," 25.

45. McGuckin, "Moses and the 'Mystery of Christ'," 30–32.

46. Here reference is made to the Byzantine liturgical tradition for several reasons. First, it reflects the author's religious background as a Byzantine Catholic. Second, the use of the book of Exodus and of these specific passages, has its roots in the Antiochene practice of the fourth century. Third, the interpretation of Cyril of Alexandria of Exod 2:11–22 is similar to how this text is interpreted in the liturgical context of Holy Week in the Byzantine liturgical tradition.

47. Meyer, *Critical Realism and the New Testament*, 46.

about this text and its use in the context of worship is that it is one of the Old Testament readings during Great Lent. This fact provides the interpretative key for the use of this Pentateuchal passage in worship. The passages for this liturgical season are continuous readings from the Pentateuch and Wisdom books, from Genesis and Proverbs in the forty-day fast and from Exodus and Job in Holy Week. Thus Exodus 2:11–22 is read on this specific day because it is the *lectio continua* of the Old Testament readings for the Great Lent:[48] just as Genesis and Proverbs are read from the beginning of Lent, so the reading continues with Exodus and Job. The book of Genesis is read in Lent because of its focus on the fall of man, and return to paradise, which is the theme of the journey of Lent. Thus, the *lectio continua* goes on with the book of Exodus, once the reading of Genesis is over, and it finishes at chapter 2 of Exodus simply because this is the last Liturgy of the Presanctified Gifts. There is also another aspect to consider here: the beginning of the book of Exodus announces the great story of freedom, and thus Exodus 1:1–20; 2:5–10; and 2:11–22 are read at the liturgies of the Presanctified Gifts. In these passages two topics are announced: the oppression of the people, and the rise of a leader through whom deliverance of the oppressed people will be carried out. The liturgy of Holy Week presents another story of deliverance carried out by Christ on the cross and, through resurrection, deliverance from the slavery of sin and death. If in Exodus 2 the rise of the "savior"[49] is announced, the liturgy of Holy Week points to the salvific work of the Savior of the world, carried out not only for the sons of Israel, but for all humanity, accomplished at the Feast of Feasts, Holy Resurrection. In this way, Exodus 2:11–22 receives, once again, this Christological interpretation, or in other words, the liturgical context presents Moses as a figure of Christ. Such a reading, that is in the light of the salvific work of Christ, is also found in Cyril's interpretation of this episode: Christ who places Satan, the oppressor of man, in Hades,[50] offers deliverance to humanity.

---

48. Stefanos Alexopoulos, *The Presanctified Liturgy in the Byzantine Rite: A Comparative Analysis of its Origins, Evolution, and Structural Components* (Leuven: Peeters, 2009), 166–67.

49. Cassuto refers to Exod 2 as "the birth of the savior," see Umberto Moshe David Cassuto, *A Commentary on the Book of Exodus*, trans. I. Abrahams (Skokie, IL: Varda), 17.

50. Cyril of Alexandria, *Glaphyra on the Pentateuch*, 8.7.

Conclusions, Challenges, and Perspectives

This study considered one pericope, viewed from four perspectives: the context of the book of Exodus, two Antiochene Fathers, two Alexandrine interpreters, and liturgy. A complete hermeneutic of the use of the Pentateuch in the light of a synthesis between Antioch and Alexandria cannot be presented in a full or systematic way in one study, nor can the view of one passage by four authors provide conclusions for all of the Pentateuch. Yet, and this is the hope here, they represent a case study that helps us to enter the world of the exegetical procedures of some ancient authors. The details of hermeneutics can indeed be observed when they are applied to the biblical text. Typological reading, focus on the literal sense, the use of allegory, the unity of both Testaments—all these procedures have been brought to light when looking at the exegesis of Exodus 2:11–22 by the above-mentioned authors.

A major challenge is the scarcity of commentaries on the Pentateuch from the early Church.[51] As specifically related to the Antiochene and Alexandrian interpreters, the number is even lower: *Commentary on the Octateuch* by Eusebius of Emesa, *Commentary on the Octateuch* by Theodoret of Cyrus, and *Adoration and Worship in Spirit and in Truth* and *Glaphyra on the Pentateuch* by Cyril of Alexandria. Origen's commentary on Genesis in thirteen books is lost, but his homilies on the books from Genesis through Numbers survive, and there are also Chrysostom's homilies on Genesis. Granted that there are references to the Pentateuch outside the commentaries on the five books of Moses, it still shows that authors commented much more on some books and paid less attention to others. A related difficulty is the disproportion of these commentaries. While the authors focus a lot on the book of Genesis, minor attention is paid for example to Numbers, and even less to Leviticus. Hence, it is especially when dealing with the legal parts of the Pentateuch, that one will find very few texts. Another challenge is to provide some guidelines that would establish principles for how to speak about the whole Pentateuch in the light of a synthesis between Alexandria and Antioch. The Pentateuch includes the most disparate texts, and, when it comes to allegory, "clearly articulated rules governing its use [allegory] and detecting its abuse are absolutely necessary."[52]

There is an important question: to what degree can one read *all* Pentateuchal passages in the light of Christ? Meyer states: "By the resurrection of

---

51. Lienhard, *Exodus, Leviticus, Numbers, Deuteronomy*, xx–xxiii.
52. Hall, *Reading Scripture with the Church Fathers*, 156.

Christ Christianity was bound to the scriptures of Israel, for the resurrection vindicated Jesus' election-historical mission, which supposed and climaxed the election history of biblical Israel."[53] If all is fulfilled in Christ, can all the Scriptures be read in this light? On the one hand, if limited to the literal sense, few Pentateuchal texts would point to Christ; on the other hand, the Christian reading of the Old Testament includes a Christological approach: "The scriptures of Israel were both the word of God and an indispensable source of the understanding of salvation in Christ."[54] There are already important guidelines in a text prior to the authors of two schools: the letter to the Hebrews offers examples of how to look at some Pentateuchal texts (especially ritual texts) and interpret them in the light of Christ.

To work within the horizons of the synthesis between the two schools would mean also to appreciate more the approach of the Antiochene school. It seems to be less known than its counterpart in Alexandria and even more neglected.[55] In addition, it would also help to value the Antiochene θεωρία. This term refers to the exegesis of this school as the "spiritual meaning of a text which both inheres in the historical framework and also takes the mind of the reader of scripture to higher planes of contemplation."[56] That is to say, a correct view of Antioch and its θεωρία saves it from the prejudice of being a literalist school. Moreover, this term has been and continues to be one of the major focuses in scholarship on early biblical interpretation.[57]

A final hint about understanding Scripture can come from the conclusion of the Gospel of Luke. Before the brief narrative of the Ascension in the Gospel of Luke, Jesus appears to the disciples (Luke 24:36-49). Among other things, Jesus refers to the Old Testament: "These are my words which I spoke to you, while I was still with you, that everything written about me in the law of Moses

---

53. Meyer, *Critical Realism and the New Testament*, 29.

54. Meyer, *Critical Realism and the New Testament*, 30.

55. Nassif, "Antiochene Θεορία in John Chrysostom's Exegesis," 53.

56. Joseph W. Trigg, *Biblical Interpretation*, MFC 9 (Wilmington, DE: Michael Glazier, 1988), 32.

57. To mention only a few contributions, past and recent: Francisco A. Seisdedos, "La 'teōria' antioquena," *Estudios Bíblicos* 11 (1952): 31-67; Paul Ternant, "La 'theōria' d'Antioche dans le cadre des sens de l'Écriture [Part I]," *Biblica* 34 (1953): 135-58; "La 'theōria' d'Antioche dans le cadre des sens de l'Écriture [Part II]," *Biblica* 34 (1953): 354-83; "La 'theōria' d'Antioche dans le cadre des sens de l'Écriture [Part III]," *Biblica* 34 (1953): 456-86; John Breck, "Theoria and Orthodox Hermeneutics," *Saint Vladimir's Theological Quarterly* 20, no. 4 (1976): 195-219; Walter C. Kaiser, Jr., "Psalm 72: An Historical and Messianic Current Example of Antiochene Hermeneutical Theoria," *Journal of the Evangelical Theological Society* 52, no. 2 (2009): 257-70; Perhai, *Antiochene Theōria*.

and the prophets and the psalms must be fulfilled" (Luke 24:44 RSV). Christ thus presents himself as the one in whom the Scriptures of Israel are fulfilled. In addition, an important note of the narrator follows: "Then he [Jesus] opened their minds to understand the Scriptures." When it comes to some Pentateuchal texts, it is sometimes difficult to see Christ there, but these words should probably remain on the interpretative horizons in any approach that tries to keep both Antioch and Alexandria, the literal and the spiritual sense, history and theology. It is with Christ, who opens our minds to its understanding, that one understands Scripture.

CHAPTER 5

The Book of Psalms: Challenges from the Past for Future Biblical Exegesis

Maurizio Girolami

The long process of the formation of the book of Psalms must be understood in the context of the Second Temple period, when Judaic and Hellenistic cultures meet, especially in the study of sacred texts. Exegesis is an ancient science and, in the Hellenistic period, was believed to be one of the best intellectual tools to reach the truth. Other important tools were philosophy and philology. Since the foundation of the Mouseion in Alexandria by Ptolemy I Soter (323–285) and his son Ptolemy II Philadelphus,[1] the scholars who worked there developed a careful attitude toward catalogues, archives, and collections of ancient works. Past knowledge could be transmitted through a systematic method of copying, gathering, and classifying, in order to teach to new generations the wisdom of life and a logical method worthy of the divine gift of rationality. The Homeric writings and Plato's works, for example, were copied in their entirety, but some of their important passages were also collected in anthologies. What was the logic of these collections? Was it respectful of the order given by the author or did the collector change the meaning of some passages because he put them in a different order?

This phenomenon was also important for early Christian authors, who were educated in these intellectual circles. Faced with the Bible, they asked themselves the meaning of the collected books of the whole of Holy Scripture

---

1. Ada Caruso, "Ipotesi di ragionamento sulla localizzazione del 'Mouseion' di Alessandria," *Archeologia Classica* 62, no. 1 (2011): 77–126, at 79; Gabriele Marasco, "Alessandria nascita e morte di una Biblioteca," *Studi sull'Oriente Cristiano* 15, no. 2 (2011): 5–16.

and, in a special way, about the shape of the book of Psalms, a collection of one hundred and fifty songs or hymns.

To interpret the Bible, the poets or the philosophers were not useful and could not serve as a model. No rational logic or narrative coherence could be seen in the Bible. They took from the Bible itself, which consisted of both the Jewish Scriptures and the memories of the apostolic preaching, the patterns with which to interpret and to understand God's Word.

We know that Paul's letters and the Gospels were written in Greek and that in the synagogues of the diaspora the Pentateuch, the prophets, and the wisdom literature, like the book of Psalms, were read in Greek according to the Septuagint version. What about the Hebrew text?

If we ignore the controversy between Justin and Trypho, who accused each other of having changed the biblical texts (Justin accused Trypho of changing the Hebrew text and Trypho accused the Philosopher of using a modified Greek version), we have to wait till the middle of the third century in Alexandria for Origen to compose the Hexapla, which was the first attempt at an agreed text. For the first time, the various versions of the Jewish Scriptures were put together in six columns: the Hebrew text, a transliteration of the Hebrew text in Greek letters,[2] and the four Greek versions of Aquila, Symmachus, the Septuagint, and Theodotion.

We know from the *Ecclesiastical History* of Eusebius that Origen added two additional Greek columns to the Hexapla, found respectively in Greece and in a jar in Jericho.[3] Despite this huge exegetical work, the Hebrew text was not read in Christian gatherings and it was not considered by Christian authors as an inspired text. They always read and explained the Greek version of the Septuagint, the best known Greek version of the Jewish Scriptures in the Second Temple period.

Introduction

My first purpose in this paper is to present questions regarding the text (or texts) of the book of Psalms and the interpretative keys used in early Christianity.[4] Beginning with the psalms and hymns in the Jewish Scriptures, I will

---

2. According to Benjamin Paul Kantor, "The Second Column (Secunda) of Origen's Hexapla in Light of Greek Pronunciation" (PhD diss., University of Texas, Austin, 2017), 11–37, Origen did not compose directly the second column, but received it from some Jewish circle.

3. Cf. Eusebius, *Ecclesiastical History*, 6.16.3.

4. Except for a brief mention of Augustine at the end of this contribution, there will be no mention of other authors who wrote on the book of Psalms, such as Didymus the Blind

show the use of the psalms in Paul's letters and in the Gospels, and then move on to the earlier Christian commentators, who showed a keen understanding of some problems that even nowadays are not clearly resolved. I think that retracing the ancient trails of exegesis will be a good exercise to improve our effort to find an even more precise method to understand and to explain the Bible.

Psalms in the Jewish Scriptures

The Term Psalm/Psalter

The Greek term "psalm" (ψαλμός)[5] probably occurs for the first time in Amos 5:23 with the meaning of "sound." In Job 21:1 and 30:31 it is an instrumental sound, perhaps that of a flute. In 1 Samuel 16:18 it is referred to as the ability to play an instrument; it is strictly linked to the praise of God in thanksgiving for his works (Jdt 16:1).[6] In Lamentations 3:14 (נְגִינָתָם) this word expresses a mocking song against the just man, and a sound in 5:14 (from the same Hebrew root נגן) and, as synecdoche, an instrument (see Ps 4:1). In 3 Maccabees 6:35 (only in

---

or the fifth-century Greek fathers Hilary, Ambrose, Jerome, and Augustine. A brief summary of the history of the psalms' interpretation can be found in Charles Kannengiesser, *Handbook of Patristic Exegesis*, BAC 1 (Leiden: Brill, 2004), 297–301; Bruce K. Waltke and James M. Houston, *The Psalms as Christian Worship: A Historical Commentary* (Grand Rapids, MI: Eerdmans, 2010), 1–112. A more extensive presentation of the Latin Fathers can be found in Marie-Josèphe Rondeau, *Les commentaires patristiques du Psautier (IIIe-Ve siècles)*, 2 vols. (Rome: Pontificium Istitutum Studiorum Orientalium, 1985), 2:323–88. For a *status quaestionis* about the patristic interpretation of the psalms see Susan Gillingham, "The Messiah in the Psalms: A Question of Reception History and the Psalter," 209–37 in *King and Messiah in Israel and the Ancient Near East: Proceedings of the Oxford Old Testament Seminar*, ed. John Day (Sheffield: Sheffield Academic, 1998); John H. Eaton, *The Psalms: A Historical and Spiritual Commentary with an Introduction and New Testament* (London: T&T Clark, 2003), 51–58; Susan Gillingham, "Studies of the Psalms: Retrospect and Prospect," *The Expository Times* 119, no. 5 (2007): 209–16; Prosper Grech, "L'interpretazione patristica dei Salmi," *Augustinianum* 48, no. 1 (2008): 221–35; Brian E. Daley, "Finding the Right Key: The Aims and Strategies of Early Christian Interpretation of the Psalms," 11–28 in *The Harp of Prophecy: Early Christian Interpretation of the Psalms*, ed. Brian E. Daley and Paul R. Kolbet (Notre Dame, IN: University of Notre Dame Press, 2015).

5. In the MT the Hebrew word is זִמְרָת. Ψαλτήριον occurs in the LXX in Ps 80:3 (כִּנּוֹר), but not in the New Testament. Other recurrences: Gen 4:21; Neh 12:27; Pss 32:2; 48:5; 56:9; 80:3; 91:4; 107:3; 143:9; 149:3; 150:3; 151:2; Job 21:12; Wis 19:18; Sir 40:21; Isa 5:12; 38:20; Ezek 26:13; 33:32; Dan 3:5, 7, 10, 15; Ode 7:20.

6. In Zech 6:14 LXX εἰς ψαλμόν translates the Hebrew לְזִכָּרוֹן. In Isa 66:20 μετὰ ψαλμῶν translates בִּכְלִי טָהוֹר.

the LXX, probably first century BCE) a "psalm" is a song to be sung. The term is used in the headings of psalms.[7]

The "Book of Psalms"

The expression "the book of Psalms" never occurs in the MT or in the LXX. In fact, we find it for the first time in Luke 20:42, where Jesus himself quotes Psalm 109:1 saying that it belongs to the "book of Psalms," and in Acts 1:20, where Peter combines Psalm 69:26 and Psalm 109:8 as a fulfilment of the prophecy about Judah.

With the discoveries in the Judean Desert in 1947, we know that the expression "book of psalms" was used in 4Q491 (War Scroll),[8] a fragment dated to the Herodian period.[9] Qumran is also important for the huge quantity of manuscripts of psalms: forty scrolls on the psalms bear witness that they were studied, prayed and copied many times.[10] Only twenty-four psalms of the 150, known in the MT, are missing in the Dead Sea Discoveries, probably because of the deterioration of the scrolls: nineteen were missing from the first three books of the psalms (Ps 1–89), and from Psalms 90–150 (fourth and fifth books) only five are missing (Pss 90; 108; 110; 111; 117).

Among the scrolls of the psalms, 11QPs[a] is the longest (probably written in the middle of the first century AD, containing thirty-eight psalms known from the MT with the addition of a part of Psalm 151,[11] transmitted only in the Septuagint, and not present in the MT. The order of the psalms is quite different from that of the MT. Despite the absence of some psalms and the different

---

7. In 67 psalms' headings we find the term; of these 54 times it translates the Hebrew term מִזְמוֹר.

8. Katell Berthelot, "Les titres des livres bibliques: Le témoignage de la Bibliothèque de Qumrân," 127–40 in *Flores Florentino: Dead Sea Scrolls and Other Early Jewish Studies in Honour of Florentino García Martínez*, ed. Anthony Hilhorst, Émile Puech, and Eibert Tigchelaar (Leiden: Brill, 2007), 132–33.

9. Katherine Dell, "Psalms," 37–51 in *The Oxford Handbook of the Reception History of the Bible*, ed. Michael Lieb, Emma Mason, and Jonathan Roberts (Oxford: Oxford University Press, 2011), 37: "The book has no title as such, but at the end of Psalm 72 'the prayers of David' is a key phrase. Rabbinic tradition, however, has preferred *tehillim*, 'praises,' and, interestingly, 'praise' and 'prayer' together describe the contents of the Psalter. The title *tehillim* is thus what one finds in Hebrew Bibles today." See also Peter W. Flint, "Five Surprises in the Qumran Psalms Scrolls," in *Flores Florentino*, 183–95.

10. 39 scrolls from Qumran, 1 from Nahal Hever, and 2 from Masada.

11. Natalio Fernández Marcos, "David the Adolescent: On Psalm 151," 205–17 in *The Old Greek Psalter*, ed. Robert J. V. Hiebert, Claude E. Cox, and Peter J. Gentry (Sheffield: Sheffield Academic, 2001).

order of those that remain, scholars claim the existence of a book of Psalms in Qumran. This confirms the Lukan information. Furthermore, it is plausible that at Qumran the group of Psalms 1–89 (first–third books) was known to be established already. Do not forget that in the Dead Sea desert other psalms were found, classified as apocryphal, or other biblical and non-biblical hymns. This highlights even more the importance of a book's existence and not only of loose sheets of psalms, hymns, or songs.

The main feature of the apocryphal compositions is the complete absence of David's mention as author or singer, whereas David's name occurs 103 times in the MT Psalter, especially in the headings of the psalms.[12] In 11QPs[a] we find a clear Davidic authorship too, and moreover we find a Davidic superscription in Psalm 123 ("Ascension Song. Of David") and in Psalm 145 we read "of David" in its superscription.

Davidic Authorship

The authorship of David is a common characteristic between the Dead Sea texts and early Christian writings. At the ending of 11QPs[a] (col. 27:2–11), we read:

> And David, son of Jesse, was wise, a luminary like the light of the sun, learned, [3] knowledgeable, and perfect in all his paths before God and men. And to him [4] YHWH gave a wise and enlightened spirit. And he wrote psalms: [5] three thousand six hundred; and songs to be sung before the altar over the perpetual [6] offering of every day, for all the days of the year: three hundred [7] and sixty-four; and for the sabbath offerings: fifty-two songs; and for the offering for the beginning [8] of the month, and for all the days of the festivals, and for the day of atonement: thirty songs. [9] And all the songs which he composed were four hundred and forty-six. And songs [10] to be sung over the possessed: four. The total was four thousand and fifty. [11] He composed them all through the spirit of prophecy which had been given to him from before the Most High.[13]

The wise son of Jesse wrote 3,600 psalms and songs with a total of 4,050 hymns. The mention of the prophetic gift given to him by God is very important for understanding the psalms' reception. David was not only a king, but a wise man, a singer, a composer of the liturgy in the Temple, and a prophet.[14]

---

12. The mentions of David are always in the psalms' headings, except: Pss 17:51; 51:2; 53:2; 71:20; 77:70; 88:4, 21, 36, 50; 121:5; 131:10–11, 17; 143:10; 144:1; 151:1.

13. Trans. Florentino García Martínez, ed., *The Dead Sea Scrolls Translated: The Qumran Texts in English* (Leiden: Brill, 1994), 309.

14. According to Peter W. Flint, "The Prophet David at Qumran," 158–67 in *Biblical Interpretation at Qumran*, ed. Matthias Henze (Grand Rapids, MI: Eerdmans, 2005), 161: "The noun

Even in the biblical Jewish writings we find the presentation of David as a singer (1 Sam 16:16–23; 2 Sam 23:1; Sir 47:8) and as a composer (2 Macc 2:13).[15] In Psalm 72:20 we read: "The prayers of David the son of Jesse are ended," but the heading of Psalm 72 says: "A Psalm of Solomon."[16] We probably have here a sign of the Psalter's first edition. Even after Psalm 72 we find David's name in the headings: Psalms 93, 97, etc. until Psalm 142 and even in Psalm 151 (LXX). Davidic authorship was important not only for the first three books of Psalms, but, as time went on, his patronage was extended to the whole Psalter too. Why was David so important for this particular part of the wisdom literature? Is it important for understanding the meaning of the psalms, their order in the Psalter and their interpretation? Or can we consider the Davidic authorship in the headings of the psalms superfluous and an editorial addition?[17] The early Christian commentators gave different answers.[18]

'prophecy' (*hawbn*) occurs only once in the Qumran corpus: in the prose epilogue of the Great Psalms Scroll (11QPs^a 27:11) as the means by which David composed his liturgies, and which is given to him by God."

15. David is first mentioned as the author of Psalms in 1 Chr, in the second century BCE. See Gary A. Anderson, "King David and the Psalms of Imprecation," 29–45 in *The Harp of Prophecy: Early Christian Interpretation of the Psalms*, ed. Brian E. Daley and Paul R. Kolbet (Notre Dame, IN: University of Notre Dame Press, 2015).

16. Waltke and Houston, *The Psalms as Christian Worship*, 101 and note 58, about Ps 72:20 as conclusion of the earlier collection of psalms: "'This concludes the prayers of David the son of Jesse' is "the eggshell" of an earlier collection. The notice in 2 Chronicles 29:30 suggests that two collections, 'the words of David' (Psalms 3–41) and 'the words of Asaph' (50, 72–82), existed in Hezekiah's time. Psalms by the sons of Korah (42–49, 84–88 [not 86]) probably constituted another collection. Whether the 'Elohistic Psalter' (Psalms 42–83), which bridges Books II and III, ever constituted a separate collection is unknown." Note 58: "Whereas in Psalm 1–41 and 84–150, *YHWH* occurs 584 times and *Elohim* 94 times, in 42–83 *YHWH* occurs 45 times and *Elohim* 210 times. Moreover, *YHWH* usually occurs elsewhere in verset 'a' and *Elohim* in verset 'b,' but in 42–83 the situation is reversed. . . . The number 42 figures prominently in this collection. . . . Elsewhere, in the Old Testament the numeral 42 is used in the contexts of judgment (Num 35:6; Judg 12:6; 2 Kings 2:24; 10:14; Rev 13:5)."

17. David's name occurs 84 times in the LXX in the *Inscriptiones psalmorum*: cf. Pss LXX 3–40; 42; 50–64; 67–70; 85; 90; 92–98; 100; 102–3; 107–9; 130; 132; 136–44 and the "idiographic" Ps 151. In the MT it occurs only 73 times. See Susanne Gillmayr-Bucher, "The Psalm Headings: A Canonical Relecture of the Psalms," 247–54 in *The Biblical Canons*, ed. Jean-Marie Auwers and Henk Jan De Jonge (Leuven: Leuven University Press, 2003); Martin Meiser, "David and Psalms in Ancient Christian Exegesis," 282–318 in *David, Messianism, and Eschatology: Ambiguity in the Reception History of the Book of Psalms in Judaism and Christianity*, ed. Erkki Koskenniemi and David Willgren Davage (Turku, Finland: Åbo Akademi University, 2020).

18. Eusebius, *In Psalmos* in *Patrologia Graeca*, 23.65 wrote that the book of Psalms contains a new teaching. After Moses and Joshua, David, as father of the Savior, invented psalmody as a new liturgy to praise God. David surpassed Moses.

The Early Christian Writers' Use of the Psalms

Before we consider the patristic use of the Psalter, we have to consider the heritage of the New Testament's writers. They are not only the first witnesses of Christian theology, but they also give us a look, probably the most ancient one, into Second Temple Judaism.[19]

Paul

Paul is the first Christian writer, and he quotes the Greek Scriptures many times in his letters. According to Moisés Silva there are 107 quotations, of which one third comes from Isaiah and twenty-four from the psalms. The Psalter is the second most quoted book in the New Testament.[20] Of the twenty-four psalm quotations in the Pauline corpus, sixteen are in the epistle to the community of Rome to whom the Apostle had never preached before. The quotations are from across the whole book of Psalms. The majority of these quotations are introduced with the formula "as it is written" (καθὼς γέγραπται),[21] and only twice are they introduced with the expression "David says" (Rom 4:6 quoting Ps 31:1–2 and Rom 11:9 quoting Ps 68:23–24).[22] In the Pauline corpus David's name occurs only one other time, in Romans 1:3, the pre-Pauline fragment where the twofold condition of Jesus Christ is presented: "Born of the seed of David according to the flesh . . . declared to be the Son of God with power,

---

19. About Philo, see David T. Runia, "Philo's Reading of the Psalms," 102–21 in *The Studia Philonica Annual: Studies in Hellenistic Judaism. Volume XIII 2001*, ed. David T. Runia and Gregory E. Sterling (Providence, RI: Brown Judaic Studies, 2001). Flavius Josephus did not quote Psalms, but uses the terms "psalm" (*Antiquitates Judaicarum*, 6.214; 7.80; 9.35; 12.323), "psalter" (*Antiquitates Judaicarum*, 1.64), "psalmist" (*Antiquitates Judaicarum*, 11.72), and "psalming" (*Antiquitates Judaicarum*, 6.166–68; 9.35, 9.269; 11.67; 12.349). About the use of Psalms in the synagogue, see John Maier, "Zur Verwendung der Psalmen in der synagogalen Liturgie (Wochentag und Sabbat)," 55–90 in *Liturgie und Dichtung: Ein interdisziplinäres Kompendium II*, ed. Hansjakob Becker and Reiner Kaczynski (St. Ottilien: Eos Verlag Erzabtei St. Ottilien, 1983).

20. Moisés Silva, "The Greek Psalter in Paul's Letters: A Textual Study," 277–88 in *The Old Greek Psalter*, ed. Robert J. V. Hiebert, Claude E. Cox, and Peter J. Gentry (Sheffield: Sheffield Academic, 2001); Manlio Simonetti, "I 'Salmi' nel Nuovo Testamento," *Orpheus* 9, no. 1 (1988): 1–20.

21. Rom 3:4.20; 8:36; 11:9; 15:3.9; 1 Cor 3:20; 2 Cor 9:9.

22. Subject of "says" (λέγει), in quoting the Scripture, is "the law" (ὁ νόμος): Rom 3:19; 1 Cor 9:8; 14:34; "the Scripture" (ἡ γραφή): Rom 4:3; 9:17; 10:11; 11:2; 1 Cor 9:10; Gal 4:30; 1 Tim 5:18; "Isaiah": Rom 10:16.20; 15:12; "Moses": Rom 9:15; 10:6.8.19; "Hosea": Rom 9:25, etc. ; "the spirit": 1 Tim 4:1; "God": Rom 10:21; 11:4; 12:19; 14:11; 15:10; 2 Cor 6:2.16–18; Eph 5:14; "Christ himself": Eph 4:7, many times in Hebrews.

according to the spirit of holiness, by the resurrection from the dead." No other mention of David occurs in the Pauline corpus. According to these three texts, David is the author/speaker of the Psalter, and he is the ancestor of Jesus ("according to the flesh").

Gospels

The same Davidic authorship is found in the Gospels.[23] A clear example is the controversy between Jesus and the Pharisees (according to Matt 22:41) or scribes (according to Mark 12:35 or Luke 20:39) regarding the Davidic descent of the Messiah. Jesus says: "How then does David in the Spirit call him Lord, saying, The Lord said unto my Lord." David, the speaker of Psalm 109:1, calls the Messiah his Lord; so, his son, according to the promise of 2 Samuel 7:14, is greater than he: David is the king, but his son is the son of God. In the controversy with his opponents, Jesus wisely uses this psalm's quotation to show that the messianic identity is greater than Davidic descent, because David himself could have never called his offspring "Lord." We ought to note that in the LXX David is never mentioned with the divine title of "Lord" (Κύριος, the Septuagint translation of the Hebrew tetragrammaton YHWH). For his explanation, Jesus used the exegetical rule called "prosopological," a term from the Greek word "prosopon" (πρόσωπον), that could be translated as "face," namely "person." Identifying the speaker allows the true meaning of a text to be determined. *Tis legei pros tina kai peri tinos*: who is speaking, to whom, and about whom?[24] Because David is the speaker and he is never acknowledged as a lord, he must be speaking about another greater than he. The prosopological use of the psalm and its affinity to the literal sense permit Jesus to claim that he is more than the Messiah.[25]

---

23. James L. Mays, "The David of the Psalms," *Interpretation* 40, no. 2 (1986): 143–55, at 145–46.

24. Acts 8:34: περὶ τίνος ὁ προφήτης λέγει τοῦτο; περὶ ἑαυτοῦ ἢ περὶ ἑτέρου τινός; about whom is the prophet speaking?: Theophilus, *Ad Autolycum*, 2.18: Οὐκ ἄλλῳ δέ τινι εἴρηκε· "ποιήσωμεν," ἀλλ' ἢ τῷ ἑαυτοῦ Λόγῳ καὶ τῇ ἑαυτοῦ Σοφίᾳ; Hippolytus, *Contra Noetum*, 4.

25. Anthony Giambrone, "Prosopological Exegesis and Christological Anagnorisis in Jesus's Reading of Psalm 110," *Nova et Vetera* 18, no. 4 (2020): 1267–1284; Rondeau, *Commentaires*, 2:20–21: "Nous nous limitons donc sans scrupules aux commentaires qui appliquent la méthode prosopologique, et même à ces commentaires en tant seulement qu'ils l'appliquent, laissant tomber tout ce qui, en eux, relève aussi de l'allégorie et de la typologie. Ces commentaires sont ceux d'Origène, d'Eusèbe, 'd'Athanase,' de Didyme, de Diodore, de Théodore de Mopsueste, de Théodoret, de Cyrille d'Alexandrie, d'Hésychius de Jérusalem, chez les Grecs; d'Hilaire, d'Ambroise, d'Augustin chez les Latins."

Challenges from the Past for Future Biblical Exegesis

The discussion about the messianic identity of Jesus is close to the passion narratives, in which we find an intensification of the psalm quotations.[26] Among them, the most important is that on the cross, when Jesus cries out with the words of Psalm 21:2, according to Matthew and Mark, or with the words of Psalm 30:6, according to Luke. Jesus's last words are not his own words, but are from the Psalter.

Jesus himself expresses his mortal destiny when he enters the city of Jerusalem for the Passover. With the quotation of another psalm, Psalm 117:25-26, he concludes the vineyard parable by claiming that his rejection is according to the prophetic Scriptures. To Jesus the psalms are prophetic, they are Davidic, and they are prayers to invoke God's help.[27]

This memory of Jesus's use of the psalms is probably the historical background of the theological affirmation we read in Luke 24:44: "the law of Moses, and the prophets, and the psalms" find their true meaning in the person of Christ, because the whole of Scripture speaks about him. Note that this Lukan sentence is uttered by the risen Lord himself, "about me." The later Christian writers will say that Jesus Christ is not only the objective content of the Scriptures, but he always has been and he is the main speaker and the principal subject of every word of God.[28] According to John 1:1, he is the Word of God and, consequently, every word of Scripture is spoken by him (Heb 1:1-2).

We cannot deduce from the sequence Law – Prophets – Psalms described in Luke 24:44 an acknowledged scriptural canon.[29] We can only say that there

---

26. Balthasar Fischer, "Le Christ dans les Psaumes: La dévotion aux Psaumes dans l'Église des martyrs," *La Maison-Dieu* 27, no. 1 (1951): 86–113; Karl Löning, "Die Funktion des Psalters im Neuen Testament," 269–95 in *Der Psalter in Judentum und Christentum*, ed. Erich Zenger (Freiburg im Breisgau: Herder, 1998); Douglas J. Moo, *The Old Testament in the Gospel Passion Narratives* (Sheffield: The Almond Press, 1983), 225–300.

27. Enrico Norelli, "Introduzione: La Bibbia come problema alle origini del cristianesimo," 9–33, 199–233 in *La Bibbia nell'antichità cristiana*, vol. 1, *Da Gesù a Origene*, ed. Enrico Norelli (Bologna: Edizioni Dehoniane Bologna, 1993), 14; Vittorio Fusco, "Gesù e le Scritture di Israele," in *La Bibbia nell'antichità cristiana*, 35–63.

28. See Origen, *De principiis*, 4.2.1.

29. Sir, prol. 1.8-10: "ΠΟΛΛΩΝ καὶ μεγάλων ἡμῖν διὰ τοῦ νόμου καὶ τῶν προφητῶν (2) καὶ τῶν ἄλλων τῶν κατ' αὐτοὺς ἠκολουθηκότων δεδομένων, (8) εἴς τε τὴν τοῦ νόμου (9) καὶ τῶν προφητῶν (10) καὶ τῶν ἄλλων πατρίων βιβλίων ἀνάγνωσιν"; Philo, *De Vita Contemplativa* 25: "ἀλλὰ νόμους καὶ λόγια θεσπισθέντα διὰ προφητῶν καὶ ὕμνους καὶ τὰ ἄλλα"; Flavius Joseph, *Contra Apionem*, 1.8 (38–41): "(38) οὐ μυριάδες βιβλίων εἰσὶ παρ' ἡμῖν ἀσυμφώνων καὶ μαχομένων, δύο δὲ μόνα πρὸς τοῖς εἴκοσι βιβλία τοῦ παντὸς ἔχοντα χρόνου τὴν ἀναγραφήν, τὰ δικαίως πεπιστευμένα. (39) καὶ τούτων πέντε μέν ἐστι Μωυσέως, ἃ τούς τε νόμους περιέχει καὶ τὴν ἀπ' ἀνθρωπογονίας παράδοσιν μέχρι τῆς αὐτοῦ τελευτῆς· οὗτος ὁ χρόνος ἀπολείπει τρισχιλίων ὀλίγῳ ἐτῶν. (40) ἀπὸ δὲ τῆς Μωυσέως τελευτῆς μέχρι τῆς Ἀρταξέρξου τοῦ μετὰ

were some written books already collected in three main groups and mentioned in this precise order: the Law, the Prophets, and the Psalms (/Writings). Luke is the first to highlight the Psalms as a collected book as well as the Law of Moses and the Prophets. Moreover, he adds the hermeneutical content concerning the paschal figure of Jesus risen from the dead. The paschal mystery and the Scriptures are inseparably intertwined, according to Luke and according to 1 Corinthians 15:3-5, where we read that Christ is dead and he is risen "according to the Scripture." The psalms (i.e., the book of Psalms, cf. Luke 20:42) are not only prophetic regarding Christ's Passover but they also interpret and explain the person of Jesus.

Short Conclusion

This very short survey on the psalms' use in the New Testament writings shows at least three elements. Firstly, before his death Jesus used the psalms very often as prayers and as prophecies of his death and his messianic identity. No other Jewish prophecy from the Torah or from the Prophets had the same importance.[30] Secondly, in order to explain the meaning of the psalms, the speaker emerges as very important, because the speaker's identity gives the true meaning of the sentence, according to the prosopological technique that we find many times in other New Testament writings (i.e., Hebrews). This technique probably became very popular with Aristarchus of Samothrace (second century BCE) with his Alexandrian Homeric commentaries. In the early Christian centuries, prosopology would become the main theological tool to explain the relationship between the Son and the Father in the Trinity,[31] and hence, the surest criterion to understand the book of Psalms in the Greek and in the Latin Christian literature.[32] Thirdly, the evangelists, especially Luke, wanted to

---

Ξέρξην Περσῶν βασιλέως οἱ μετὰ Μωυσῆν προφῆται τὰ κατ' αὐτοὺς πραχθέντα συνέγραψαν ἐν τρισὶ καὶ δέκα βιβλίοις αἱ δὲ λοιπαὶ τέσσαρες ὕμνους εἰς τὸν θεὸν καὶ τοῖς ἀνθρώποις ὑποθήκας τοῦ βίου περιέχουσιν. (41) ἀπὸ δὲ Ἀρταξέρξου μέχρι τοῦ καθ' ἡμᾶς χρόνου γέγραπται μὲν ἕκαστα, πίστεως δ' οὐχ ὁμοίας ἠξίωται τοῖς πρὸ αὐτῶν διὰ τὸ μὴ γενέσθαι τὴν τῶν προφητῶν ἀκριβῆ διαδοχήν."

30. On the prophetic use of Isa 53, note that is a redactional assessment (Luke 22:37). The only prophet quoted by Jesus is the three days and nights of Jonah in the fish's belly as prophetic announcement of his death and resurrection.

31. Tertullian, *Adversus Praxean*, 1159-1205 in *Quinti Septimi Florentis Tertulliani Opera*, Pars 2, ed. Aemilius Kroymann and Ernest Evans, CCSL 2 (Turnholt: Brepols, 1954), chapter 2; Giambrone, "Prosopological Exegesis and Christological Anagnorisis," 1267-1284.

32. Rondeau, *Commentaires*, 2:7-40; Maurizio Girolami, *La recezione del Salmo 21 (LXX) agli inizi dell'era cristiana: Cristologia ed ermeneutica biblica in costruzione* (Rome: Istituto Patristico Augustinianum, 2011), 220-30; on Augustine's interpretation of the psalms see Michael

transmit the risen Christ's command to read the whole Scripture not only in order to understand his paschal mystery as the true meaning of the Scriptures, but also in order to fulfil their apostolic duty. It would be impossible to preach God's Gospel without continuous reference to the Jewish Scriptures.[33] Therefore, we can say that for the early Christian writers the apostolic activity, the Church's growth, and the paschal mystery's fulfilment would only be possible with and according to the Jewish Scriptures (translated in Greek).

Before we move on to speak about the earliest commentators on the Psalter, we have to mention other not inconsiderable facts that happened in the second century. At the beginning of the second century, in the time of Trajan's reign (98–117), we have a famous letter from the governor of Bithynia, Pliny the Younger, addressed to the emperor, which describes the Christian liturgy with songs to Christ as a God.[34] Based on this witness, we cannot identify the Jewish Psalter with Christian songs, and neither can we imagine that these songs were new Christian compositions. It should be highlighted that this evidence, very ancient and non-Christian, attests to a liturgy with *"carmina."*[35]

Fiedrowicz, *Psalmus vox totius Christi: Studien zu Augustinus "Ennarrationes in Psalmos"* (Freiburg: Herder, 1997); Anthony Dupont, "The *Enarrationes in Psalmos* by Augustine of Hippo: The Psalms as the Voice(s) of the Church and Christ," 319–36 in *David, Messianism, and Eschatology: Ambiguity in the Reception History of the Book of Psalms in Judaism and Christianity*, ed. Erkki Koskenniemi and David Willgren Davage (Turku, Finland: Åbo Akademi University, 2020).

33. Charles H. Dodd, *According to the Scriptures: The Substructure of New Testament Theology* (London: Nisbet & Co., 1952), 96–103.

34. Pliny the Younger, *Epistula* 96.7, in *Lettres. Livre X. Panégyrique de Trajan*, ed. Marcel Durry (Paris: Les Belles Lettres, 1959), p. 96: "adfirmabant autem hanc fuisse summam vel culpae suae vel erroris, quod essent soliti stato die ante lucem convenire carmenque Christo quasi deo dicere secum invicem seque sacramento non in scelus aliquod obstringere, sed ne furta, ne latrocinia, ne adulteria commiterent, ne fidem fallerent, ne depositum appellati abnegarent." It is not certain that "carmen" means "psalm." "Carmen" also referred to prophecies, magic formulas, and spells: cf. *Lexicon Totius Latinitatis*, ed. Egidio Forcellini et al. (Patavii: Gregoriana, 1965), 1:539.

35. The first mention of the psalms' use in the liturgy comes from Tertullian, *De anima*, 779–869 in *Quinti Septimi Florentis Tertulliani Opera*, Pars 2, ed. Jan. H. Waszink, CCSL 2 (Turnholt: Brepols, 1954), 9.4.29–31: "iamvero prout scripturae leguntur aut psalmi canuntur aut allocutiones proferuntur aut petitiones delegantur, ita inde materiae visionibus subministrantur"; *De oratione*, 255–74 in *Quinti Septimi Florentis Tertulliani Opera*, Pars 1, ed. Gerardus F. Diercks, CCSL 1 (Turnholt: Brepols, 1954), chapters 27–28: "diligentiores in orando subiungere in orationibus alleluia solent et hoc genus psalmos, quorum clausulis respondeant qui simul sunt. Et est optimum utique institutum omni quod praeponendo et honorando Deo competit saturatam orationem velut opimam hostiam admovere. (28) Haec est enim hostia spiritalis, quae pristina sacrifice delevit. . . . Hanc de toto corde devotam, fide pastam, veritate curatam, innocentia integram, castitate mundam, agape coronatam cum pompa operum honorum inter

The first Christian composition of new psalms is mentioned in the Muratorian fragment, among the list of Christian writings where we read about Valentinus, the famous gnostic thinker, who wrote some psalms for Marcion.[36] Although the Muratorian fragment should not be considered as giving an acknowledged canonical list of New Testament books, we must note that this new book of Psalms was included among the others Christian writings as if it had the same authority because they had been read in the Christian gatherings.

Another case is that of the first Syriac author Bardaisan (154–222, according to Eusebius, *Ecclesiastical History*, 4.30: ἱκανώτατός τις ἀνήρ), who wrote some new psalms as well. Did Valentinus and Bardaisan write new psalm compositions in order to supersede the Jewish Scriptures or to add to the new Scriptures? Sadly, not very many of these works are extant, probably because they were considered heretical and, above all, the Council of Laodicea (Phrygia Pacatiana) forbade the writing of new psalms because the only Psalter should be that of the Jewish Psalter (of the LXX).[37]

---

psalmos et hymnos deducere ad Dei altare debemus omnia nobis a Deo impetraturam." Susan Gillingham, "From Liturgy to Prophecy: The Use of Psalmody in Second Temple Judaism," *Catholic Biblical Quarterly* 64, no. 3 (2002): 470–89.

36. "Pastorem vero nuperrime temporibus nostris in urbe Roma Hermas conscripsit sedente cathedra urbis Romae ecclesiae Pio episcopo fratre eius: et ideo legi eum quidem oportet, se publicare vero in ecclesia populo neque inter prophetas completo numero neque inter apostolos in fine temporum potest. Arsinoi autem seu Valentini vel Miltiadis nihil in totum recipimus, qui etiam novum Psalmorum librum Marcioni conscripserunt una cum Basilide Asiano, Cataphrygium constitutore." *Das Muratorische Fragment und Die Monarchianischen Prologe zu den Evangelien*, ed. Hans Lietzmann (Bonn: Marcus & Weber, 1921), 9–11, lines 73–85. Even Tertullian, *De carne Christi*, 871–917 in *Quinti Septimi Florentis Tertulliani Opera*, Pars 2, ed. Aemilius Kroymann, CCSL 2 (Turnholt: Brepols, 1954), 17.1 writes about Valentinus's psalm. In *De carne Christi*, 20.3 he writes: "nobis quoque ad hanc speciem psalmi patrocinantur, non quidem apostatae et haeretici et Platonici Valentini, sed sanctissimi et receptissimi prophetae David." The author of *Elenchos* refers to the Valentinian psalm composition too: Hippolytus, *Elenchos*, 134–89 in *Hippolytus Werke*, vol. 3, *Refutatio Omnium Haeresium*, ed. Paul Wendland, GCS 26 (Leipzig: J.C. Hinrichs'sche Buchhandlung, 1916), 6.37.6. *Elenchos*, 5.6.5 uses the term ὕμνοι. Cf. Adolf von Harnack, *Marcion: Das Evangelium vom Fremden Gott. Eine Monographie zur Geschichte der Grundlegung der Katholischen Kirche*, 2nd ed., TU 45 (Leipzig: J.C. Hinrichs'sche Buchhandlung, 1924), 29: "Dass Marcion sich persönlich (in Rom?) mit Valentin und Basilides berührt hat („wie ein Älterer mit Jüngeren"), kann man mindestens nicht mit Wahrscheinlichkeit aus einer Stelle bei Clemens (Stromata VII,18,107) schließen, und die abgerissene Nachricht im Muratorischen Fragment, Valentin und noch ein anderer hätten für M. ein neues Psalmbuch geschrieben, bleibt ganz dunkel." See also 315. In Beilage III, 174–76, Harnack writes that the Marcionite church used this non-Davidic Psalter.

37. Cf. Carlo Nardi, "Laodicea (concili)," 2735–2736 in *Nuovo Dizionario Patristico e di Antichità Cristiane*, ed. Angelo Di Berardino (Rome: Marietti, 2008). It seems that this Council

According to Eusebius (*Ecclesiastical History*, 4.18.5), even Justin (100–167) wrote a lost work called *Psaltes* (Ψάλτης). In the second century we note a relative freedom to write and to use some new compositions, probably as a substitution for the Jewish psalms. In that century the most important Christian institutions, like the hierarchy, the biblical canon, the annual feast of Easter, and apologetic theology, were forged. We have too few sources from this period to have a clear picture of the variety and, at the same time, of the harmony of Christian faith. We have to wait for the third century to see a new stage of theological development, when the Jewish Scriptures and the Christian writings were considered as a whole. Even if there were no official list of canonical books, with Origen the Bible was commented upon book by book, verse by verse, word by word. This new way to interpret the biblical writings grew within the Alexandrian milieu, where the philological sense and Platonic thinking conditioned the "new"[38] literary genre of biblical commentary.

The Early Commentators on the Psalter

According to Jerome (*Epistle* 112.20), the first Christian commentators on the psalms were Origen, Eusebius of Caesarea, Theodorus of Heraclea, Asterious of Scythopolis, Apollinaris of Laodicea, and Didymus of Alexandria. Among the Latin authors, Jerome mentions Hilary, bishop of Poitiers, Eusebius, bishop of Vercelli, and Ambrose, bishop of Milan. The monk of Bethlehem notes that these last Latin writers translated (*transtulerunt*) the Origenian works, but they did not write their own. We know some of these works through direct tradition (manuscripts) confirmed and enriched by the huge work of the "chains" (*catenae*), begun by Procopius of Gaza in Palestine in the sixth century.[39] Through the latter, we can read part of the lost work of Hippolytus on the psalms (first two decades of the third century).

---

was summoned by Theodosius (between 379 and 395), but Theodoret writes about this Council as if it were at his time, immediately after Ephesus. On the canon 59, see *Die Kanones der wichtigsten altkirchlichen Concilien nebst den apostolischen Kanones*, ed. Friedrich Lauchert (Freiburg: Mohr Siebeck, 1896), 78: "ὅτι οὐ δεῖ ἰδιωτικούς ψαλμούς."

38. It was new for the Christian world, but it was well known for the Homeric works.

39. René Cadiou, *Commentaires inédits des Psaumes: Etude sur le textes d'Origène contenus dans le manuscrit Vindobonensis 8* (Paris: Les Belles Lettres, 1936); Robert Devreesse, "Chaînes exégétiques grecques," 1084–1233 in *Dictionnaire de la Bible: Supplément*, vol. 1 (Paris: Letouzey et Ané, 1926); Robert Devreesse, *Les anciens commentateurs grecs des Psaumes* (Vatican City: Biblioteca Apostolica Vaticana, 1970); Marguerite Harl, *La chaîne palestinienne sur le psaume 118 (Origène, Eusèbe, Didyme, Apollinaire, Athanase, Théodoret)*, vol. 1 (Paris: Cerf, 1972).

Jerome's witness is well supported not only by the biblical manuscript tradition, but also by the high esteem that these patristic works on the psalms had for the better understanding of the Psalter. In fact, at the beginning of the fifth century and probably in Alexandria, a biblical manuscript was composed with the Septuagint version of the Old Testament and the New Testament, today known as the Codex Alexandrinus. Between the apocryphal books of 3 and 4 Maccabees and the book of Psalms we find Athanasius's *Epistle to Marcellinus* (ff. 522–530),[40] written probably after his fifth exile (366), some years before his death (373). After this, there are three introductory works to the psalms by Eusebius of Caesarea: *Hypothesis* (f. 531r), *Periochae* (ff. 531v–533r), and *Canones* (f. 533r). The first work deals with the Psalter's division and the authorship of the psalms; the second is a short presentation of each psalm's importance for the Christian life; *Canones* is a table in which Eusebius, noting the headings, organized the 150 Psalms in groups following the prosopological rule: the first "canon" enumerates the Davidic psalms (72); the second one the Solomonic psalms (2), then those without inscription (19), of the sons of Korah (11); of Asaph (12); anonymous psalms (17), and Alleluia psalms (15). At the end Eusebius mentions the unique Psalm of Ethan (88) and that of Moses (89). Athanasius's and Eusebius's works became part of a biblical manuscript which help the reader understand the importance of the Psalter and to have a sure guide in reading each psalm in an appropriate way. Athanasius's and Eusebius's works were original, but they would have been incomprehensible without the pioneering and extensive study of Origen.

The Works of Origen on the Psalter

Being in Rome in 385, Jerome wrote a letter to Paula (*Letter* 33) in which he explains the genius of Origen, whom he compared to the great Latin writer Varro. Jerome's purpose is to claim that with Origen's works, Christianity would no longer be considered inferior to the huge heritage of ancient authors. In order to show the quality and the quantity of the Origenian writings, Jerome, who had gone to Bethlehem in 386, tried to list Origen's works for the first time.

Jerome probably had access to the library of Caesarea,[41] where Origen lived

---

40. Facsimile by the British Museum available at https://archive.org/details/TheCodexAlexandrinusV.4/page/n165/mode/2up. On Athanasius's Epistle to Marcellinus see Everett Ferguson, "Athanasius' *Epistula ad Marcellinum* in interpretationem Psalmorum," 295–308 in *Studia Patristica* 16, part 2, ed. Elisabeth A. Livingstone, TU 129 (Berlin: Akademie Verlag, 1985).

41. Cf. Jerome, *Contra Rufinum*, 242–51 in *Saint Jérôme: Apologie contre Rufin*, ed. Pierre Lardet, SC 303 (Paris: Cerf, 1983), 3.12–13; Jerome, *Commentarioli in Psalmos*, 163–245 in S.

and taught from 232 until his death. Jerome mentioned three categories: *tomoi* or books, homilies, and *scholia*, which are short explanations of difficult biblical passages. About the book of Psalms, he mentions *Excerpta in Psalmos a primo usque ad quintum decimum*, a lost commentary on the first 15 (or 25) psalms; a Commentary in forty-five books about non-continuous psalms, from 1 to 103; 120 homilies on 63 psalms, that were transcribed after he was sixty years old, i.e., AD 245, according to Eusebius (*Ecclesiastical History*, 6.36.1).[42] Jerome also mentioned *Excerpta in totum Psalterium*, which perhaps were the *scholia*.[43] The exegetical endeavor of Origen began with the Psalter and continued through all his life. About the homilies, we have to remember that in 2012 in Munich a medieval manuscript was discovered with twenty-nine unknown homilies on the psalms, only five of which were known to us previously in a Latin translation by Rufinus of Concordia.[44] Jerome himself, in *Letter* 34.1, wrote that Pamphilus, the successor of Origen in Caesarea, could not find the Origenian commentary on Psalm 126 or his homily on the letter *Phe* of Psalm 118 (cf. *Ecclesiastical History*, 6.36.2). Origen's exegetical work was so huge that even immediately after his death some works could not be traced. Some fragments were kept in the anthology called *Philocalia*, traditionally attributed to Basil and Gregory, but probably composed in Caesarea far earlier: the introduction

Hieronymi Presbyteri Opera, Pars 1, *Opera Exegetica* 1, ed. Germanus Morin, CCSL 72 (Turnholt: Brepols, 1959), 1.4.46–47 and 4.8.27–31.

42. On the chronology of Origen's work on the Psalter, according to *Ecclesiastical History*, 6.24.2, he would have composed the Commentary on the first 25 psalms in Alexandria between 222 and 225; then in Caesarea between 245 and 249. The homilies, probably, could date back a few years earlier (239–242). See Pierre Nautin, *Origène: sa œuvre et sa vie* (Paris: Beauchesne, 1977), 261–92.

43. According to Rondeau, *Commentaires*, 1:49. Probably *Excerpta in totum Psalterium* corresponds to what Jerome in *Commentaroli* (cf. Jerome, *Commentarioli*, prologue) calls *Enchiridion*. According to Franz X. Risch, "Das Handbuch des Origenes zu den Psalmen: Zur Bedeutung der zweiten Randkatene im Codex Vindobonensis theologicus graecus 8," *Adamantius* 20 (2014): 36–48, *Enchiridion* would have been a preliminary work before the Commentaries.

44. We knew nine homilies in Latin translation on Pss 36 (5), 37 (2), 38 (2). In *Monacensis Graecus 314* we can read in Greek four homilies on Ps 36. In Greek we also know the homily on 1 Sam 28 (the Witch of Endor) and twenty homilies on Jeremiah. Origen, *Homélies sur les psaumes 36 à 38*, ed. Emanuela Prinzivalli, Henri Crouzel, and Luc Brésard, SC 411 (Paris: Cerf, 1995); Antonio Grappone, "Omelie tradotte e/o tradite?," 59–115 in *L'Oriente in Occidente: l'opera di Rufino di Concordia*, ed. Maurizio Girolami (Brescia: Morcelliana, 2014); Origen, *Die neuen Psalmenhomilien: eine kritische Edition des Codex Monacensis Graecus 314*, ed. Lorenzo Perrone et al., GCS 19, *Origenes Werke* 13 (Munich: De Gruyter, 2015); Origen, *Homilies on the Psalms: Codex Monacensis Graecus 314*, trans. Joseph W. Trigg, FaCh 9 (Washington, DC: Catholic University of America Press, 2020).

to the commentary on Psalm 1 (*Philocalia*, 2–3),[45] the commentary on Psalm 50 (*Philocalia*, 1, 29),[46] and the commentary on Psalm 4:7 (*Philocalia*, 26).[47] In the introduction to the commentary on Psalm 1 (Origen, *Philocalia*, 2–3) we read the famous metaphor of the Scriptures as a house with many rooms. Each room has a key inside it to open a door to another room (Epiphanius, *Panarion*, 64.5–7). It is an image to explain the ancient principle "Scriptures explain Scriptures," what today, with some important differences, we could call "intertextuality."

In other passages of his works Origen mentioned his study on the psalms (see Eusebius, *Ecclesiastical History*, 6.24.2).[48] We have already mentioned that, according to Jerome, Origen was the first to comment on the Psalter. However, we cannot forget that his exegetical project to explain the Scriptures was always based on a profound study of the biblical text, as we can see in his composition of the Hexapla. Only for the psalms did he add a fifth column, discovered at Nicopolis, near Actium in western Greece, and a sixth column discovered in a jar in Jericho from the time of Severus's son, Caracalla (198–217). Eusebius also wrote that he probably added a seventh column (*Ecclesiastical History*, 6.16.3). We have very few fragments regarding these additions.

We move on to speak about another of Origen's contributions to the exegetical work on the psalms, namely the prologues and the introductory prefaces. In them the Alexandrian author gathers the preliminary discussion on the number of the psalms, their order, and their authorship, the value of the titles/headings, the diacritical signs, and the presence of *diapsalma*.[49]

We cannot present here the analytical reconstruction of Origen's and Eusebius's introductory works to the psalms made by Cordula Bandt, Franz Xaver Risch, and Barbara Villani in a book edited six years ago. They collected nine texts of Origen and eight of Eusebius, in which we find some preliminary

---

45. Origen, *Philocalia*, 238–68 in *Philocalie, 1–20: Sur les Écritures; La Lettre à Africanus sur l'histoire de Suzanne*, ed. Marguerite Harl, SC 302 (Paris: Cerf, 1983), 2–3; Ronald E. Heine, "Restringing Origen's Broken Harp: Some Suggestions Concerning the Prologue to the Caesarean Commentary on the Psalms," in *The Harp of Prophecy*, 47–74.

46. Origen, *Philocalia*, 209–28 in *Philocalie, 1–20*, sections 1, 29.

47. Origen, *Philocalia*, 234–67 in *Philocalie, 21–27: Sur le libre arbitre*, ed. Éric Junod, SC 226 (Paris: Cerf, 2006), section 26.

48. See John A. McGuckin, "Origen's Use of the Psalms in the Treatise on First Principles," 97–118 in *Meditations of the Heart: The Psalms in Early Christian Thought and Practice, Essays in Honour of Andrew Louth* (Turnhout: Brepols, 2011).

49. On the Hebrew column in Origen's Hexapla see Epiphanius, *Panarion*, 403–524 in Epiphanius, *Panarion, Haer. 34–64*, ed. Karl Holl, GCS 31 (Leipzig: J.C. Hinrichs'sche Buchhandlung, 1922), 64.3.5–7.

problems that show how these ancient authors were attentive to understanding the biblical text from many points of view. We will only focus on the text called "Catholica in Psalmos," where Origen deals with the majority of the themes named elsewhere in his works.

Origen begins by saying that the book of Psalms has no title and that the Jews call it *"sefra tellim"*; only in Acts do we find the expression "book of Psalms" (Acts 1:20). Then the question about the redactor of the Psalter follows. For Origen there is no doubt that the main author is David, but he claimed that Ezra collected the psalms after the return from the exile.[50] At the time of Origen there is a clear understanding that the order of the psalms is a very complicated question, and the difficulty in conceiving an order could be attributed to the hastiness of a collector such as Ezra would have been, living in perilous times.

The next theme is about the titles of the psalms.[51] Some of them bear the name of David, others of Solomon, Asaph, Idithum, Korah, or Moses. Other psalms are without headings. Asking himself why there is such a lack of titles, Origen refers to a Jewish tradition according to which the psalms without titles have to be ascribed to the previous one with a title. The title of the psalms may seem to us to be a question of little importance, however in the eyes of the ancient authors, great attention was paid because they also saw in it the question of the authorship of the psalm itself.[52] Without a specific author the possibility of identifying the speaker is compromised and with that the possibility to reach the true meaning of the text. The prosopological key remains the guide to understanding the psalms.

After that, Origen moves to the question of the number 150, the number of the psalms in the LXX.[53] He thinks that 150 is the number 50 multiplied by

---

50. The same idea is in Hilary, *Instructio Psalmorum*, 126–67 in SC 515, ed. Jean Doignon and Patrick Descourtieux (Paris: Cerf, 2008), sections 4 and 8. See also Enzo Cortese, "Sulle redazioni finali del Salterio," *Revue Biblique* 106, no. 1 (1999): 66–100 considers the possibility of a redaction at the beginning of the fourth century BCE.

51. Gilles Dorival, "Les titres des psaumes en hébreu et en grec: les écarts quantitatifs," 58–70 in *L'écrit et l'esprit: études d'histoire du texte et de théologie biblique en hommage à Adrian Schenker*, ed. Dieter Böhler, Innocent Himbaza, and Philippe Hugo (Göttingen: Vandenhoeck & Ruprecht, 2005).

52. Hilary, *Instructio Psalmorum*, 17–18.

53. In *De Psalmi Moysis*, Origen describes the discussion with Jewish scholars about the number of Moses's psalms: see *Die Prologtexte zu den Psalmen von Origenes und Eusebius*, ed. Cordula Bandt, Franz X. Risch, and Barbara Villani, TU 183 (Berlin: De Gruyter, 2018), 50–57. Origen put that number at 11, while Iullus 13.

3, the symbol of the Trinity.[54] Firstly, he finds in the Bible an explanation of the number 50 in the Hebrew feast of Pentecost and, looking into the Gospels, he finds that same number in the parable of Luke 7:41–42 that expresses the forgiveness of sins. Multiplied by the number of the Trinity, there is the complete gift of godly forgiveness. Numbers are very important for Alexandrian exegesis, as we know from Philo, Clement, and Origen himself.

A further and relevant question is the relationship between the content of the psalm and actual history, because it is sometimes difficult to understand the historical background of the psalms. We should not forget that generally what is written in the Bible also really happened, according to the ancient authors. To Paul, for example, Adam really existed (Rom 5:12).

The final themes deal with the musical signs and the question of *diapsalma*, which are interpreted as a musical sign. These detailed questions mentioned by Origen can be summed up in three main topics: author, number, and music. The other texts of Origen reiterate the themes covered in *Catholica in Psalmos* with some minor variations.

The work of Origen on the preliminary questions about the Psalter is the starting point for further studies. Some of the above issues are simply reiterated with few variations. For Eusebius, for instance, there are nineteen psalms without titles, but for Origen there are eighteen. This is because Psalm 32 is Davidic for the Alexandrian author but without a heading for the bishop of Caesarea.

Eusebius of Caesarea

The eight texts published in the book of Bandt, Risch, and Villani can underline two main contributions: the division of the book of Psalms into five books,[55] according to the blessing we find at the end of each book, and the *Canon of the*

---

54. Hilary, *Instructio Psalmorum* seems to oppose a division into five books, and explains a threefold partition disposed like a stair from the conversion from sin (Pss 1–50), through the virtues of a saintly life (Pss 51–100), in order to reach the praise of God (Pss 101–150). *Tractatus in Psalmos* 150.1 (PL 9:889): "cum prima nos libri huius quinquagesima regeneret ad innocentiam, sequens ad iudicium innocentiae resurrectio perducat, tertia in naturam spiritus et laudem constituat."

55. Cf. Bandt, Risch, and Villani, *Die Prologtexte*, 162–73 (the same text is in PG 23:66C–68A). Jerome, *Commentaroli in Psalmos*, 163–245 in *S. Hieronymi Presbyteri Opera*, Pars 1, *Opera Exegetica*, CCSL 72 (Turnholt: Brepols, 1959), section 40; and Jerome, *Tractatus sive Homiliae in Psalmos*, 3–447 in *S. Hieronymi Presbyteri Opera*, Pars 2, *Opera Homiletica*, CCSL 78 (Turnholt: Brepols, 1958), *Tractatus de Psalmo 89*, vers. 1; Hilary of Poitiers, *Instructio Psalmorum*, 1. See Jean-Marie Auwers, "L'organisation du psautier chez les Pères grecs," in *Le Psautier chez les Pères* (Strasbourg: Centre d'Analyse et de Documentation Patristiques, 1994), 37–54.

Psalms.[56] The latter is a table with seven columns (plus one),[57] where Eusebius collects the psalms according to the author mentioned in the title. This *Canon* is a type of map, like the *Canones* on the Gospels that the bishop of Caesarea composed for Carpianus. Eusebius was nurtured in the school of Pamphilus, the disciple of Origen who had collected and ordered the huge library in Caesarea and educated his students to read, copy, summarize, and list the literary works. It is little wonder that Eusebius tried to provide a map to reading the fourfold Gospel and that he also tried to do so with the book of Psalms.

Regarding the division of the book of Psalms into five books, he simply noted the number of the psalms where each book ends, but he does not provide a literary or theological reason, as Gregory of Nyssa will do. We also can mention *Periochae*, a list of short Christian meanings to each of the 150 Psalms. It is the first attempt to express clearly and briefly the spiritual meaning of each psalm for the Christian life. This work could be seen as a polemic against those who were writing new psalms to substitute for the Jewish Psalter and against those who did not accept the Old Testament. If the Christian reader could immediately find a Christian meaning in each psalm, he would not have to invent new compositions.

The main contribution of Eusebius's interpretation of the psalms is his effort to find the historical background for each psalm.[58] To him, history is a place where God reveals himself. In fact, Eusebius was a great theologian of history, as he showed in his *Ecclesiastical History*. To him the Bible is mainly a historical book, and he did not doubt that the facts related in it truly happened. However, he found many obstacles to linking each psalm to a historical event. For example, on Psalm 62 he wrote:

> The order of the psalms does not follow the sequence of the historical phases, on the contrary, as far as dating is concerned, they are very mixed.

---

56. To clarify, the term "canon" does not mean "canonical book," but simply a list or a table.

57. Canon I: seventy-two psalms of David; Canon II: two psalms of Solomon; Canon III: nineteen psalms without headings; Canon IV: eleven psalms of the sons of Korah; Canon V: twelve psalms of Asaph; Canon VI: seventeen anonymous psalms; Canon VII: fifteen Alleluia-psalms; outside these columns are mentioned Psalm 88 of Ethan and Psalm 89 of Moses. The same division is present in *De divisione psalmorum* (Bandt, Risch, and Villani, *Die Prologtexte*, 172). See the study of Matthew R. Crawford, *The Eusebian Canon Tables* (Oxford: Oxford University Press, 2019).

58. Dell, "Psalms," 38: Thirteen of the seventy-three "Davidic" psalms are linked to particular historical events in David's life. Some psalms have a double attribution (e.g., to David and Jeduthun, Pss 39 and 62).

The history immediately places, precisely, first, the account of Saul's sending messengers to David's house to kill him, and tells how his wife Melchol lowered him from the window, while in the psalms the mention of this fact is found in Psalm 58.[59]

Furthermore, Caesarea's bishop claims, "You see how the first events are placed after, and the subsequent ones before? . . . It is then logical to ask the reason for all this. There is in fact no reason for such an arrangement, unless some absolute necessity arises."[60] After some examples drawn from the Bible, he gives a historical reason: Ezra collected disjointed psalms in no historical order. According to Eusebius, the historical order had to be the principle of the unity of Scripture. Origen claimed that the Holy Scriptures sometimes lack a literal sense, but they always have a spiritual sense (*De principiis*, 4.2.9).

From Origen to Eusebius, we note a significant trajectory: for Origen the unity of Scripture is in its Christological sense, in each detail, even when the reader finds a lack of meaning; for Eusebius we see an attempt to find the sense of Scripture on the literal level, where "literal" means "historical," as something that truly happened. Eusebius tried to find a coherent sense on the level of history, but the text of Scripture does not completely allow this historical method because the biblical narrative does not support a literal coherence in every case. In Eusebius's exegetical work we glimpse, in another time and with other exegetical categories, Gunkel and Mowinckel's earnest efforts to describe the historical backgrounds of the psalms.

Athanasius and the Epistle to Marcellinus

From the Alexandrian school we have two important documents on the exegesis of the psalms: the *Epistle to Marcellinus* by Athanasius and *On the Titles of Psalms* of Gregory of Nyssa.[61]

Athanasius was a deacon under the bishop Alexander at the time of the Council of Nicaea (325). He became his successor in 328, and undeterred by the five exiles that he suffered, he tenaciously defended the profession of faith of the first Council. In fact, these experiences allowed him the opportunity to

---

59. Eusebius of Caesarea, *Commentaria in Psalmos*, In Psalmum 62, PG 23:600 (author's translation).

60. Eusebius of Caesarea, *Commentaria in Psalmos*, In Psalmum 62, PG 23:600 (author's translation).

61. We do not address here the discovery in 1941 in Tura, Egypt of the commentary on Pss 20–44:4 attributed to Didymus the Blind (313–398): see Didymus the Blind, *Lezioni sui Salmi. Il Commento ai Salmi scoperto a Tura*, with introduction, translation, and annotation by Emanuela Prinzivalli (Milan: Paoline, 2005).

spread the Alexandrian creed to the West, sharing Greek thought about the Arian teaching. Probably at the end of his very troubled life, he wrote a letter to Marcellinus, an unknown friend of his, regarding the importance and the use of the psalms. In only thirty-three short paragraphs, he showed the importance of the psalms for the Christian life. They are like a garden with various and multiple flowers, with many colors and with many powers to heal the wounds of the soul. According to Athanasius, the Psalter is a mirror of the soul, because in the Davidic compositions every believer can find his own feelings. A garden of beauty (par. 1) and a mirror of the soul (par. 12): these are truly powerful images to depict the usefulness of the psalms. We owe to Athanasius two other important considerations: the understanding of the Psalter as a sum of all Scripture, and the identification of literary genres. According to Athanasius the Law of Moses, the prophets, history, and the wisdom of David and Solomon are included in the book of Psalms, so that this book becomes a companion to all that is written in both the Old and the New Testament (par. 2–9). Athanasius is the first in early Christianity to express this synthesis of the book of Psalms. We can suppose that it was not his own thought, but that he only presented a conviction of the Christian life, probably under the influence of monasticism (cf. par. 9; he wrote the *Life of Anthony*).

Regarding the question of literary genres, his sensitivity to the inner speech of the human person leads him to closely link the variety of states of mind to the varieties of literal expressions of sacred authors. He attempts to list the different literary genres of the psalms: historical, parenetic, prophetic, pleading, praise confession, individual and collective lamentation, prayer (par. 14).[62]

In his epistle, we find the first attempt to collect the psalms in groups of different literary genres. In my opinion, it does not depend on a strictly literary method but on the need to link each divine expression of Scripture with human situations, in order to be useful and salvific for humankind. Athanasius's exegesis is not an academic exercise but a pastoral tool to encourage his people to use the Word of God as a good guide for the Christian life.

Gregory of Nyssa and the Titles of the Psalms

Holy Scripture and the Christian life are well combined in Gregory of Nyssa's work too. It is supposed that his *On the Titles of Psalms* was written in his early

---

62. Eusebius attempted to give a classification of the literary genres of the psalms based on their titles with his work *Hypomnema*: see Bandt, Risch, and Villani, *Die Prologtexte*, 218–72.

years, because, as noted by Rondeau,[63] we do not find the two characteristic themes of his old age: σκότος (darkness) and ἐπέκτασις (*progressio ad infinitum*, continuing attention or infinite progress to God). His work on the titles of the psalms has three main ideas: the unique σκοπός or unifying theme, ἀκολουθία or the connection of each part, and the idea that the beginning of a part is like the summary of the whole. According to this last idea, the book of Psalms has five books and each opening psalm (1; 41; 72; 89; 106) is the interpretative key of the book (1:5–9). Psalms 1 and 2 are the entrance to the whole Psalter because they present blessedness as the σκοπός and the fullness of the Christian life. Hilary and Augustine, as well as Jerome, refuse to accept five books, because they were rooted in the idea of a unique book as described in the Acts of the Apostles. It is not too hypothetical to think that the idea of five books was too close to Jewish thought, but to divide the Psalter into three parts of fifty psalms was nearer to the symbolic view of the Trinity, a Christian characteristic.

Gregory sees in the five books a spiritual progression.[64] The first step is to turn away from evil and adhere to good: it is the meaning of Psalm 1. The second step is the desire for participation in God (Ps 41). The third is the discernment of the true good among the evil deeds of men (Ps 72). The fourth is a contemplation of the immutability of God's nature and a meditation on human instability (Ps 89). The last step is a summary of salvation history in order to praise God (Ps 106). Gregory captured important themes of each of the five opening psalms based on their literal meaning, but nowadays we probably have difficulty in accepting that the opening psalms are a summary of the following psalms in each book.

In order to understand the exegetical mind of the Cappadocian theologian, we must explain the meaning of ἀκολουθία (2.16).[65] It is a Stoic word which means no part of the world is unrelated to any other and the order among the

---

63. Marie-Josèphe Rondeau, "Exégèse du Psautier et anabase spirituelle chez Grégorie de Nysse," 517–31 in *Epektasis: Mélanges patristiques offerts au Cardinal Jean Daniélou*, ed. Jacques Fontaine and Charles Kannengiesser (Paris: Beauchesne, 1972).

64. On spiritual progression see also Hilary, *Tractatus in Psalmos* (see note 51) and his vision of the three parts of the Psalter as the three steps of Christian life: penitence (Pss 1–50); acquiring virtues (Pss 51–100); praise of God (Pss 101–150).

65. Ἀκολουθία is used by Clement, *Stromata*, 1.28 *passim*, but not for the Psalter: see Marie-Josèphe Rondeau, "D'où vient la technique exégétique utilisée par Grégoire de Nysse dans son traité 'Sur les titres des Psaumes'?," 263–87 in *Mélanges d'histoire des religions offerts à Henri-Charles Puech* (Paris: Presses Universitaire de France, 1974). Eusebius uses the word but without true interest; Athanasius never does. See Rondeau, *Commentaires*, 1:113.

parts is a harmonic principle, such that each part finds its place within the relationship with the whole. According to Gregory, this philosophical idea is also valid for the Psalter. There is a harmony that links each part. In a remarkable way he tries to see the ἀκολουθία in the succession of the titles of the psalms, even if they are barely related in meaning. It is a different technique from that of Eusebius's *Periochae*. By it Gregory tries to explain the Christian meaning of each psalm in order to illuminate the relevance of the whole Psalter. Gregory does not shy away from the literal sense of each title and tries to see its purpose and its relevance for the spiritual life.

Ἀκολουθία would not be possible without the idea of the unity of the Psalter, which Gregory wants to find in the allegorical explanation of the literal sense of the title of the psalms. This unity pertains not only to the spiritual meaning (i.e., blessedness), but also to the immediate literal meaning, because the first psalm and the ending verse of each of the five books of the Psalter have the same theme of blessedness. Thus, the Psalter has no other aim other than that of leading humankind to true happiness. The spiritual meaning is not separable from the literary one because the creator of man is the same author of the Bible, and this Bible was given by God as an instrument to help man to reach blessedness.[66]

Conclusion

Our journey through the centuries led us to encounter the Latin authors like Hilary, the first commentator on the psalms in the middle of the fourth century, and Jerome and his enormous work of translation from the Septuagint and the Hebrew texts. His was the first attempt in Christianity to read a *Hebraica veritas*, although this latter translation was never used in the liturgy of the Church. We ought not to forget the *Enarrationes in Psalmos* of Augustine, who began to preach in 391 (*enarrationes* are homilies), collecting the previous exegetical

---

66. According to Augustine Christ is the purpose of the Psalter; *Enarratio in Psalmum* 16.51: "totus enim Christus hic loquitur, in quo sunt omnia membra eius"; *In Psalmum* 96.2: "totum ad Christum revocemus, si volumus iter rectae intellegentiae tenere"; *In Psalmum* 98.1: "quando psalmus audimus, quando prophetam, quando lege, quae omnia antequam venire in carne Dominus noster Iesus Christus, conscripta sunt, Christum ibi videre, Christum ibi intellegere": Augustine, *Enarrationes in Psalmos*, ed. Eligius Dekkers and Johannes Fraipont, CCSL 38-39 (Turnhout: Brepols, 1956). According to Hilary the purpose is blessedness; *Instructio Psalmorum*, 11: "et hoc ratione ac numero beatae illius nostrae expectationis existit." Cf. Fiedrowicz, *Psalmus vox totius Christi*, 15; Domenico Marafioti, "Sant'Ilario e il libro dei Salmi," *Rassegna di Teologia* 48, no. 3 (2007): 455-66.

contributions to the Psalter and promoting the Christian life through the use of psalms. His hermeneutical key of *Christus totus* will remain, on the one hand, the most advanced development of the prosopological technique and, on the other, the most useful method for reading the psalms in the medieval age.[67]

With the works of Basil, Gregory of Nyssa, Hilary, Jerome, and Augustine, we can say that the fourth century, especially its second half, was the stage of the most important studies regarding the psalms. This is not surprising if we consider how widespread monasticism was in the West and in the East. Evagrius of Pontus testifies that the psalms are the best tool for fighting evil thoughts; Basil builds his *Ascetikon* by putting the psalms at the heart of daily community life. After the period of the persecutions, becoming a monk would mean belonging to a truer form of the Christian life, and the book of Psalms became the most used handbook to attain the virtues, to dialogue with God, to preserve peace of heart, and to promote brotherly love.

Our presentation stops at the border with Greek literature, because our purpose is to show the continuity between the apostolic age and the further developments in the exegetical techniques that we find in the first commentaries on the psalms. The extensive use of the psalms in the Second Temple period, at Qumran and in the New Testament writings, witnesses to the importance of these prayers and songs but also to the need of true explanations of their composition, their origin, their place in the history of salvation, and their role in the life of believers.

With this heritage, we can try to sum up a few themes that, in my opinion, would be useful for modern exegesis. While admiring the efforts of modern exegesis, we cannot forget past attempts. Patristic exegesis was and remains the first, and sometimes the best, effort to understand Scripture in its inner unity and in its relationship with the Christian life. We can speak of the meaning of Scripture, especially the psalms with their titles; the methodological principle of reading the Scriptures with the Scriptures; the question of the unity of the Scriptures strictly linked to the principle of its usefulness to the reader; and the prophetic sense of the book of Psalms.

Regarding its meaning, we have to say that this is the major question of exegesis: what is the true meaning of the Scriptures? Where can I find it? On the literal level or on a deeper level that is hidden to the simple reader? And, there is another major question: what is the literal sense? Regarding the psalms, we have noted that the prosopological technique was the consistent focus of the earlier commentators' interpretation, starting with Jesus himself.

---

67. Augustine, *Enarrationes in Psalmos*, 85.1.

After him, through Origen and Eusebius, up till Gregory of Nyssa, a psalm is well understood if its author or its speaker is identified. This was (and perhaps is?) the background to fathoming the importance of the titles, because we can read the assumed author in them. The presence of David in more than half of the psalms encouraged the commentators to find references to the events of Israel's king in the historical books of 1–2 Kings. This was the aim of Eusebius. David was a king, but also a prophet, because God promised him a permanent line of descendants and the Messiah as his offspring. Jesus knew that very well. The presence of other authors or speakers of the psalms ought always to be explained in relation to history. The lack of titles for some psalms was problematic, but Origen postulated the idea that the speaker of a psalm without a heading was the same speaker as the previous and immediate psalm with a title. What is the value of the headings in modern exegesis? Are they only editorial elements, as Diodorus of Tarsus suggested,[68] or are they really part of the psalms?[69] Only Gregory of Nyssa tried to focus the attention of the reader on the possible coherent unity of these seemingly unnecessary headings. His effort was guided by spiritual interest, but the playing field was the biblical text as it is, in its literal sense. In fact, he never changed the text of the Bible or ignored it. The biblical text is important in each part, and every detail is worthy of study. Origen was the master of this attentive reading of the Scriptures in every small detail, so much so that when the meaning of the text is obscure or lacking, there is always, according to Origen, a meaning on the spiritual level, which is the Christological sense. I think that we must consider this Christological interpretation as an extension of the evangelical use of the psalms: Christ is the speaker, the subject, and the object of each psalm (cf. Luke 24:44).

---

68. Diodorus of Tarsus, *Diodori Tarsensis Commentarii in Psalmos: I. Commentarii in Psalmos I–L*, ed. Jean-Marie Olivier (Turnhout: Brepols, 1980), 6: "'Ἐντεῦθεν καὶ αἱ ἐπιγραφαὶ αἱ πλείους ἐσφαλμέναι εἰσί, τῶν συνθεμένων τοὺς ψαλμοὺς ἐπὶ πολὺ στοχασαμένων τῆς ἐννοίας καὶ οὐ κατ'ἐπιστήμην τεθεικότων," trans. Louis Mariès, "Extraits du commentaire de Diodore de Tarse sur les Psaumes," *Recherches de Science Religieuse* 9, no. 1 (1919): 79–101, at 87: "De là aussi vient que les inscriptions sont pour la plupart fautives, ceux qui avaient réuni les Psaumes ayant cherché le plus souvent à les comprendre, sans les avoir [au préalable] classés correctement." Eustathius of Antioch wrote *In stelographiam* about the titles (PG 18:685–86, 695–98). According to Augustine (*Enarrationes in Psalmos*, 55.1 and 58.1) the titles of the psalms are like a nameplate of a house where the owner's name is written.

69. Cf. Waltke and Houston, *The Psalms as Christian Worship*, 87, which presents the results of the studies of Ernst Wilhelm Hengstenberg (1802–1869), Franz Delitzsch (1813–1890), John S. Perowne (1823–1904), Alexander F. Kirkpatrick (1849–1940) and Derek Kidner (1913–2008). According to them the superscript establishes a psalm's historical context.

With Eusebius there was a shift in focus: the prophetic meaning of the Psalter had to be verified in the events of history. Thus, the historical meaning became the foundational layer of reality on which texts could be properly interpreted. Prophecy and history are linked, and their mutual relationship determines the divine origin of the biblical word because only God is the creator of the world and of its history. To the Christological and historical aspects, Athanasius, Basil, and Gregory of Nyssa added an anthropological interpretation following the Origenian assumption that everything in Scripture is useful. The aim of the Christian life is the happiness of man. It is announced at the beginning of the Psalter and at the end of each of its five books. From the Christological sense of Origen, going through the historical and prophetic sense of Eusebius, the anthropological interpretation was the practical sense linked to the Christian life. The Psalter had to be useful to its reader. Origen had already highlighted the strict link between Scriptures and its reader: the simple person understands the basic meaning; the one who makes some progress can reach the moral meaning; and the perfect reader finds the spiritual sense of the text, that is the divinity of Christ, the incarnate Word of God. The greater the spiritual effort of its reader, the richer the meaning of the Bible becomes.

The main methodological assumption of this view is expressed in Latin: *Scriptura Scripturae interpres*: Scripture explains itself. This is a Hellenistic conviction we find in the commentaries on Homer,[70] which was applied to the Scriptures for the first time by Origen, before the canonical list was necessary.[71] It probably was the use and the interpretation of some books of the Jewish Scriptures and Christian writings that determined the later canonical list.[72] After the studies of Brevard Childs, we are acquainted with the canonical reading, and many studies on the Psalter utilize this method. Historically speaking, we must keep in mind that the canon does not precede the exegetical method, but the exegetical methods led to the creation of a canon. Scripture is the Word of God, and God spoke through Moses, through the prophets (David

---

70. See Benjamin Sargent, "'Interpreting Homer from Homer': Aristarchus of Samothrace and the Notion of Scriptural Authorship in the New Testament," *Tyndale Bulletin* 65, no. 1 (2014): 125–39, esp. 137–38. See also Philip S. Alexander, "'Homer the Prophet of All' and 'Moses Our Teacher': Late Antique Exegesis of the Homeric Epics and the Torah of Moses," in *The Use of Sacred Books in the Ancient World*, ed. Tjitze Baarda, Aire van der Kooij, and Adam S. van der Woude (Leuven: Peeters, 1998), 127–42.

71. Cf. Origen, *Contra Celsum*, 153–220 in *Gegen Celsus Buch V–VIII*, ed. Paul Koetschau, GCS 3 (J. C. Hinrichs'sche Buchhandlung, 1899), 7.11.

72. Eusebius, *Ecclesiastical History*, 3.25 does not write about "canonical" or "apocryphal" but uses ὁμολογούμενοι, ἀντιλεγόμενοι, νόθοι.

and Solomon were also prophets), through the witness of the Gospels, and the writings of the apostles.

This assumption also influenced the concept of the Psalter as a literary unit. Gregory of Nyssa attempted to find a single purpose for the Psalter through the explanation of the ἀκολουθία or connection of the single parts with others. Once again: at what level can we reach the true meaning of the Psalter? On that spiritual meaning, which is hidden and deep, or on the immediate meaning, i.e., literal one? Should we understand "spiritual" according to the Christological sense or according to the anthropological one? Do we intend "literal" to mean philological, the meaning of single words and their connection, or historical, i.e., the facts as they truly happened? Origen, when he began his exegetical work on the Psalter, had the clear idea that the guideline was the usefulness (ὠφέλεια) to the reader.[73] According to Origen, "usefulness" means to reach the Christological meaning; according to Athanasius and Gregory of Nyssa, "usefulness" means to attain the virtues in order to have communion with God. I think we can explain the concept of usefulness as strictly bound to the soteriological purpose of the incarnation. For the reader, to seek the usefulness of Scripture means to appropriate the gift of salvation brought by the incarnate Word of God.

The basic importance of the Psalter is its prophetic meaning:[74] prophetic regarding the person of the Son of God, as Jesus himself shows in the Gospels, but also prophetic regarding the total body of Christ. According to Hilary, Christ is the key to the whole Psalter (*Instructio* 3). As Augustine wrote:

> When the Body of the Son prays, it separates not its Head from itself: and it is one Saviour of His Body, our Lord Jesus Christ, the Son of God, who both prays for us, and prays in us, and is prayed to by us. He prays for us, as our Priest; He prays in us, as our Head; He is prayed to by us, as our God. Let us therefore recognise in Him our words, and His words in us. Nor when anything is said of our Lord Jesus Christ, especially in prophecy, implying a

---

73. Cf. 2 Tim 3:16; Origen, *De principiis*, 4.2.6–9; Gregory of Nyssa, *Prologus in Canticum Canticorum*, 3–13 in *Gregorii Nysseni Opera*, vol. 4, ed. Hermannus Langerbeck (Leiden: Brill, 1960).

74. Hans Boersma, "The Church Fathers' Spiritual Interpretation of the Psalms," 41–55 in *Living Waters from Ancient Springs: Essays in Honor of Cornelis Van Dam*, ed. Jason van Vliet (Eugene, OR: Wipf & Stock, 2011), 50: "According to the Fathers' interpretation, the Spirit has so shaped the contents of the Old Testament that it already bespeaks New Testament christological realities. This confidence in divine inspiration is what allows the Fathers to read the book of Psalms prophetically. The notion that the Psalter is a book of prophecy is perhaps one of the distinguishing characteristics of pre-modern exegesis. Interpreters like Augustine will often refer to the psalmist as 'the prophet'."

degree of humility below the dignity of God, let us not hesitate to ascribe it to Him who did not hesitate to join Himself unto us.[75]

It is prophetic again because it is the Psalter of David, the king of Israel and the prophet of the future Messiah.[76] David is the ancestor of him who will call God his father (2 Sam 7:14 and Ps 89:25–27), but David is also remembered as a true man of prayer, who is not afraid of God's judgment but trusts him in every circumstance. The Davidic attribution of the Psalter is not only a historical matter. If he is the true speaker of the psalms, his figure cannot be forgotten in the theological interpretation of his songs. We can find this idea in Qumran and in the mouth of Jesus. Thus, in the person of David, we can find the messianic promise of God accomplished in Jesus but also in every believer who trusts in God. In my opinion, David creates an inseparable link between a Christological and an anthropological interpretation that makes the Psalter a summary of the Holy Scriptures and an unfailingly useful tool for understanding the greatness of the human being face to face with God.

---

75. Augustine, *Enarrationes in Psalmos*, 85 (trans. NPNF 1/8:410).

76. James L. Kugel, "Topics in the History of the Spirituality of the Psalms," 113–44 in *Jewish Spirituality: From the Bible through the Middle Ages*, ed. Arthur Green (New York: Crossroad, 1986), 134–36.

Appendix: The Canons of Eusebius

CANON I	CANON II	CANON III	CANON IV	CANON V	CANON VI	CANON VII
72 David	**2** Solomon	**19** without headings	**11** sons of Korah	**12** of Asaph	**17** anonymous	**15** Alleluia
3 4 5 6 7 8 9 10 11 12 13 14 15 16 17 18 19 20 21 22 23 24 25 26 27 28 29 30 31 33 34 35 36 37 38 39 40		1 2 32 42	41 43 44 45 46 47 48	49		
50 51 52 53 54 55 56 57 58 59 60 61 62 63 64 67 68 69	71	70	a 83 84 86 87 90 92 93 94 95 96 98	72 73 74 75 76 77 78 79 80 81 82	65 66 91 97 99 101	
85			103 114		119 120 121 122 124 125 127 128 129	104 105 106 110 111 112 113 115
100 102 107 108 109 123 130 132 137 138 139 140 141 142 143 144	126	116 118 136 146 147 Of Ethan: 88 Of Moses: 89			131 133	117 134 135 145 148 149 150

99

CHAPTER 6

The Alexandrian and Antiochian Method of Exegesis of Psalm 75[74]: Toward a Rebalancing of Both Methods of Exegesis

Juana L. Manzo

Introduction

For the early Church, the prophetic books of the Old Testament predicted the coming of Christ fulfilled in the New Testament. The Old Testament and early Christian writings provided the kerygma and ethical instruction for the pastoral needs of the community. At the same time, Christian apologetics were becoming more aware of the necessity of developing biblical interpretative methods to defend the unity of both Testaments. The intellectual centers of Alexandria and Antioch established their own schools with their own traditions and methods of biblical interpretation between AD 325 and 451. The difference in their approaches has been characterized as allegorical or spiritual in Alexandria and literal or historical in Antioch. This period became known as the "golden age of patristic exegesis."[1] But even given that this was a "golden age," there are only rare occasions where we are able to examine more than one patristic interpretation of the same text.

During my research, I was pleased to discover that two patristic commentaries, namely those by Origen and Theodoret of Cyrus, representatives of the Alexandrian and Antiochian schools respectively, are extant on Psalm 75[74].[2]

---

1. For the historical background of the school of Alexandria in Egypt, see Gerald Brey, *Biblical Interpretation: Past and Present* (Downers Grove, IL: InterVarsity Press, 1996), 451.

2. The brackets designate the LXX numbering of the Hebrew text.

The Alexandrian and Antiochian Method of Exegesis of Psalm 75 [74]

My present purpose is to compare both interpretative approaches to gain a clearer understanding of the theological and pastoral motives of each author, as well as the advantages and limitations of each approach, all with the hope of striking a balance or synthesis between spiritual and historical exegesis. The essay is divided into two sections. In the first section, I consider Origen's pedagogy of the Logos for preaching conversion and the spiritual journey of the soul in the sacramental life of the Church. In the second section, I consider the theological dimensions of Theodoret of Cyrus's historical exegesis.

Origen's Exegetical Principle

The most prolific Christian writer of antiquity is Origen (AD 203–?). St. Epiphanius credits Origen with the composition of six thousand works.[3] He is the greatest exegete of the Antiochian school and "the most influential early Christian interpreter of the Bible."[4] Origen's exegetical method has been traditionally associated with the three-fold sense of Scripture: the literal, the moral, and the mystical or allegorical sense.[5] In a study of Origen's use of the three-fold senses, Karen Jo Torjesen finds in her work, *Hermeneutical Procedure and Theological Method in Origen's Exegesis*, that the three-fold sense of Scripture does not function as Origen's principle of biblical exegesis since it

---

3. John A. McGuckin, *The Westminster Handbook to Origen* (Louisville: Westminster John Knox, 2004), 26.

4. Manlio Simonetti, *Biblical Interpretation in the Early Church: An Historical Introduction to Patristic Exegesis*, trans. John A. Hughes, ed. Anders Bergquist and Markus Bockmuehl (Edinburgh: T&T Clark, 1994), 67. Joseph W. Trigg, *Biblical Interpretation*, MFC 9 (Wilmington, DE: Michael Glazier, 1988), 23.

5. The literal sense was referred to as historical (the narrative of events and characters) and included the following grammatical analysis: *diorthōtikon*, textual criticism; *glōssēmatikon*, word meaning; *historikon*, the setting of historical events, characters, and geography; *tecknickon*, literary genre and *krisis* or judgment, which included identification of the speaker (*propōsa*) to determine the weight of the argument: see Origen, *On First Principles* (Notre Dame, IN: Ave Maria Press, 2013), 4.3–4; Joseph W. Trigg, "Introduction" to Origen, *Homilies on the Psalms: Codex Monacensis Graecus 314*, FaCh 9 (Washington, DC: Catholic University of America Press, 2020), 13; Origen, *Homily on Psalm 75*, 228–37 in FaCh 9; Frances Young, "Alexandrian and Antiochene Exegesis," 334–54 in *A History of Biblical Interpretation*, vol. 1, *The Ancient Period*, ed. Alan J. Hauser and Duance F. Watson (Grand Rapids, MI: Eerdmans, 2003), 12–13. For a discussion of the moral and allegorical senses see Henri de Lubac, *History and Spirit: The Understanding of Scripture According to Origen*, trans. Anne Englund Nash (San Francisco: Ignatius, 2007), 161–64; R. P. C. Hanson, *Allegory and Event: A Study of the Sources and Significance of Origen's Interpretation of Scripture* (Louisville: Westminster John Knox, 2002), 235.

is not used systematically for textual arguments or as a tripartite structure of his exegesis.[6]

Modern scholars have proposed different theories for Origen's exegesis and in particular for his understanding of the historical ("the letter") and spiritual ("the spirit") dimensions of Scripture. Among these scholars stand the contributions of R. Gögel and W. Gruber.[7] Gögel suggests that Origen's exegesis is based on a Christological structure in which Scripture is a manifestation of the *kenosis* of the Word for the revelation of salvation to humanity.[8] Origen's exegesis is grounded on the encounter with the Word (analogous to the theology of the Incarnation) by moving from the letter (historical) to the spirit of the message or the revelation of the power of God for salvation. Gögel argues that Origen sees the Word as the objective content of Scripture as well as the interpreter of the spiritual sense.[9] In other words, the Word is both "revelation and redemption."[10] Gruber sees in Origen's exegesis a pedagogical structure of the Word in which the movement from letter (historical) to spirit is grounded in a theological understanding of the soul's redemption.[11] There are two points to be made regarding this statement. First, the pedagogy of the Word for the salvation of souls is fundamentally realized as salvation history—an encounter between revelation and faith. Second, Origen's approach for biblical interpretation begins with the understanding of the Holy Spirit as the principal agent of inspiration at work in the Word itself to challenge those who hear it to accept it as the Word of salvation. Allegory (*allēgoria*) and its cognates *súmbolon* and *sēmeion* were terms denoting an authoritative symbolic interpretation for Scripture and tradition and the means by which Origen arrives at Scripture's spiritual meaning—the encounter with the Word through the active participation of the Holy Spirit.[12] Based on Gögel's and Gruber's contributions,

---

6. Karen Jo Torjesen, *Hermeneutical Procedure and Theological Method in Origen's Exegesis* (Berlin: De Gruyter, 1985), 41.

7. R. Gögel, *Zur Theologie des biblischen Wortes bei Origenes* (Dusseldorf, 1963); W. Gruber, *Die peneumatiche Exegese bei den Alexandrimen: Ein Beitrag zur Noematik der heiligen Schrift* (STFG Reihe D, Heft 3/4, 1957). Cited by Torjesen, *Hermeneutical Procedure*, 8–9.

8. Cited by Torjesen, *Hermeneutical Procedure*, 8–9.

9. Cited by Torjesen, *Hermeneutical Procedure*, 8–9.

10. Cited by Torjesen, *Hermeneutical Procedure*, 8–9.

11. Cited by Torjesen, *Hermeneutical Procedure*, 8–9.

12. "On this account we must explain to those who believe that the sacred books are not the works men, but that they were composed and have come down to us as a result of the Holy Spirit by the will of the Father of the universe through Jesus Christ." Origen, *On First Principles*, 4.2.2. For a study of the allegorical method see Henry Chadwick, ed. and trans., *Origen: Contra Celsum*, vol. 2 (Cambridge: Cambridge University Press, 1980), 69; Hanson, *Allegory and Event*,

The Alexandrian and Antiochian Method of Exegesis of Psalm 75 [74]

Torjesen's extensive study of Origen's exegesis of Psalm 37 led her to proposes a three-step process for Origen's exegesis: "The text, the means of its interpretation and the hearer."[13]

Origen first identifies the theme(s) from the text, next, he provides an interpretation, and lastly, he relates the interpretation to the spiritual journey of the hearers. Each aspect of interpretation is interwoven to present two main exegetical points. Torjesen identifies them as "the original, historical pedagogy of the Logos represented in the literal sense of Scripture and a contemporary pedagogy of the Logos directed for the *hearer* given in a spiritual sense."[14] Let us look now at how this approach is found in Origen's exegesis of Psalm 75[74].

Origen's Exegesis of Psalm 75[74]

Joseph W. Trigg's work on Origen's *Homilies on the Psalms* will be the basis for our commentary on Origen's exegesis of Psalm 75[74].[15] Origen's interpretation was delivered as a sermon during the Christian liturgy to a diverse audience at Caesarea between AD 239–242.[16]

39, 117; Peter W. Martens, *Origen and Scripture: The Contours of the Exegetical Life* (Oxford: Oxford University Press, 2012), 64.

13. Torjesen, *Hermeneutical Procedure*, 13, 22–28.
14. Torjesen, *Hermeneutical Procedure*, 13.
15. Origen, *Homily on Psalm 74* (trans. Trigg, 220–27). The translation is as follows:

> [1]To the end. Do not destroy. A Psalm of a song for Asaph.
> [2]We shall confess to you, God. We shall confess to you and we shall call upon your name.
> [3]I shall recount your marvelous deeds, whenever I receive an occasion. I shall judge straight judgments.
> [4]The earth melted and all who dwell on it. I have strengthened her pillars.
> [5]I said to those who violate the Law and to sinners, "Do not violate the law," and to the sinners, "Do not lift up a horn."
> [6]Do not raise up on high your horn. Do not speak injury against God.
> [7]Because neither from the sunrises nor from settings nor from the desert mountains, because
> [8]God is judge. He humbles this one and raises up this one.
> [9]A cup is in the Lord's hand full of unmixed wine of mixed, and he moves it aside this way and that, except that its dregs have not been emptied out. All sinners of the earth shall drink.
> [10]But I shall proclaim to the age, I shall make music to the God of Jacob.
> [11]And all of the horns of sinners I shall smash, but the horns of the just ones shall be lifted up.

16. Trigg, "Introduction," 3, 7; Joseph T. Lienhard, "Origen as Homilist," 36–72 in *Preaching in the Patristic Age: Studies in Honor of Walter J. Burghardt, S.J.*, ed. David G. Hunter (New York: Paulist, 1989), 43.

In the first exegetical step, Origen identifies the subject of the psalm and the speaker(s) (*propōsa*). Ignorant that the title is a clue to the psalm's melody, he interprets it literally and sees in the title ("do not destroy," v.1) the psalm's theme: "indestructability,"[17] that is, human behaviors that lead to the *indestructability* (i.e., the salvation) of God's people. Identifying the psalm's theme allows Origen to establish a relationship between the text and the listener who will be instructed on the indestructible behavior Scripture prescribes for their salvation. From the outset, Origen presents to his hearers the text's significance for their journey of salvation. Next, the offer of salvation is cast within the life of the Church and salvation history through the identification of the psalm's first speakers—"we shall confess to you, God, we shall confess, and we shall call upon your name" (v. 2)— as the members of the Gentile Church who promise to repent of their sins.[18] In this way, Origen establishes a theological connection between the psalmist's words and his audience and then moves to explain the meaning. Salvation requires not only a first confession of sins by the Church but a continual confession of its transgression, as indicated by the double repetition of "we shall confess," so that they may be found among those who can call upon the Lord's name and be saved. A first important step for the salvation and perfection of the soul is the frequent confession of sins.

In the second step, Origen entertains the historical reality or the letter of the text.[19] As indicated previously, Origen's understanding of the historical reality is not the study of past events, but the history of the "pedagogy of the Logos" found in the written word of Scripture or in a process of encounter with the Logos—that is, redemption.[20] Origen's understanding of salvation history as an encounter with the Logos permits him to identify Christ as the speaker in vv. 2–10 (and not as YHWH) and bypass the exilic setting of the psalm and its original Jewish historical context. Therefore, Origen attributes to *Christ* the phase, "I shall recount your marvelous deeds, whenever I receive an occasion" (v. 3a). Origen interprets this to mean that Christ awaits the Gentile Church's promise to confess her sin (v. 2), and then conveys its significance to the hearer: "Each of us, if he wants to hear Jesus recounting the marvelous deeds of the Father, let him give him an occasion in himself."[21] The attitude of the faithful

---

17. Origen, *Homily on Psalm 74*, 1 (trans. Trigg, 220).
18. For Origen identification of *propōsa*, speaker and the *anaphora*, the repetition of words and phrases, were essential for proper interpretation of the text: see Trigg, "Introduction," 13; Origen, *Homily on Psalm 74*, 1 (trans. Trigg, 220).
19. Torjesen, *Hermeneutical Procedure*, 138.
20. Torjesen, *Hermeneutical Procedure*, 140.
21. Origen, *Homily on Psalm 74*, 1 (trans. Trigg, 221).

believer is acknowledgment of his/her sins to Christ while the one who "tarries in sin" will not confess, thereby placing himself/herself within the sphere of forgiveness or condemnation. For Origen salvation history remains a mixture of salvation and condemnation until its completion at the end of time. Therefore, salvation is placed in relationship to Christ and the sacramental life of the Church. Beyond this, salvation history is for Origen the working of God the Father, to whom Christ attributes salvation. Christ as the center of salvation history and the setting in which Christ's judgment is announced and accomplished is taken up next.

In the third step, Jesus places himself as the center of the psalm's messages as the righteous judge ("I shall judge straight judgments," v. 3b) and omnipotent Lord who vanquishes all sins ("the earth melted and all who dwell on it," v. 4). Origen allegorizes the latter using 1 Corinthians 15:49, "Just as we have borne the image of the *earthly* man," and equates "the earth" (v. 4) with the earthly man, the man created out of dust and thus corrupted because of sin (Rom 8:13). Origen then actualizes the text for his audience, telling them of the need to put off the image of the earthly man by putting to death the deeds of the body with the help of the Spirit, followed by the theological reason: Christ has melted the earth, meaning he has destroyed sinners, conveyed by the reference to the earthly man (1 Cor 15:49); additionally, Christ's judgment on sin is universal. According to Origen, the phrase, he melts "all" (*pantēs*), refers to the hostile powers responsible for sin on earth (v. 4b).[22]

Between the time of the personal and universal judgments, Christ teaches: "I have strengthened her pillars" (v. 4c). Origen identifies "her" with the Church, and not with the earth, as intended by the author. He first asks, who are the pillars of the Church? Origen has very little difficulty in identifying them with the early church leaders (Peter, Andrew, James, and John, cf. Matt 4:18–45; Gal 2:9). He then observes that the Church is the pillar of truth (1 Tim 3:15), and adds that anyone who overcomes sin will become a pillar ("be secured") in God's Church (Rev 3:12). By identifying the Church as the pillar of truth, Origen is in essence telling his audience that the Church is the earthly source of spiritual knowledge and salvation.

In the fourth step, Origen transitions to the pedagogy of the Logos within Israel's history.[23] As Origen understands Christ as the author of history, Christ states: "I said to those who violate the law, 'Do not violate the law,' and to the

---

22. Origen, *Homily on Psalm 74*, 2 (trans. Trigg, 222).
23. Torjesen, *Hermeneutical Procedure*, 146.

sinners, 'Do not lift up a horn. Do not speak injury against God'" (vv. 5–6). Origen interprets Christ's words as follows:

1) "Those who violate the Law" are the Israelites who have received the Torah by divine revelation;
2) "The sinners" are the Gentiles. Since they are not under the Law (1 Cor 9:21) they do not violate the Law. But they "lift up their horn," a symbol of idol worship, and thus speak "injury against God."

While Jews and Gentiles alike are sinners and subjected to divine judgment, Origen finds in the reiteration of God as judge (v. 8a) and in view of Deuteronomy 38:43: "But you should descend down, down," that the statement, "He [God] humbles this one," refers to the Jews. Origen does not identify the reason for the Jews having been humbled; perhaps he has in mind the exile as punishment for their idolatry or for their refusal to accept Christ as their savior. What is certain is that Origen sees in the phrase, "and raises up this one" (v. 8b), the salvation of the Gentiles. He states:

> "The proselyte who is among you shall ascend up, and up, upon you," for this is the one he raises. . . . In keeping with "the earth melted, and all who dwell on it," we have interpreted "he humbles this one and raises up this one." He humbles this one, the thinking of the flesh and the flesh. . . . He raises this one: the soul and spirit. The opposite, the soul of sinners, has been humbled by sin, but the other is raised up, that of the just, who are fasting, laboring, staying awake, putting to death the [bodily] parts on earth. The body has been humbled, but the soul is always renewed according to the inner human being [Rom 7:22; 12:2].[24]

When Origen states God has humbled the thinking of the flesh, he is not only affirming the inability of human beings (especially the Jews) to do the good prescribed by the Law, but also shows that fasting, laboring, and staying awake represent the way the listener can put aside the works of the flesh and experience greater spiritual transformation.

Christ's own teaching on divine judgment is expanded with the metaphor of the cup of wine. The cup full of unmixed wine in the Lord's hand that he tips from one side to the other is a dark symbol of God's fierce condemnation on sinners (v. 9; cf. Jer 25:15–16). But Christ, who desires to save (vv. 2–3), offers the cup of salvation as a counterpart to the cup of wrath (Ps 115:4). Origen offers this explanation:

---

24. Origen, *Homily on Psalm 74*, 3 (trans. Trigg, 223–24).

Thus always, understand with me, there are two drinks in the Lord's hand for each of us; and whenever we sin, according to the degree of the sin, we insert our sinful deed into the cup of sinful deeds, but when we do well, into the cup of upright deeds. Next, each of us is going to drink; if he has both sinful and upright deeds, he will not drink the sin straight, but mixed according to the proportion of things that were produced before the sin.[25]

The cup, a metaphor of an individual's fate, can be filled with wrath or blessings according to the degree of sin or righteous deeds. Origen understands that the life of most individuals is a mixture of good and evil, and therefore, the cup the Lord offers to drink as punishment will be filled in proportion to those deeds.[26] According to Origen, Christ's words, "But I shall proclaim to the ages, I shall make music to the God of Jacob" (v. 10a), affirm Jesus's teachings as endless, unlike worldly wisdom, and his eternal commitment to praise his Father. The overriding motif of Christ as divine judge makes the final point that the condemnation of evil ("And all the horns of the sinners I shall smash," v. 11a) and the vindication of the righteous ("the horns of "just ones shall be lifted up" (v. 11b) are both inescapable and unassailable. Finally, Christ reaffirms his divine power as judge over sinners and righteous alike (v. 11).

We have now seen that Origen's interpretation of Psalm 75[74] follows a series of repetitive steps: analysis of the text's message, interpretation of the message, and actualization of the message in a way that is meaningful to the listener's journey of faith. In his efforts to share and strengthen the faith of his Christian audience, Origen reads the psalm Christologically to show that Christ's judgment in history over human sin demands a personal response of faith and repentance within the sacramental life of the Church.[27]

The School of Antioch

The literal approach of the school of Antioch was a response to the excessive use of Alexandrian allegory.[28] During the Council of Nicaea (AD 325), Eustathius accused the Alexandrian school of allegorizing passages that ought to be read in a literal sense: "Come now, let us interpret the text (*gramma*) of the account (*historia*) to the extent that it is accessible."[29] Sound interpretation

---

25. Origen, *Homily on Psalm 74*, 4 (trans. Trigg, 225).
26. Origen, *Homily on Psalm 74*, 4 (trans. Trigg, 226).
27. Torjesen, *Hermeneutical Procedure*, 140, 143.
28. The school of Antioch spans the period between AD 325–460.
29. Robert C. Hill, *Of Prophets and Poets: Antioch Fathers on the Bible* (Brookline, MA: Holy Cross Orthodox Press, 2007), 28.

lies in determining what facts (*historia*) and events (*pragmata*) the words of the text denote to arrive at its truth (*aletheia*). Diodore of Tarsus (AD 394) accepted Eustathius's principles as normative for the school of Antioch and sought to explain the biblical text based on the historical and textual sense. In *Commentary on the Psalms*, he states: "The historical sense . . . is not in opposition to the more elevated sense [*theoria*]; on the contrary, it proves to be the basis and foundation of the more elevated ideas."[30] The interpreter must never let *theoria* subvert the historical sense, since it would turn into allegory.[31] The Anthiochians' emphasis on the literal or historical sense did not keep them from promoting the idea of *theoria*, or insight to arrive at the deeper meaning of Scripture. For them, *theoria* maintains the historical sense, and makes it possible to see certain people and events of the Old Testament as *typoi* or types of persons or events in the New Testament. The Antioch approach differentiates itself from the Alexandrians' by bringing forth *theoria* without forsaking the "literal historical sense of the text."[32] One of the noted Antiochene exegetes is Theodoret of Cyrus, whose reading of Psalm 75[74] adheres to the historical letter.

Theodoret of Cyrus

Theodoret, who was born in Antioch in AD 393, was a prolific writer, authoring twenty-five books and hundreds of letters.[33] Preserved is his commentary on the psalms, which he wrote between AD 441–448.[34] In the nineteenth century, it was published in J. P. Migne's *Patrologiae Cursus Completus: Series Graeca* (1857–1866). The first English translation, by Robert C. Hill, *Theodoret of Cyrus: Commentary on the Psalms*, consists of vol. 1, *Psalms 1–72* and vol. 2, *Psalms 73–150*. The latter volume contains the translation of the psalm that is the basis

---

30. Diodorus of Tarsus, *Commentary on the Psalms 1–51*, trans. Robert C. Hill (Atlanta: SBL Press, 2005), xxv.

31. Diodorus of Tarsus, *Commentary on the Psalms 1–51*, xxv.

32. Bernard McGinn and Susan E. Schreiner, "According to the Scriptures: Biblical Interpretation Prior to 1600," 1891–1922 in *The Jerome Biblical Commentary for the Twenty-First Century*, ed. John J. Collins et al. (London: T&T Clark, 2022), 1902.

33. Robert C. Hill, "Introduction," 1–36 in Theodoret of Cyrus, *Commentary on the Psalms, 1–72*, trans. Robert C. Hill, FaCh 101 (Washington, DC: Catholic University of America Press, 2000), 3.

34. Hill, "Introduction," 4; for Theodoret's understanding of the Psalter as a prophetic text predicting the Jews' future salvation and the advent of Christ see G. W. Ashby, *Theodoret of Cyrrhus as Exegete of the Old Testament* (Grahamstown: Rhodes University, 1972), 27.

of our commentary.³⁵ Unlike Origen, whose audience is the ordinary churchgoer, Theodoret's work is that of a "desk theologian."³⁶ He writes for monastics so that they can "profit from what lies hidden in its [Scripture's] depths."³⁷ In the prologue to the commentary, he identifies his exegetic principles:

> Now, let no one think any less of our efforts for the reason that others have produced a commentary on this before ours. I have, in fact, encountered various such commentaries: some I found taking refuge in allegory with considerable relish, while others make the inspired composition resemble historical narratives of a certain type with the result that the commentary represents a case rather for Jews than the household of the faith. In my opinion, it is for a wise man to shun the extreme tendencies of both the former and the latter: the things that are relevant to stories of the past should be applied to them even today, whereas the prophecies about Christ the Lord, about the Church from the nations, the evangelists' lifestyles, and the apostolic preaching should not be applied to anything else, as Jews with their proclivity to malice love to do and contrive a defense for their disbelief.³⁸

35. Theodoret of Cyrus, *Commentary on Psalm 75*, 18–21 in *Commentary on the Psalms, 73–150*, trans. Robert C. Hill, FaCh 101 (Washington, DC: Catholic University of America Press, 2001). The translation of Psalm 75[74] reads:
> ¹To the end. Do not destroy. A Psalm of a song for Asaph.
> ²We shall confess to you, God, we shall confess to you and we shall call upon your name.
> ³I shall narrate all your wonders, when I take the opportunity. I shall deliver upright judgements.
> ⁴The earth was wasted, and all its inhabitants in it. I shall strengthen its pillars.
> ⁵I said to the transgressors, Do not transgress, and to the sinners, Do not raise your horn.
> ⁶Do not lift up your horn on high. Do not speak inquiry against God
> ⁷Because it is not from the dawn nor from the west nor from desert mountains.
> ⁸Because the Lord is judge: He humbles one and elevates another.
> ⁹Because in the Lord's hand there is a cup full of pure wine well mixed, and he moved from one to the other. But its dregs will not be emptied: all the sinners of the earth will drink.
> ¹⁰As for me, on the contrary, I shall rejoice forever, I shall sing to the God of Jacob.
> ¹¹I shall break all the horns of sinners, and the horn of the righteous will be exalted.

36. Hill, "Introduction," 7.

37. Hill, "Introduction," 13–14.

38. Theodoret of Cyrus, *Commentary on the Psalms, 1–72*, Preface (trans. Hill, 41–42). Theodoret's use of the "Jews" to condemn all Jewish people for rejecting Jesus as Savior poses a contradiction. It allows his readers to ignore the fact that Jesus, his disciples, his mother, and the earliest believers in Jesus were all Jews (John 11:45). Even given the constraints of Theodoret's negative profile of the "Jews" as those who refuse to believe in Jesus, the reality does not fit. It is best to consider Theodoret's commentary within intra-ecclesial tensions that arose

Theodoret's exegesis seeks to find the middle ground between a purely historical approach and an excessive allegorical interpretation of Alexandria. In his reading of Psalm 75[74], he relies on the *historia*: the setting of historical events, characters, and geography for its interpretation.

Let us begin with the interpretative challenge of the psalm's title, "Do not destroy" (v. 1). Like Origen, he is ignorant of its musical meaning but aware that the psalm's theme is a prophecy on the divine judgment on the wicked. He sees Symmachus's translation of the title ("A triumphal psalm about the *incorruption* for Asaph," v. 1) as an appropriate introduction exhorting the believer not to "destroy [their] pious thoughts" so as to be found worthy of incorruption.[39] The future tense of the Jewish people's proclamation ("We shall confess to you, O God, . . . and call upon your name," v. 2) suggests for Theodoret that the Jewish exiles are pledging to identify themselves as God's people again by calling on his name (in worship) after having been resettled in Jerusalem. When taking up the meaning of "I will narrate . . . your wonderful deeds, when I take the opportunity" (v. 3a–b), Theodoret adapts Aquila and Symmachus's alternative reading, "when I take the assembly," for the latter phrase to say that the exiles once repatriated into the Holy Land and gathered in the Temple in worship will "*instruct*" others about God's great salvific deeds.[40]

Inspired by God's Word ("How shall we sing the Lord's song in a foreign land," Ps 134:4) into repentance (v. 1), God responds to the return of the exiles to Jerusalem with a promise of judgment and mercy: "I shall deliver upright judgment" (v. 3c). "The earth was wasted, and all its inhabitants in it. I shall strengthen its pillars" (v. 4). As mentioned above, Theodoret's biblical interpretation has been as classified as historical, but in what follows he strongly resembles Origen's divine pedagogy, although unlike Origen, he identifies the speaker as God, not the Logos. He presents God (YHWH) as the interpreter of his own revelatory word (vv. 3c–4):

> I am judge of all the world and shall inflict due punishment on all. *I shall strengthen its pillars*: I am master of all in being creator of all; I made the earth and establish it, supporting it on my boundaries like pillars. After all, I gave the order, and it shall not lapse. Hence, though I am also judge, I do not choose to punish, but foretell retribution so as by the threat to render the sinners more

within the Church to defend the Church's orthodoxy from heretical teachings and that often led authors to redefine the Church position in opposition to the synagogue.

39. Theodoret of Cyrus, *Commentary on Psalm 75*, 18–21 in *Commentary on the Psalms, 73–150*, trans. Robert C. Hill, FaCh 101 (Washington, DC: Catholic University of America Press, 2001), 1 (trans. Hill, 18).

40. Theodoret of Cyrus, *Commentary on Psalm 75*, 2 (trans. Hill, 18).

moderate; I urge and advise them to loathe every form of iniquity, on the one hand, and on the other to have a care for a righteous and balanced attitude.[41]

God declares having the right to judge all, by virtue of being the Creator, but chooses instead to exercise divine forbearance. In his mercy he defers the full measurement of his judgment to give his creatures the opportunity to reject sin and embrace virtue.[42] Therefore, God teaches: "Do not transgress, and to the sinners, do not raise your horn" (vv. 4–6). Theodoret comments that the transgressors not only sin, but also take pride in their wickedness, as illustrated by the image of the horn. "From the dawn [east] . . . west . . . desert mountains [north and south]" (v. 7) covers the four cardinal points of the earth from which none can escape God's judgment. In fact, God's judgment has already been manifested over Israel. God gave the cup of his fury and judgment (v. 9; Jer 25:15–28) to Israel by weakening it with the exile ("He humbles," v. 8). According to Theodoret, the metaphor of wine as retribution is appropriate because "it [divine retribution] undermines strength in a manner like inebriation," weakening the limbs of those who consume it.[43] God has chosen to raise another, Babylon, to punish Israel for its sins. God repeats this cycle of humbling and elevating by later giving Babylon the dregs, the most bitter sediments of wine, by raising Cyrus to defeat them, and simultaneously restoring Israel's freedom (vv. 1–2). In the uncertainties of life, Theodoret then exhorts the reader not to mock the bitter destiny of the nations, but to praise God for his favor (v. 9). In the concluding statement, "I shall break the horns of the sinners and the horn of the righteous will be exalted" (v. 11), Theodoret argues God has foretold through the prophets (Ezekiel, Micah, and Zechariah) that the "horns," a symbol of the strength and power of the nations, will be broken, and the exiles will in the end be victorious under the leadership of the "horn of righteousness": Zerubbabel, the Davidic heir, who many Jews believed would restore Israel's former glory.

Theodoret reads Psalm 75[74] in the context of *historia*, which permits him to interpret the psalm within the context of historical events and within God's (YHWH's) historical intervention in Israel without compromising the moral and doctrinal message of the text. But unlike Origen, he presents the message without endeavoring to enter the spiritual life of the reader and without attributing the psalm to the direct teaching of Jesus Christ, the Logos, to the Gentile Church.

---

41. Theodoret of Cyrus, *Commentary on Psalm 75*, 3 (trans. Hill, 19).
42. Theodoret of Cyrus, *Commentary on Psalm 75*, 3 (trans. Hill, 19).
43. Theodoret of Cyrus, *Commentary on Psalm 75*, 5 (trans. Hill, 20).

Conclusion and Implications

At the conclusion of this brief comparison between Origen's allegorical exegesis and Theodoret's of Cyrus use of *historia* for the interpretation of Psalm 75[74], we can make the following observation. Origen's understanding of Scripture as the pedagogy of the Logos is the basis of his exegesis, and consequently, he glosses over the literal sense of the text in favor of the spiritual sense.[44] As a priest, his sermon is meant to lead the congregation to an encounter with Christ by disclosing the truth about themselves—the need to confess their sins in a personal encounter with the Lord. By exposing the reality of sin, Origen explains how Christ offers a choice between two stark alternatives: salvation and condemnation. The effects of encountering Jesus sacramentally are relevant to their existential reality. Jesus does more than forgive their sins, he justifies them by transforming their sinful nature. He offers them a secure place, that is, salvation within the embrace of his Church. In contrast, the sinner will inevitably experience God's punishment according to his or her deeds. In presenting the two ways of life, Origen, by engaging the community directly at the personal level, implicitly explains how Christ seeks a free response to the question: Do you wish to have life in me by renouncing sin and embracing a life of virtue? This is a question that a purely scientific or historical approach cannot offer. Origen's desire to bring Christ to the faithful echoes in Church documents:

> The Gospel preached by the Church is not just a message but a divine and self-giving experience for those who believe, hear, receive and obey the message.... In hearing the Word, the actual encounter with God himself calls to the heart of man and demands a decision which is not arrived at solely through the intellectual knowledge but which requires conversion of the heart.... The proclamation of the Gospel by the sacred ministers of the Church is, in a certain sense, a participation in the salvific character of the Word itself.[45]

But Origen's approach to Scripture also allowed him to remove the psalm from its historical context and to divorce the passage from its Jewish setting, both of which could promote anti-Jewish readings. By focusing on the Gentile Church to the exclusion of the Jews, Origen could identify the speaker not as YHWH, but as Jesus Christ, the Logos.

---

44. Torjesen, *Hermeneutical Procedure*, 140, 143.
45. Congregation for the Clergy, *The Priest and The Third Christian Millennium: Teacher of the Word, Minister of the Sacraments, and Leader of the Community* (Vatican City: Libreria Editrice Vaticana, 1999), 2.1.

The Alexandrian and Antiochian Method of Exegesis of Psalm 75 [74]

Theodoret's approach on the *historia* (historical setting) and *lexis* (literary sense) overlaps with Origen's in the following themes: God's universal verdict against the wicked, God's warning of punishment on sinners, and God's own teaching on his forbearance and love for humans despite sin. Theodoret's explanation is not void of theological or spiritual content. Additionally, he interprets the psalm within the history of the Jewish people in exile—the first hearers and readers of this psalm. But Theodoret's reading lacks the personalistic approach so characteristic of Origen, an approach that speaks directly to those who have come to Church to be transformed by the Word of God. Undoubtedly this is due to Theodoret's historical approach to Scripture.

When considering both approaches, the tendency with the approach found in Theodoret, representing "Antioch" then and now, may be to employ the historical approach without personalizing the spiritual dimension of the text and allowing Scripture to speak to the hearts of contemporary hearers. In the case of Origen, representing "Alexandria" then and now, the tendency is often to allegorize or "spiritualize" a text so that it might speak to a contemporary audience without considering the essential contribution of a historical analysis. Especially when reading Old Testament texts, to divorce texts dealing with the Jewish people from their historical context can inadvertently lead to anti-Jewish readings or omit Jews from their own Scriptures in order to insert the hearers in the Church alone. One cannot gloss over one aspect of the scriptural text or the other in our interpretive practices. "Antioch," the historical approach, is a critical step in understanding Scripture's theological message in context before moving to "Alexandria" and the application of Scripture's theological (spiritual) message to the lives of individuals today.

CHAPTER 7

At the Jordan Christ Deposited for Us the Robe of Glory: Unjustified Hiatus between the Historical Event and the Theological Interpretation of the Baptism of Jesus[1]

Marcin Kowalski

Tertullian once asked what Athens and Jerusalem had in common, suggesting falsification of the truth by philosophy that, based on limited rational premises, denies revelation.[2] The same objection seems to be raised against contemporary exegesis by Ben F. Meyer, who claims that it has lost the sense of the mystery of salvation, not only opting for a historical-critical method, but also embracing its historicizing, rationalist, and naturalistic methodological premises.[3] The author juxtaposes "Antioch" and "Alexandria," two important

---

1. My heartfelt thanks goes to Kevin Zilverberg and John Martens, the organizers of the 2022 Quinn Conference, The Transcendent Mystery of God's Word: A Critical Synthesis of Antioch and Alexandria. Thank you for the wonderful community of prayer and scholarly discussions, out of which this paper is born. To John Martens and the anonymous reviewers, I am very grateful for all the comments and questions that helped me to hone and clarify my argumentation. In this paper, I am expanding and elaborating on some ideas that can be found in my earlier article, M. Kowalski, "Baptism – the Revelation of the Filial Relationship of Christ and the Christian," *The Biblical Annals* 11 no. 3 (2021): 459–95.

2. Tertullian, *Praescr.* 7.9. On the meaning of this well-known statement, see Eric Osborn, *Tertullian, First Theologian of the West* (Cambridge: Cambridge University Press, 2001), 27–47.

3. Ben F. Meyer, *Critical Realism and the New Testament* (Allison Park, PA: Pickwick, 1989), 43. On the (more or less moderate) critique of the historical-critical method from the Catholic point of view, see Joseph Ratzinger, *Behold the Pierced One: An Approach to a Spiritual Christology* (San Francisco: Ignatius, 1986), 15–17, 33, 41; Joseph Ratzinger, *Principles of Catholic Theology: Building Stones for a Fundamental Theology* (San Francisco: Ignatius, 1987), 315–33; Pontifical Biblical Commission, *The Interpretation of the Bible in the Church* (Vatican City: Libreria Editrice Vaticana, 1993), §I.A; Joseph Ratzinger, *Truth and Tolerance: Christian Belief*

cities of early Christianity, symbolizing two different approaches to the analysis of the biblical text. Antioch can be associated with modern historical-critical exegesis, seeking the original meaning of the text by embedding it firmly in its original context. Alexandria embodies a once popular allegorical reading, seeking a deeper, spiritual and theological message contained in the Bible.[4] Each of these approaches has its own merits and shortcomings. Antioch's flaw—here Meyer follows John Henry Newman—consists in losing the sight of the mystery of salvation unfolding in the Scriptures. Alexandria's weakness, in turn, manifests itself in its tendency to disregard the principles of historical analysis.[5] According to Meyer, only the combination of these two perspectives will enable us to escape the aporia and sterility of modern exegesis, which clearly leans toward the Antiochian approach.[6]

The description of Jesus's baptism in the Jordan is a perfect example of the contemporary clash occurring between the Antiochian (radical historical-critical) and Alexandrian (theological-spiritual) exegesis. On the one hand, the

---

and World Religions (San Francisco: Ignatius, 2004), 132–33; Albert C. Vanhoye, "The Reception in the Church of the Dogmatic Constitution 'Dei Verbum'," 104–25 in *Opening up the Scriptures: Joseph Ratzinger and the Foundations of Biblical Interpretation*, ed. José Granados, Carlos Granados, and Luis Sánchez-Navarro (Grand Rapids, MI: Eerdmans, 2008) esp. 120–24; Marcin Kowalski, "Meditatio of Lectio Divina Following upon Exegesis-Informed Lectio: The Test Case of Romans 7:7–25," 82–97 in *Piercing the Clouds: Lectio Divina and Preparation for Ministry*, ed. Kevin Zilverberg and Scott Carl (Saint Paul, MN: Saint Paul Seminary Press, 2021), esp. 84–85. See also Vernon K. Robbins, "Divine Dialogue and the Lord's Prayer: Socio-Rhetorical Interpretation of Sacred Texts," *Dialogue* 28, no. 3 (1995): 117–46; Joel B. Green, "Scripture and Theology: Uniting the Two So Long Divided," 23–43 in *Between Two Horizons: Spanning New Testament Studies and Systematic Theology*, ed. Joel B. Green and Max Turner (Grand Rapids, MI: Eerdmans, 2000), esp. 27–30; Fernando F. Segovia, *Decolonizing Biblical Studies: A View from the Margins* (Maryknoll, NY: Orbis, 2000), 148–50; Anna Runesson, *Exegesis in the Making: Postcolonialism and New Testament Studies* (Leiden: Brill, 2011), 61–67.

4. Such a division clearly presupposes a simplification, also present in Meyer. In fact, the ancient Antiochian school did not shy away from allegory and theological conclusions, while the Alexandrian school also relied on a historical and literal reading. Here, however, we are not comparing the Antiochian and Alexandrian schools as they presented themselves in antiquity, but rather, using them after Meyer as a generic reference point, we are attempting to show the sterility of historical-critical exegesis in its radical form, which excludes texts in which a theological interpretation is found. According to the position taken in this paper, the theological or sacramental interpretation, which, following Meyer, we symbolically associate with the Alexandrian school, in biblical texts naturally merges with the historical interpretation, symbolically referred to as Antiochian. Only their combination makes it possible to discover both the history and its meaning, intrinsically related for the biblical authors.

5. Meyer, *Critical Realism and the New Testament*, 45–48.
6. Meyer, *Critical Realism and the New Testament*, 33, 49.

historical-critical school separates the event of baptism and the theophany that followed it, considering the latter a literary construct and a secondary interpretation of the former. Moreover, according to *Formgeschichte*, which we will treat here as a contemporary incarnation of the Antiochian school, there is no parallel between the baptism of Jesus in the Jordan and the baptism of believers. Such a connection is absent from the New Testament texts and was created later by imposing a Christian baptismal praxis upon the Jordan event. On the other hand, in the Fathers of the Church quoted below, whom we shall make symbolic representatives of the Alexandrian school, Jesus's baptism in the Jordan and the theophany that follows it are inextricably linked. The Fathers also see a profound analogy between Christian baptism and the baptism of Jesus. Referring to the title of this paper, they speak of Christ who, emerging from the waters of the Jordan, left us on its shore the baptismal robe of glory.[7] Unfortunately, the Fathers do not explicate exegetically the bond they perceive, operating on the general level of a canonical approach and the spiritual sense of the Scriptures. Therefore, it will be our task to substantiate their reading by trying to unite Antioch and Alexandria, the historical and theological readings of Jesus's baptism in the Jordan. In fact, we are not inventing anything new here, because this combination is already present in the baptismal pericopes and is intended by the evangelists. We will also refer to Paul, suggesting that in his description of the Christian's new life in Jesus in Romans, the apostle could also be inspired by the event that took place at the Jordan. The connection between Jesus's baptism and the Christian baptismal experience, so dear to the Fathers of the Church, can be spotted already in Paul. Ultimately, the New Testament authors testify to a profound unity between the historical and theological readings of Jesus's baptism, which will be the focal point of the analyses carried below.

The Meaning of Jesus's Baptism in the Jordan

Jesus's baptism in the Jordan belongs to the few New Testament events whose historicity is almost unanimously held as undisputable.[8] The factuality of the

---

7. On the baptismal robe of glory left by Christ for the catechumens, see Kilian McDonnell, "Jesus' Baptism in the Jordan," *Theological Studies* 56, no. 2 (1995): 209–36, esp. 232–35.

8. John P. Meier, *A Marginal Jew: Rethinking the Historical Jesus*, vol. 2, *Mentor, Message, and Miracles* (New Haven: Yale University Press, 1994), 100. See also Ed P. Sanders, *Jesus and Judaism* (London: SCM, 1985), 11; Robert L. Webb, "Jesus' Baptism: Its Historicity and Implications," *Bulletin for Biblical Research* 10, no. 2 (2000): 261–309, esp. 261; Ulrich Luz, *Matthew*

At the Jordan Christ Deposited for Us the Robe of Glory

story is strongly defended on the basis of the combined classical criteria of embarrassment, multiple attestation, and discontinuity.[9] The character of John's baptism has also been studied in detail in terms of its relationship with other similar rituals in the Greco-Roman and Jewish world.[10] Thus, John Meier, citing Rudolf Bultmann and many other representatives of the historical-critical school, concludes that there is no reason to doubt the historicity of Jesus's baptism.[11]

1–7: A Commentary on Matthew 1–7, Hermeneia (Minneapolis: Fortress, 2007), 144; Daniel J. Harrington, *The Gospel of Matthew*, SP 1 (Collegeville, MN: Liturgical Press, 2007), 63; Robert H. Stein, *Mark*, BECNT (Grand Rapids, MI: Baker Academic, 2008), 56; Craig S. Keener, *The Gospel of Matthew: A Socio-Rhetorical Commentary* (Grand Rapids, MI: Eerdmans, 2009), 131; M. E. Boring, *Mark: A Commentary*, NTLi (Louisville: Westminster John Knox, 2012), 44. See, however, the works of earlier authors, who claim that Jesus's baptism in the Jordan is an early Christian creation: Ernst Haenchen, *Der Weg Jesu: Eine Erklärung des Markus-Evangeliums und der kanonischen Parallelen*, 2nd ed., De Gruyter Lehrbuch (Berlin: De Gruyter, 1968), 60–63; Morton S. Enslin, "John and Jesus," *Die Zeitschrift für die Neutestamentliche Wissenschaft und die Kunde der älteren Kirche* 66, nos. 1–2 (1975): 1–18.

9. Meier, *A Marginal Jew: Rethinking the Historical Jesus*, 2:101–5; Webb, "Jesus' Baptism," 261–74. On the usability of the criteria and the model on which they are based, see Tobias Hägerland, "The Future of Criteria in Historical Jesus Research," *Journal for the Study of the Historical Jesus* 13, no. 1 (2015): 43–65 (the author speaks in favor of the nuanced use of the criteria); Chris Keith, "The Narratives of the Gospels and the Historical Jesus: Current Debates, Prior Debates and the Goal of Historical Jesus Research," *Journal for the Study of the New Testament* 38, no. 4 (2016): 426–55. Keith makes a negative assessment of the form-critical model and its criteria which aim at seeking a pure, devoid of interpretation version of the historical event. In its stead, he proposes studies and models related to collective memory (social memory theory), which in his view are incompatible with form-critical categories.

10. On John, his prophetic mission, and the character of his baptism, see among others, Robert L. Webb, *John the Baptizer and Prophet: A Socio-Historical Study*, JSNTSup 62 (Sheffield: JSOT Press, 1991), 179–205; Webb, "Jesus' Baptism," 278–94 (John is a prophet, his rite is of initiatory and eschatological character and is related to God's forgiveness, purification, and even to a protest against the temple establishment); Joan E. Taylor, *The Immerser: John the Baptist within Second Temple Judaism*, SHJ (Grand Rapids, MI: Eerdmans, 1997) (the baptism by John as a repeatable purification rite); Bruce Chilton, "John the Baptist: His Immersion and his Death," 25–44 in *Dimensions of Baptism: Biblical and Theological Studies*, ed. Stanley E. Porter and Anthony R. Cross, JSNTSup 234 (London: Sheffield Academic, 2002) (John is not a prophet, his baptism exhibits the traits of Jewish purification rites); Craig A. Evans, "The Baptism of John in a Typological Context," 45–71 in *Dimensions of Baptism: Biblical and Theological Studies*, ed. Stanley E. Porter and Anthony R. Cross, JSNTSup 234 (London, New York: Sheffield Academic Press, 2002) (John as a prophet of eschatological transformation, his rite being of an initiatory, eschatological, and purifying character).

11. Meier, *A Marginal Jew: Rethinking the Historical Jesus*, 2:105, with reference to Rudolf Bultmann, *Jesus and the Word* (London: Collins, 1934), 26, 110–11; Ernst Käsemann, "On the Subject of Primitive Christian Apocalyptic," 108–37 in *New Testament Questions of Today*, ed. Ernst Käsemann, NTLi (London: SCM Press, 1969), esp. 112; Günther Bornkamm, *Jesus of*

Doubts, however, begin to multiply when the discussion about its literary construction and meaning is undertaken.

The Historical-Critical Interpretation of Jesus's Baptism in the Jordan

When examining the events connected with Jesus's baptism in the Jordan, modern exegesis basically asks itself two questions. First, why did Jesus enter the waters of the Jordan?[12] Second, how is Jesus's baptism related to the theophany which follows: the vision of the open or torn heaven, the Spirit, and the voice of the Father? John Meier, reading the baptism of Jesus with the use of the historical-critical tools, points at several aspects which define it.[13] *First*, it is a real turning point in the life of Jesus, which, according to the author, can be referred to as his "conversion" in the basic sense of the word. Jesus embarks on a public mission, which nothing had heralded previously, and turns completely to God from then on.[14] Did he make this decision earlier or was he led to it by his baptism in the Jordan? According to Meier, these questions cannot be answered if the theophany is removed as an early Christian interpretation of the figure of the Messiah.[15] At the Jordan, Jesus, together with all Israel, simply declares that he will give up his old way of living.

Second, according to Meier, Jesus knew John's message and agreed with him on the following points: the end of Israel's history was approaching, the people had gone astray and were in danger, they needed conversion, and John was an eschatological prophet sent by God. By his baptism, then, Jesus confirmed John's authority and accepted his message. *Third*, Jesus embraced John's eschatological ritual as necessary for salvation. *Fourth*, the ritual was associated with conversion and forgiveness of sins. Did Jesus need them? This is the opinion of Friedrich Strauss and Paul Hollenbach, according to whom Jesus received baptism from John because, like everyone else, he considered himself a sinner.[16] As Meier rightly points out, this is not a problem to be solved in

---

Nazareth (New York: Harper & Row, 1960), 54; Hans Conzelmann, *Jesus* (Philadelphia: Fortress, 1973), 31.

12. A comprehensive list of reasons given by scholars can be found in W. D. Davies and Dale C. Allison, *A Critical and Exegetical Commentary on the Gospel According to Saint Matthew*, ICC (Edinburgh: T&T Clark, 1988), 321–23.

13. Meier, *A Marginal Jew: Rethinking the Historical Jesus*, 2:106–16, 129.

14. Webb fundamentally agrees with Meier in this and other aspects of Jesus's baptism. See Webb, "Jesus' Baptism," 294–300, 305–7.

15. Meier, *A Marginal Jew: Rethinking the Historical Jesus*, 2:109.

16. Paul Hollenbach, "The Conversion of Jesus: Jesus the Baptizer to Jesus to Healer," 196–219 in *ANRW* 25.1, ed. Wolfgang Haase (Berlin: De Gruyter, 1982), esp. 199–201. Furthermore, Hollenbach considers Jesus to be a representative of the middle class, who feels guilty for being

a *strictly* historical perspective, as Hollenbach postulates, because it concerns theological categories. In view of the uniform testimony of the entire New Testament and the Christian tradition about the sinlessness of Jesus, Hollenbach's position should also be considered with skepticism.[17]

Fifth, finally, the descent of Jesus into the waters of the Jordan, according to Meier, must have had something to do with sin. Confession of sins was part of public rituals in postexilic Israel. It did not necessarily signify a direct involvement in wrongdoing but a recognition that a believer was part of the nation of sinners, which was in need of conversion. This is how Ezra prayed, having discovered the sins of his people (Ezra 9:6-15; Neh 9:6-37). Also, other great leaders of Israel, such as Daniel, prayed in solidarity with sinners (Dan 3:29; 9:5, 15). A similar prayer can also be found in the Qumran community, whose members profess (1QS 1:24-25): "We have acted sinfully, we have transgressed, we have sinned, we have committed evil, we and our fathers before us."[18] Jesus could have shown a similar solidarity with sinful Israel by immersing himself in the waters of the Jordan and asking God to restore his chosen people.[19]

James D. G. Dunn also finds in the baptism of Jesus a penitential rite, practiced by the prophets who identify themselves with the sins of the people. The author additionally qualifies the ritual as Jesus's submission to God's will and a commitment to fulfill the mission entrusted to him by the Father.[20] The idea of the solidarity of the Messiah, entering the waters of the Jordan, finds many sympathizers and takes many forms. Edward Burrows argues that Jesus at his baptism likely represents a converting community, the first fruit of God's new

---

part of the system that persecutes and oppresses the poor. Cf. Meier, *A Marginal Jew: Rethinking the Historical Jesus*, 2:111-13.

17. For a critical evaluation and response, see Carl R. Holladay, "Baptism in the New Testament and Its Cultural Milieu: A Response to Everett Ferguson, Baptism in the Early Church," *Journal of Early Christian Studies* 20, no. 3 (2012): 343-69, esp. 353.

18. Florentino García Martínez and Eibert J. C. Tigchelaar, eds., *The Dead Sea Scrolls Study Edition (Translations)* (Leiden: Brill, 1997), 71.

19. See also William L. Lane, *The Gospel of Mark*, NICNT (Grand Rapids, MI: Eerdmans, 1974), 54; John R. Donahue and Daniel J. Harrington, *The Gospel of Mark*, SP 2 (Collegeville, MN: Liturgical Press, 2002), 65; Keener, *The Gospel of Matthew*, 132; Boring, *Mark*, 44. Meier does not answer the question of whether Christ was confessing his sins at the same time. According to him, this issue is beyond the reach of a historian. See Meier, *A Marginal Jew: Rethinking the Historical Jesus*, 2:115.

20. James D. G. Dunn, *Baptism in the Holy Spirit: A Re-Examination of the New Testament Teaching on the Gift of the Spirit in Relation to Pentecostalism Today* (Philadelphia: Westminster, 1970), 36.

people. The Messiah reinterprets the rite by applying it to himself; there is nothing he needs to be cleansed of, but he renews his dedication to do God's will.[21] In turn, Jeffrey Gibbs, following the Gospel of Matthew, argues that Jesus by the Jordan represents Israel, but also the Gentiles, and as the Servant of the Lord fulfills God's saving plan—he is the one on whose behalf the nations will be baptized.[22]

In the latter interpretation, history is closely intertwined with Matthew's theological message, which the historical-critical school tries to avoid on methodological grounds. Its austere reconstruction leads to the conclusion that Jesus, upon his baptism in the Jordan, severs ties with his former life, recognizes himself as a member of the sinful people, turns to God with all his heart, acknowledges John as an eschatological prophet, and probably stays with him for some time, becoming his disciple.[23] Where is the baptismal theology that the tradition of the Church derived from this scene? It remains beyond the

---

21. Edward W. Burrows, "Baptism in Mark and Luke," 99–115 in *Baptism, the New Testament and the Church: Historical and Contemporary Studies in Honour of R. E. O. White*, ed. Stanley E. Porter and Reginald E. O. White, JSNTSup 171 (Sheffield: Sheffield Academic, 1999), esp. 101–3. With regard to the Gospel of Matthew, similar views are held by David L. Turner, *Matthew*, BECNT (Grand Rapids, MI: Baker Academic, 2008), 119, who also claims that Jesus identifies with the rest of Israel, being repentant and righteous.

22. Jeffrey A. Gibbs, "Israel Standing with Israel: The Baptism of Jesus in Matthew's Gospel (Matt 3:13–17)," *Catholic Biblical Quarterly* 64, no. 3 (2002): 511–26.

23. Meier, *A Marginal Jew: Rethinking the Historical Jesus*, 2:129; Webb, "Jesus' Baptism," 261, 301–5. In this strand of scholarship one can also place Joel Marcus, *John the Baptist in History and Theology*, SPNT (Columbia, SC: University of South Carolina Press, 2018), 81–97 and Tucker S. Ferda, "The Historicity of Confusion: Jesus, John the Baptist, and the Construction of Public Identity," *Journal of Biblical Literature* 139, no. 4 (2020): 747–67. Marcus speaks of John's identity and relation to Jesus in a typically historical-critical way. According to the author, Jesus was John's disciple who outgrew his master. If John regarded himself as Elijah, Jesus might have been regarded by him as Elisha, who outranked his predecessor. John realized this only in the further course of his mission. According to Ferda, Jesus intentionally constructs his mission and identity by referring to John, his former master. Both authors attempt at historical-critical reconstruction, excluding the data coming from the baptismal theophany and downplaying the context of John's mission, which is to prepare for the revelation of Christ. Ferda's approach ultimately gives less value to the Gospel texts and their theology than to the speculative historical-critical reconstructions supported by contemporary social identity theories: "As noted above, it is clear that the gospels have framed the story of John the Baptist from their view of Jesus at the center, which means that John functions almost entirely as a forerunner. But if, as I have argued, the reality is that John was first, John was (initially at least) more popular, and John did not publicly point to Jesus as the fulfillment of his work, we can see that Jesus had a lot to gain by 'constructing' his own identity and message in relation to John's" (765).

grasp of much historical-critical research, which does not accept this scene's connection with the theophany.[24]

According to researchers such as Meier and Dunn, it is naive to look for Jesus's understanding of baptism in the theophany that follows.[25] Why is it so? First, because attempting to penetrate the psychology of Jesus was a path trod by nineteenth-century biographies and has little to do with contemporary research, as identified by the criteria of historicity.[26] Second, in the Jordan theophany the reader is likely dealing with a Christian midrash, not a description of a historical fact. Meier discerns in the pericope allusions to Isaiah 11:2 and 61:1 (the Spirit resting upon the Messiah), a reference to Psalm 2:7 (divine filiation), to the story of Abraham from Genesis 22 (the beloved son), to the Song of the Servant of the Lord from Isaiah 42:1 (the theme of God's will and the gift of the Spirit for the Servant), to Ezekiel 1:1 (the location of the vision by the river), and finally to Isaiah 63:19 (the tearing of the heavens).[27]

In this view, the theophany does not reflect the experience of the historical Jesus, but what the early Church knew and thought about him, taking into account his entire mission.[28] It demonstrates the fulfilment of the Old Testament prophecies in Jesus, the true Son of God, the messianic descendant of David, the eschatological prophet, and the Servant of the Lord, who surpasses John in power and dignity. The theophany arose out of the need to cover the confusion that resulted from the baptism of Jesus in the Jordan and to emphasize the superiority of Jesus over the Baptist.[29] In Meier's opinion, the very nature of the theophany as a later Christian composition disqualifies it in the eyes of a historian.[30]

Meier is essentially supported by Dunn, whose stance evolved somewhat in the course of his research. In *Jesus and the Spirit*, the author draws attention

---

24. On the historicity of the theophany, see Webb, "Jesus' Baptism," 274–78. The author ultimately decides to analyze it separately from the ritual of baptism itself, treating it as a foreign entity.

25. Meier, *A Marginal Jew: Rethinking the Historical Jesus*, 2:106; James D. G. Dunn, *Jesus Remembered*, CM 1 (Grand Rapids, MI: Eerdmans, 2003), 374–47.

26. See also similar skepticism toward the psychological analyses of Jesus in Donald H. Juel, *Mark*, ACNT (Minneapolis: Augsburg, 1990), 37; Stein, *Mark*, 60.

27. Meier, *A Marginal Jew: Rethinking the Historical Jesus*, 2:106–7. Similarly, Dunn, *Jesus Remembered*, 374, and virtually all commentators analyzing the baptism of Jesus in the synoptic Gospels.

28. Meier, *A Marginal Jew: Rethinking the Historical Jesus*, 2:107; Dunn, *Jesus Remembered*, 374. Juel, *Mark*, 36: "There are hints that the story of Jesus has 'been written'."

29. Meier, *A Marginal Jew: Rethinking the Historical Jesus*, 2:107.

30. Meier, *A Marginal Jew: Rethinking the Historical Jesus*, 2:108.

to the gradual development of the tradition discernible in the baptismal pericopes. First, from a private scene, which is how the baptism is portrayed in Mark, we move on to a public, verifiable event in Matthew and later Christian authors like Justin, who mentions the fire in the Jordan, a visible sign of Jesus's baptism (*Dial.* 88.3).[31] Second, the shape of the story, in which the actual events are retold from the perspective of the narrator, not Jesus, indicates that we are dealing with an early Christian creation, not a record of the Messiah's own experience.[32] There is no doubt that Jesus's whole life and activity are marked by his awareness of the gift of the Spirit and special relationship with the Father. According to Dunn, if the early Christian tradition linked these two elements to the baptism in the Jordan, it must have had good reasons for doing so. Baptism may have been the moment when Jesus's identity was crystallized, providing him with a meaningful experience of the Spirit and Fatherly love.[33]

According to Dunn, Jesus did not share this personal experience with his disciples, but he could have alluded to it, on the basis of which the Jordan theophany was created.[34] The very fact that Christian communities practiced baptism could have also originated from the fact that Christ indicated the importance of this ritual for himself.[35] The author here allows linking the baptism in the Jordan with the experience of the historical Jesus and emphasizes its "epochal significance" for the Master, along with the two most significant elements: the Spirit and sonship.[36] At the Jordan, Jesus experienced an increase in spiritual power, was anointed with God's eschatological Spirit, and was chosen to fulfill a special divine mission. In his later book, *Jesus Remembered*, Dunn, building on what was said above, emphasizes much more strongly that the theophany reflects the disciples' perception of the identity and work of the Master. It can be said that the Jordan scene contains a reference to the filial consciousness of Jesus and his special gift of the Spirit (a historical element),

---

31. Dunn, *Baptism in the Holy Spirit*, 63; Dunn, *Jesus Remembered*, 375–76. Joel Marcus, *Mark 1–8: A New Translation with Introduction and Commentary*, AncB (New Haven: Yale University Press, 2008), 164 recognizes that the public form might have arisen from the apologetic purpose of later Gospels, but the private form may also be a Markan invention in accordance with the so-called "Messianic secret." Similar views are held by Boring, *Mark*, 45.

32. James D. G. Dunn, *Jesus and the Spirit: A Study of the Religious and Charismatic Experience of Jesus and the First Christians as Reflected in the New Testament* (London: SCM, 1975), 63; Dunn, *Jesus Remembered*, 374–75.

33. Dunn, *Jesus and the Spirit*, 63.

34. Dunn, *Jesus and the Spirit*, 64–65.

35. Dunn, *Jesus and the Spirit*, 65.

36. Dunn, *Jesus and the Spirit*, 65.

but ultimately everything else is a construct of the tradition.[37] Dunn no longer repeats his observations about the importance of the baptismal event for Jesus's mission and is cautious even of stating that Christ understood the moment of baptism as anointing for his mission.[38] Ultimately, the author clearly separates the fact of baptism in the Jordan from its later interpretation, which we find in the theophany.[39]

The Unjustified Separation of Jesus's Baptism from the Theophany

Is the abyss dug between the historical event and its interpretation justified from the point of view of the Gospel text? I find this to be unlikely for a number of reasons. The first one is the nature of ancient texts, which never present themselves as bare, factual descriptions. This feature of ancient historiography has already been emphasized by biblical scholars, challenging strict historical-critical methodology during past stages of historical Jesus research. According to Charles Dodd, the Gospels are interested in the historical Jesus, who is the starting point of the Church's faith. His event is given an interpretation that cannot be separated or even distinguished from historical facts.[40] In the same vein, Oscar Cullman described the Gospels as the community's testimony of the historical Jesus, containing both the image of the Jesus of history and its interpretation.[41] Bornkamm, in his *Jesus of Nazareth*, argued not only that there is full continuity between the kerygma of the Church and the Jesus of history, but even that the apostolic kerygma is a continuation of Christ's self-consciousness. Similar views were expressed by representatives of the so-called New Hermeneutics, critical of *Formgeschichte*. They postulated a move away from history understood anachronistically as factography, emphasizing the close connection between the apostolic kerygma, and the Jesus of history and his self-awareness.[42]

Second, the syntactic and lexical markers binding the baptism and the

---

37. Dunn, *Jesus Remembered*, 376.
38. Dunn, *Jesus Remembered*, 377. Similar views are held by Meier, *A Marginal Jew: Rethinking the Historical Jesus*, 108.
39. Dunn, *Jesus Remembered*, 371-74.
40. C. H. Dodd, *The Founder of Christianity* (New York: Macmillan, 1970).
41. Oscar Cullman, "Die neuen Arbeiten zur Geschichte der Evangelientradition," 41-90 in *Vorträge und Aufsätze: 1925 – 1962*, ed. Oscar Cullman (Tübingen: Mohr Siebeck, 1966).
42. J. M. Robinson, *A New Quest for the Historical Jesus* (London: SCM, 1959); Ernst Fuchs, *Zur Frage nach dem historischen Jesus*, Gesammelte Aufsätze 2 (Tübingen: Mohr Siebeck, 1965). Also Keith, "The Narratives of the Gospels and the Historical Jesus," 441-48, draws attention to the historical value of the descriptions of events, into which the interpretation of evangelists and their communities is integrated.

theophany also call into question the separation of these two events. In Mark 1:10, the theophany occurs the moment Jesus comes out of the water (ἀναβαίνων ἐκ τοῦ ὕδατος).⁴³ In Matthew 3:16, the vision takes place right after Jesus comes up out of the water, which is stressed by the construction καὶ ἰδού. In Luke, in turn, the theophany occurs while Jesus is still praying in the Jordan. Participles in the genitive (βαπτισθέντος καὶ προσευχομένου) describe the baptism and prayer as succeeding each other, at the same time introducing the scene in which heaven opens, the Spirit descends, and Jesus hears the voice of the Father (all these actions are described with the infinitive aorist: ἀνεῳχθῆναι τὸν οὐρανόν, καὶ καταβῆναι τὸ πνεῦμα τὸ ἅγιον, καὶ φωνὴν ἐξ οὐρανοῦ γενέσθαι) (Luke 3:21-22).⁴⁴ In all of the synoptic accounts, baptism and theophany are closely related syntactically and literarily.

Third, the separation of baptism and theophany ignores the thematic unity between the two stages of the same event. In Mark 1:5, all those who come to John confess their sins, stating that they are a community of sinners, whose relationship with God requires healing. The remedy for their dramatic departure from God is Jesus, to whom the Father confesses: "You are my Son, the Beloved; with you I am well pleased" (Mark 1:11).⁴⁵ The healer stands in front of the wounded, who seek a cure. The connecting theme is the sin that drives a person away from God, and which is overcome in the new relationship of closeness that the sinners receive in the Son.⁴⁶ In Matthew, in turn, the Baptist, resisting Jesus's desire for baptism at his hands and stating that it is he who needs baptism from Jesus, hears from him: "Let it be so now; for it is proper for us in this way to fulfill all righteousness" (Matt 3:15). "All righteousness" means the will of the Father, God's plan of salvation, and the Scriptures which are fulfilled in the mission and person of Christ.⁴⁷ The predilection of the Father, announced by the voice at the Jordan (Matt 3:17), is related to the fulfilment of

---

43. Robert A. Guelich, *Mark 1-8:26*, WBC 34A (Dallas: Word, 1989), 31: εὐθύς emphasizes the unity between baptism and theophany. Similarly, about the unity of the two scenes and about the καὶ εὐθύς functioning as a frequent link in Mark, see Stein, *Mark*, 56.

44. I. H. Marshall, *The Gospel of Luke: Commentary on the Greek Text*, NIGTC (Exeter: Paternoster, 1978), 152 rightly notes that the baptismal scene is only an introduction to the theophany, which is the real object of Luke's interest.

45. Scripture citations in this chapter are from the New Revised Standard Version.

46. Artur Malina, *Chrzest Jezusa w czterech Ewangeliach: Studium narracji i teologii*, SMWTUSK 34 (Katowice: Księgarnia św. Jacka; Wydział Teologiczny Uniwersytetu Śląskiego, 2007), 205-18, 230-37.

47. Donald A. Hagner, *Matthew 1-13*, WBC 33A (Dallas: Word, 1993), 56-57; Luz, *Matthew 1-7*, 142-43. For possible interpretations of the formula, see Davies and Allison, *A Critical and Exegetical Commentary on the Gospel According to Saint Matthew*, 325-27.

God's redeeming justice in the Son.⁴⁸ Finally, in Luke, Jesus, being baptized and praying in the Jordan, is shown in solidarity with people who also seek God's will by coming to John (Luke 3:21).

The baptismal scene is so closely related to the theophany that the former loses its meaning without the latter.⁴⁹ John in his Gospel eliminates the scene of baptism altogether, quoting only the testimony of the Baptist: "I myself did not know him; but I came baptizing with water for this reason that He might be revealed to Israel" (John 1:31). This is the evangelist's way of showing that that the baptism serves to reveal the identity of Christ, whom John calls the Lamb of God, taking away the sins of the world (1:29), the one who ranks ahead of him (1:30), on whom the Spirit rests and who baptizes with the Spirit (1:32–33). He is the Son of God (John 1:34). The revelation of the filial dignity of Christ, endowed with the Spirit, also stands at the center of the baptismal pericopes in the synoptic Gospels (Mark 1:10–11; Matt 3:16–17; Luke 3:22). It can be concluded that the historical event of baptism in the Jordan is only a time-space frame for Jesus's revelation.

Toward a Holistic, Historical-Theological Interpretation of Jesus's Baptism

Jesus comes to the Jordan to start his mission as the Messiah, the one who will cleanse Israel with the Holy Spirit and fire. At this point, one can also ask the question of whether Jesus gains any special awareness of sonship at the Jordan.⁵⁰

---

48. For the relationship between righteousness (*dik-*) and pleasing God in the Old Testament, see Ps 5:13; 50:21; Sir 9:12; Hab 2:4; Mal 2:17 (LXX).

49. See Guelich, *Mark 1–8:26*, 31: "Thus, John's baptism was the occasion rather than the means of the Spirit's coming to Jesus and the voice speaking from heaven."

50. On the various theories related to a hypothetical new consciousness and status of the Son of God that Jesus gains at the Jordan, see Ernest van Eck, "The Baptism of Jesus in Mark: A Status Transformation Ritual," *Neotestamentica* 30, no. 1 (1996): 187–215, esp. 187–88. The author, using sociological tools (the patron-client model), argues that at the Jordan Jesus experiences a status reversal, becoming a broker of the kingdom of God and enabling clients from the fringes of religious and social structures to access God, the Patron (201–11). In opposition to the various "adoptionist" theories of Jesus's status or changing condition at the Jordan, see James R. Edwards, "The Baptism of Jesus according to the Gospel of Mark," *Journal of the Evangelical Theological Society* 34, no. 1 (1991): 43–57, esp. 55–57. As a counterargument, the author provides the canonical reading of the New Testament (Paul's texts) and the testimony of the Church Fathers. On the other hand, Dunn, *Baptism in the Holy Spirit*, 28 claims that discussing baptism in the Jordan through the lens of Jesus's experience, adoption, or divine or messianic consciousness goes outside the scope and interests of the Gospel authors.

The scholars of the radical historical-critical school consider such reflections to be pointless, unscientific, and missing the interests of the evangelists. The question of Jesus's identity, as projected in the scene of baptism, however, was not disregarded by the Fathers of the Church or by modern biblical scholars, such as George R. Beasley-Murray.[51] The latter claims that the pericopes describing the baptism in the Jordan do not indicate the new filial dignity that Jesus gains there. Rather, they describe him as sure of his identity, which in turn motivates him to act.[52] Let us have a look at a couple of points emerging from a holistic reading of Jesus's baptism in the Jordan, in which the theological message is not severed from the historical event.

The Sinlessness of the Son

This sinlessness of Jesus entering the Jordan was unanimously highlighted by the Fathers of the Church and ancient writers. An anonymous patristic author, in his homily on the Gospel of Matthew, argues that "Jesus came that he might receive John's witness and confirm his preaching: Behold the Lamb of God, who takes away the sins of the world" (John 1:29). The sinless Christ was baptized "as if he were a sinner" also to motivate us to repentance.[53] Theodore of Mopsuestia similarly combines Matthew with John 1:29, claiming that the one "who takes away the sin of the world" (John 1:29) had no need of baptism.[54] The same line of argumentation with the same references to the Gospel of John is present in the commentary by John Chrysostom.[55] Chromatius, in turn, explains John's reluctance to baptize Jesus with an extended monolog of the Baptist:

> "I am a man. You are God. I am a sinner because I am a man. You are sinless because you are God. Why do you want to be baptized by me? I do not refuse the respect you pay me, but I am ignorant of the mystery. I baptize sinners in repentance. But you have no taint of sin. So why do you want to

---

51. George R. Beasley-Murray, *Baptism in the New Testament* (London, New York: Macmillan; St Martin's Press, 1962), 45. See also Dodd, Cullman, Bornkamm, and Fuchs, mentioned above.

52. Beasley-Murray, *Baptism in the New Testament*, 60. Dunn, *Baptism in the Holy Spirit*, 29 claims that Jesus is led to baptism in the Jordan by his messianic consciousness, although this is difficult to prove, according to the author.

53. PG 56:657; trans. Manlio Simonetti, *Matthew 1–13*, ACCS (Downers Grove, IL: InterVarsity Press, 2001), 50.

54. Joseph Reuss, ed., *Matthäus-Kommentare aus der griechischen Kirche* (Berlin: Akademie-Verlag, 1957), 101. Cf. Simonetti, *Matthew 1–13*, 51.

55. John Chrysostom, *Homilies on Matthew*, 12.4 (PG 57:203; cf. Philip Schaff, ed., NPNF 1/10:75).

be baptized? Why do you want to be baptized as a sinner, who came to forgive sins?" This is what John in effect was saying to the Lord.[56]

The Fathers of the Church interpret Jesus's baptism in the Jordan through the lens of the New Testament tradition that unanimously acknowledges the sinlessness of the Son. They also have no problem combining the Gospel of Matthew with the Gospel of John, a highly questionable operation from the point of view of the historical-critical approach. What they claim, however, is reasonable according to the exegetical practices of our day and can be inferred from the literal reading of Jesus's baptism. Although Jesus is baptized by John, we never hear him confess his sins or those of Israel at the Jordan. In Mark, he is not at all the recipient of a baptism of repentance for the forgiveness of sins and comes out of the water immediately, without the confession of sins (Mark 1:9; cf. also Matt 3:16). This point was raised by Cyril of Alexandria: "In the times before Christ's coming, those being baptized were held down in the water a longer time for the confession of sin. But Christ, being sinless, 'came up immediately.'"[57] One can even argue that the *primary* purpose of the Son's coming to the Jordan *was not* to sympathize with Israel's sins or to ask forgiveness for them. The evangelists portray him as separate, unrelated to the people receiving baptism from John. Mark and Matthew describe Jesus as being away from the crowd and coming from Galilee (Mark 1:9; Matt 3:13).[58] Luke also distinguishes the baptism of Jesus from the crowd, treating the latter as the background for the former (Luke 3:21).[59] What was then the *primary* purpose of Jesus undergoing John's baptism?

Jesus's Baptism and His Special Relationship with the Father

Jesus arrives at the banks of the Jordan confident of not only having committed no sin, but also of his unique relationship with the Father. This is the relationship he wants to make manifest and share with others in the course of his mission. The anonymous patristic author who we have already quoted argues that the open heavens, the Spirit, and the voice of the Father testify to the fact

---

56. Chromatius of Aquileia, *Tractatus in Matthaeum*, 185–498 in *Chromatii Aquileiensis opera*, ed. R. Étaix and J. Lemarié, CCSL 9a (Turnhout, Belgium: Typographi Brepols Editores Pontificii, 1974), at 244 (CCL 9a:244). Cf. Simonetti, *Matthew 1–13*, 52.

57. Reuss, ed., *Matthäus-Kommentare aus der griechischen Kirche*, 162. Cf. Simonetti, *Matthew 1–13*, 53.

58. R. T. France, *The Gospel of Mark: A Commentary on the Greek Text*, NIGTC (Grand Rapids, MI; Carlisle: Eerdmans; Paternoster, 2002), 75.

59. Malina, *Chrzest Jezusa w czterech Ewangeliach*, 307–8.

"that he who was baptized by John was truly more worthy than John."[60] John Chrysostom concurs, saying that being baptized by John might have "caused some to imagine that John was greater than Jesus. In order that this opinion not be entertained, when Jesus was baptized the Spirit came down, and a voice with the Spirit proclaimed the identity of the Only Begotten."[61] In fact, in the Gospel of Matthew, on which the ancient authors are commenting, the revelation is directed not to the Son but to those standing ashore: "This is my Son, the Beloved, with whom I am well pleased" (Matt 3:17). For the Syrian and Armenian Fathers, the Jordan is the beginning of the glorification of the Son and the revelation of his filial identity. According to Ephrem, the moist womb of the Jordan receives the Son in purity and lets him ascend out of the water in glory, while the *Teaching of St. Gregory* speaks of both the Father and the Spirit manifesting the glory of Jesus at his baptism.[62]

The greatness of Christ, resulting from his unique relationship with the Father, is confirmed by the title ὁ ἀγαπητός (Matt 3:17, Mark 1:11, Luke 3:22) which, apart from "beloved," can also mean the "only" Son. It communicates the unique relationship which is the foundation of Jesus's mission.[63] The Father's voice does not make the Son such, but it confirms and proclaims this truth.[64] In turn, εὐδόκησα in the aorist may suggest that divine favor was granted to Jesus much earlier in his life, preceding the baptism.[65] This is especially evident in Luke, where the identity of Jesus as the Son of God and the expected descendant of David is revealed already at his conception (Luke 1:31–35).[66]

Moreover, Mark 1:10, in contrast to Luke 3:21 and Matthew 3:16, does not describe the open (ἀνοίγω) but the torn heaven (σχιζομένους τοὺς οὐρανοὺς), which the Son sees. The same verb σχίζω appears again in Mark 15:38 as part of the narrative of Jesus's death, in which the temple curtain is torn in two, from

---

60. PG 56:657. Cf. Simonetti, *Matthew 1–13*, 50.
61. John Chrysostom, *Homilies on Matthew*, 12.2 (PG 57:204; trans. NPNF 1/10:76).
62. McDonnell, "Jesus' Baptism in the Jordan," 226–28.
63. Lane, *The Gospel of Mark*, 57; Guelich, *Mark 1–8:26*, 34; John Nolland, *Luke 1:1–9:20*, WBC 35A (Dallas: Word, 1989), 164–65; Luke T. Johnson, *The Gospel of Luke*, SP 3 (Collegeville, MN: Liturgical Press, 1991), 69; Hagner, *Matthew 1–13*, 59; France, *The Gospel of Mark*, 82; Stein, *Mark*, 59; Boring, *Mark*, 45.
64. France, *The Gospel of Mark*, 83; Boring, *Mark*, 46 (see the author's observation: if "this is my beloved Son" in Mark 9:7 is a performative language which enacts adoption, then Jesus was adopted twice in the Gospel of Mark).
65. Marcus, *Mark 1–8*, 160.
66. Nolland, *Luke 1:1–9:20*, 165; Darrell L. Bock, *Luke: 1:1–9:50*, BECNT (Grand Rapids, MI: Baker Academic, 1994), 344. A similar fact is indicated by the prophecies fulfilled in the life of the Son in Matt 1–2.

top to bottom. It is commonly interpreted as overcoming the gulf that separated God and humankind, thus signifying the full access to the Father ensured by the Son's sacrifice.[67] Edwards discerns here references to Jewish traditions (Isa 64:1; T.Levi 18.6–8; T.Jud. 24.1–3) regarding the inauguration of God's kingdom and the introduction to the revelation of the Son's dignity.[68] These would be confirmed by the descent of the Spirit, interpreted by the prophets as a gift of the eschatological times (Ezek 36–37; Joel 3:1) and a special attribute of the Messiah (Isa 11:2; 42:1; 61:1). William Lane emphasizes the cosmic significance of the baptismal event as reflected in the heaven "being torn apart."[69] Finally, Malina proposes that this vision be interpreted as a union of the Father and the Son's hearts in love for sinners.[70] This interpretation seems to concur well with the overall image of the historical Jesus in Mark. At the Jordan, the Son shows solidarity with the Father's broken heart, which suffers because of human sin. The final redemptive tearing of God's heart takes places on the cross.

Dwelling still on Jesus's filial consciousness, it should be noted that in Matthew it is expressed by the fact that the Son comes to fulfill "all righteousness," which means that already prior to the baptism he was in complete union with the Father's will and his plan for the salvation of humanity (Matt 3:15). The Father in turn affirms that the Son (in the third person) is his "beloved one" (Matt 3:17). This word, as Luz terms it, is a statement "aimed at objectivization," addressed not to Jesus but to the witnesses. It proclaims the identity of which the Son himself is certain.[71] Finally, in Luke, Jesus's prayer reveals his special bond with the Father, as testified by the descending Spirit (Luke 3:21). The motif of prayer in the Gospel of Luke is also related to the revelation of God as the Father and believers as his children. The prayer and the presence of the Spirit at the Jordan thus emphasize Jesus's special relationship with the Father and testify to his unique sonship. In all of this, we are not arguing for the complete historical accuracy of the Jordan theophany, but we are trying to show its intrinsic relation to the historical fact of Jesus's baptism. Moreover, it is the theophany that, in congruence with the image of the historical Jesus, allows us to read the meaning of the Son's baptism as the moment in which he reveals his divine identity to the world.

---

67. France, *The Gospel of Mark*, 77; Marcus, *Mark 1–8*, 165–66; Boring, *Mark*, 45.

68. Edwards, "The Baptism of Jesus according to the Gospel of Mark," 44–45. The general association is correct, although the texts referred to by the author contain the verb ἀνοίγω.

69. Lane, *The Gospel of Mark*, 55.

70. Malina, *Chrzest Jezusa w czterech Ewangeliach*, 252–58.

71. Luz, *Matthew 1–7*, 143. Similarly, Keener, *The Gospel of Matthew*, 134; Nolland, *Luke 1:1–9:20*, 165 (the author does not postulate the public nature of the event in Luke).

The Jordan and Jesus's Awareness of Mission

Jesus comes to the banks of the Jordan aware not only of his sinlessness and special relationship with the Father but also of his mission. According to Mark, the Jordan is part of Jesus's opening toward sinners, which will achieve its completion in Jerusalem. The same verb ἀναβαίνω, with which Mark describes Jesus's ascent (climbing, going up) onto the bank of the Jordan, will also describe his entry to Jerusalem (Mark 10:32-33). To sinners, separated from God, Jesus offers a new filial relationship, modeled on his relationship with the Father. The Jordan is only the first stop on his journey to preach the Good News. Likewise, in Matthew, Jesus's baptism is the beginning of his mission, consisting in the fulfillment of God's redemptive righteousness (Matt 3:15). Origen interprets Jesus's coming to John as an act of humility, foreshadowing the cross: "By this act Jesus showed himself to be 'meek and lowly in heart' [Matt 11:29], coming to those inferior to him, doing all that followed in order to humble himself and become obedient unto death."[72] Christ's response to John's objections suggests that the baptism plays an important role in fulfilling Jesus's greater mission.[73] John Chrysostom has Jesus saying to the Baptist:

> Since then we have performed all the rest of the commandments, this baptism alone remains. I have come to do away with the curse that is appointed for the transgression of the law. So I must therefore first fulfill it all and, having delivered you from its condemnation, bring it to an end.[74]

In the same vein, in Jacob of Serugh, Christ explains to John why he seeks baptism at his hands: he is trying to find the lost Adam.[75]

The Role of the Spirit

Finally, what is the role of the Spirit in Jesus's baptism? It is not described as an intermediary in the bestowal of the filial gift to Jesus, but as a participant and the one who confirms the Son's experience. Dunn also qualifies the Spirit as the one who anoints Jesus for his future mission.[76] The Spirit, of course, heralds

---

72. Origen, "Fragmenta," in *Origenes Werke*, ed. Erich Klostermann, GCS 41.1 (Leipzig: J. C. Hinrichs, 1941), p. 36; trans. Simonetti, *Matthew 1-13*, 51.

73. R. T. France, *The Gospel of Matthew*, NICNT (Grand Rapids, MI: Eerdmans, 2007), 119-20.

74. John Chrysostom, *Homilies on Matthew*, 12.1 (PG 57:203; trans. NPNF 1/10:76). On the link between Jesus's baptism and his passion in the *Teaching of St. Gregory*, see McDonnell, "Jesus' Baptism in the Jordan," 227.

75. Jacob of Serugh, *Homiliae Selectae Mar-Jacobi Sarugensis*, ed. P. Bedjan (Leipzig: Harrassowitz, 1905-1910), 1:177. Cf. McDonnell, "Jesus' Baptism in the Jordan," 234.

76. Dunn, *Baptism in the Holy Spirit*, 24, 26, 29, 32, 33; Dunn, *Jesus Remembered*, 371-74, 377.

Jesus's mission full of divine power, but that alone does not do justice to its further working in the life of Christ. Jesus is the beloved Son of God. The Spirit, having descended upon him, confirms his special relationship and union with the Father. The Church Fathers stress this fact particularly in the context of the anti-adoptionist polemics of their times. Jacob of Serugh argues that the Spirit sanctifies neither the waters nor Jesus, as it appears when the Son is already coming out of the Jordan. The Spirit is the finger of the Father, pointing to the Son. Christ is the living coal (Isa 6:6) going down into the Jordan, inflaming and sanctifying the waters.[77] Ephrem stresses an equally important fact: the Spirit abandons others to rest only on one, thus confirming Jesus's special position.[78]

The Spirit will accompany not only the powerful words and deeds of Jesus but also the revelation of his sonship in the next stages of his life. Thus, the Spirit manifests itself in the temptation scene (Matt 4:1; Mark 1:12; Luke 4:1), at the inauguration of Jesus's public activity in Nazareth (Luke 4:18-19), and at his proclamation of the kingdom of God by miracles and by casting out demons (Matt 12:28, 31-32; Mark 3:29; Luke 12:10-12).[79] In Luke, Jesus rejoices in the Spirit, glorifying the Father, who has revealed the mysteries of the kingdom to the Son (Luke 10:21-22). In the Gospel of John, the Master describes the necessary birth from water and the Spirit (John 3:5-8), depicts himself as the one sent by God, to whom the Father gave the Spirit without measure (John 3:34), and speaks of the worshipers of the Father in the Spirit and truth (John 4:23-24). Christ claims that his words are Spirit and life (John 6:63), mentions the Spirit who will flow from within him (John 7:37-39), and the Paraclete, who will remind the disciples of his words and lead them to the fullness of truth (John 14:17, 26; 15:26-27; 16:13-15). The Gospels illustrate the historical-theological rather than psychological development of Jesus's identity, which accompanies the successive stages of his mission. The Son, upon entering them together with the Spirit, shapes them and allows himself

---

77. Jacob of Serugh, *Homiliae Selectae*, 1:159, 183, 185. Cf. McDonnell, "Jesus' Baptism in the Jordan," 212-15, 219.

78. Ephrem the Syrian, *Hymns on Epiphany*, 131-77 in *Des Heiligen Ephraem des Syrers Hymnen de Nativitate (Epiphania)*, ed. Edmund Beck, CSCO 187 (Louvain: CSCO, 1959), 6.1 (CSCO 187:147). Cf. McDonnell, "Jesus' Baptism in the Jordan," 214n37.

79. Dunn, *Baptism in the Holy Spirit*, 29-31, the descent of the Spirit makes Jesus the new Adam. This is evident in Mark and Matthew, where Jesus—the new Adam—is tempted immediately after receiving the Spirit and, unlike the first Adam, emerges victorious from this trial (29-30). Likewise in Luke, who begins the story of Jesus with Adam in his genealogy (31). This analogy reflects only to a limited extent the function of the Spirit in the baptismal pericope and in the further public activity of Jesus.

to be shaped by them, experiencing an ever deeper filial relationship with the Father.[80]

One more important question to be answered is the relationship between Jesus's and a Christian's baptism. Do they really stand so far apart? The distinctive features of Jesus's baptism should not discourage us from seeing a parallel between his and our experience, a parallel pursued not only by the Fathers of the Church but probably also by Paul himself.

Paul and the Relationship between the Baptism of Jesus and the Baptism of a Christian

Historical-critical exegesis often denies a historical connection between the baptism of Jesus in the Jordan and the baptism of a Christian.[81] Bultmann finds the connection to be derivative and fabricated by Christian tradition, which created a "legend" describing a scene which took place at the Jordan. For him, it is nothing but a record of the post-paschal baptismal practices placed in a pre-paschal context. Christ's messianic identity is linked here with the gift of the Spirit, which, as argued by Bultmann, exhibits later Hellenistic influences.[82] Dunn, in turn, traces the origins of early Christian baptism to Jesus's command to go and make disciples of all nations, baptizing them in the name of the Father and of the Son and of the Holy Spirit (Matt 28:18–20).[83]

---

80. Dunn, *Baptism in the Holy Spirit*, 28–29. Dunn understands the development of Jesus's filial relationship also as a qualitative one: at each stage Jesus, being the Son and the Messiah, enters an ever deeper state of his sonship and messianic identity. In his later *Jesus and the Spirit*, Dunn maintains his statement about the Spirit anointing Jesus. On the other hand, he refrains from determining whether the descent of the Spirit at the Jordan was the summit or the catalyst of Jesus's experience and does not link it causatively with the gift of sonship, treating the Spirit and sonship as two separate phenomena. See Dunn, *Jesus and the Spirit*, 66–67.

81. See Stein, *Mark*, 56. Other scholars who deny this link are helpfully enumerated in Hans Kvalbein, "The Baptism of Jesus as a Model for Christian Baptism: Can the Idea Be Traced Back to New Testament Times?," *Studia Theologica* 50, no. 1 (1996): 67–83, esp. 80n5–6.

82. Rudolf Bultmann, *Die Geschichte der synoptischen Tradition*; 5th ed. (Göttingen: Vandenhoeck & Ruprecht, 1979), 263–65. Likewise, Hans D. Betz, "Jesus' Baptism and the Origins of the Christian Ritual," 377–96 in *Ablution, Initiation, and Baptism: Late Antiquity, Early Judaism, and Early Christianity*, ed. David Hellholm et al., BZNW 176 (Berlin: De Gruyter, 2011), esp. 392–93, who suggests Mark's Christology as the reason for placing Jesus's baptism at the beginning of the Gospel. Mark, in turn, is influenced by Paul when he describes the inauguration of Jesus's messianic mission as the Son of God according to the Spirit (Rom 1:3–4).

83. James D. G. Dunn, *Beginning from Jerusalem*, CM 2 (Grand Rapids, MI: Eerdmans, 2009), 186. Similarly, John Nolland, "'In such a manner it is fitting for us to fulfil all righteousness': Reflections on the Place of Baptism in the Gospel of Matthew," 63–80 in *Baptism, the New*

Moreover, Dunn states that what Jesus experienced was not baptism *sensu stricto*, and it cannot be compared to the baptism of a Christian.[84] For Dunn, what takes place in Jesus's baptism at the Jordan deals not so much with Christ's personal experience as with the beginning of a new era of salvation. While John still belongs to the old *aeon*, the Spirit's descent upon the Messiah inaugurates the new, long-awaited time of eschatological fulfilment.[85] Jesus is the first one to enter it, bringing others with him.[86] Second, as asserted by Dunn, the Spirit descends upon Jesus in the Jordan not in consequence of baptism, which serves as a backdrop here, but as the result of the Son's surrendering himself completely to the Father's will. The only thing that connects baptism with the descent of the Spirit is the Son's submission to God's will.[87]

Dunn emphasizes the uniqueness of Jesus's baptism in the Jordan so much that it loses any connection with the baptism of a Christian. The latter, in a common opinion, is rooted not in Jesus's experience at the Jordan, but in Jesus's death and resurrection, as described by Paul in Romans 6. The apostle in Romans 6:3–4 speaks of baptism by which believers were submerged into the death of the Son in order to rise with him to a new life. Immersion in the death signifies union with Christ and participation in resurrection similar to that of the Son (Rom 6:5; see also 1 Pet 3:21). This implies the destruction of the body of sin and liberation from its slavery (Rom 6:6–7), but also participation in the life of Christ and his resurrection (Rom 6:8–9). The connection of Christian baptism with Jesus's paschal mystery is obvious and fundamental in Paul. Through baptism, believers experience the effects of the saving work of Christ, in which their sin is erased and the prospect of resurrection opens before them. The immersion into the paschal mystery of the Son of God also motivates them to break away from sin in the present life (Rom 6:1, 14).

According to Beasley-Murray, there is no reference to Christ's death and resurrection in the scene at the Jordan, upon which the later Christian baptismal theology was built. The author, however, is inclined to recognize that the

---

Testament and the Church: Historical and Contemporary Studies in Honour of R.E.O. White, ed. Stanley E. Porter and Reginald E. O. White, JSNTSup 171 (Sheffield: Sheffield Academic Press, 1999), esp. 70, 76–80.

84. Dunn, *Baptism in the Holy Spirit*, 32–34.

85. Dunn, *Baptism in the Holy Spirit*, 24–28, 31.

86. Dunn, *Baptism in the Holy Spirit*, 32.

87. Dunn, *Baptism in the Holy Spirit*, 36–37. I express my gratitude to the anonymous reviewer, who pointed out an aversion to sacramentalism which Dunn himself acknowledged in other contexts, for instance in his commentary on Rom 6. See James D. G. Dunn, *Romans 1–8*, WBC 38A (Dallas: Word, 1988), 303–57.

baptism of Jesus and the baptism of a Christian bring about the same effects: communion with God and the Spirit, and divine filiation. Why, then, do the New Testament authors not draw a parallel between the experience of Christ and the experience of a Christian? According to Beasley-Murray, with whom Dunn agrees, the reason is the uniqueness of the baptism of the Messiah. However, Beasley-Murray claims that since the baptism of Jesus marks the beginning of his entire mission, it is here that we should look for the roots of a Christian baptism. Moreover, the Messiah, as a representative figure, foreshadows the baptism of all his followers.[88] Beasley-Murray thus argues for a link between the baptism of Jesus and the baptism of a Christian, but he does not discern it in the New Testament authors, as they present the baptism of the Messiah as unique in all respects.

Michael Labahn, in basic agreement with Beasley-Murray, perceives both continuity and discontinuity between the baptism of Jesus and the experience of a Christian.[89] However, according to the author, the foundations of early

88. Beasley-Murray, *Baptism in the New Testament*, 62–66.

89. On the origins of early Christian baptismal practices, and continuity and discontinuity between the baptism of Jesus in the Jordan and the baptism of a Christian, see Michael Labahn, "Kreative Erinnerung als nachösterliche Nachschöpfung: Der Ursprung der christlichen Taufe," 337–76 in *Ablution, Initiation, and Baptism: Late Antiquity, Early Judaism, and Early Christianity*, ed. David Hellholm et al., BZNW 176 (Berlin: De Gruyter, 2011). Among those who find a strong continuity between the early Christian practice of baptism and the baptism of Jesus, see Beasley-Murray, *Baptism in the New Testament*, 62–67; Kurt Aland, *Neutestamentliche Entwürfe*, TB 63 (Munich: Kaiser, 1979), 187–96; Gerhard Lohfink, *Studien zum Neuen Testament*, SBAB 5 (Stuttgart: Katholisches Bibelwerk, 1989), 173–98; Ludger Schenke, *Die Urgemeinde: Geschichtliche und theologische Entwicklung* (Stuttgart: Kohlhammer, 1990), 115; Knut Backhaus, *Die "Jüngerkreise" des Täufers Johannes*, PaThSt 19 (Paderborn: Schöningh, 1991), 332–23; André Benoit and Charles Munier, *Die Taufe in der alten Kirche (1.–3. Jahrhundert)*, TC 9 (Bern: Peter Lang, 1994), Introduction; Joel Marcus, "Jesus' Baptismal Vision," *New Testament Studies* 41, no. 4 (1995): 512–21, esp. 513 (admits the possibility of linking the baptism of Jesus with the baptism of a Christian through the theme of sonship in Gal 4:5–6 and Rom 8:15); Kvalbein, "The Baptism of Jesus as a Model for Christian Baptism," 67–83 plus others mentioned by the author on p. 80n8; Lars Hartman, *Into the Name of the Lord Jesus: Baptism in the Early Church*, SNTW (Edinburgh: T&T Clark, 1997), 9, 31–35; Burrows, "Baptism in Mark and Luke," 102–3, 113–15 (the author indicates three baptismal themes which gain special significance for a Christian: total devotion, total purification, and a new beginning); Bernhard Oestreich, "Die Taufe als Symbol für das eschatologische Gericht," in *Die Taufe: Theologie und Praxis*, ed. Roberto Badenas, SAE 3 (Lüneburg: Advent, 2002), 31–55, esp. 49–51; Everett Ferguson, *Baptism in the Early Church: History, Theology, and Liturgy in the First Five Centuries* (Grand Rapids, MI: Eerdmans, 2009), 100 (the gift of the Spirit, sonship, and the obedience of Jesus to be imitated by a Christian). Similarly Holladay, "Baptism in the New Testament and Its Cultural Milieu: A Response to Everett Ferguson," 351, 353.

Christian baptism are to be sought in the historical event of Jesus's baptism, transformed then into a rite of initiation. The reinterpreted ritual of John and the baptism of Jesus became a model for Christians, as evidenced by the factual and structural parallels, although the fundamental difference between them should be maintained. The starting point for early Christian baptism is the command of the risen Lord: "Go therefore and make disciples of all nations, baptizing them in the name of the Father and of the Son and of the Holy Spirit" (Matt 28:19). This new ritual instituted by the Christ introduces believers into the Church community. The old baptism by John, the baptism of repentance, is transformed into a ritual of sharing in new life in Christ, based on his death and resurrection (1 Cor 6:9-11).[90]

As one can see, Beasley-Murray and Labahn are somewhat prone to establishing a thematic and (in case of Labahn) a historical connection between Jesus's baptism in the Jordan and a Christian's baptism, without neglecting the uniqueness of the former. In the same vein, the Fathers of the Church had no problem with linking Jesus's baptism with the baptism of believers.[91] One of the most common images that appears in ancient Christian authors is that of Jesus sanctifying the waters of Christian baptism. In the words of Hilary, Christ "had no need for baptism. Rather, through him the cleansing act was sanctified to become the waters of our immersion."[92] According to Jerome, the sanctification of waters was the task of the Spirit, who in baptism also comes to believers.[93] Ephrem states: "And because the Spirit descended in his baptism, the Spirit is given by his baptism."[94] Jacob of Serugh speaks of the Jordan set ablaze like a "furnace" where Christian baptism recasts the original image marred by sin.[95] The analogy between Christ's and a Christian's baptism is also espoused by Theodore of Mopsuestia (a representative of the ancient historical Antiochian

---

90. Labahn, "Kreative Erinnerung als nachösterliche Nachschöpfung," 367-68.

91. On the programmatic function of Jesus's baptism in the Fathers, see McDonnell, "Jesus' Baptism in the Jordan," 213-14.

92. Hilary of Poitiers, *In Matthaeum*, ed. Jean Doignon, SC 254 (Paris: Cerf, 1978), 108. Cf. Simonetti, *Matthew 1-13*, 50. See also Cyril of Alexandria in Reuss, ed., *Matthäus-Kommentare aus der griechischen Kirche*, 162; Origen, "Fragmenta," GCS 41 1:37. Cf. Simonetti, *Matthew 1-13*, 53.

93. Jerome, *Commentariorum in Matthaeum libri iv*, ed. D. Hurst and M. Adriaen, *Sancti Hieronymi Presbyteri Opera: Pars 1.7*, CCSL 77 (Turnhout, Belgium: Typographi Brepols Editores Pontificii, 1969), pp. 18-19. Cf. Simonetti, *Matthew 1-13*, 51.

94. Ephrem the Syrian, *Commentary on the Diatessaron*, ed. Louis Leloir, SC 121 (Paris: Cerf, 1966), 4.3 (SC 121:95). Cf. McDonnell, "Jesus' Baptism in the Jordan," 226.

95. Jacob of Serugh, *Homiliae Selectae*, 1:181. Cf. McDonnell, "Jesus' Baptism in the Jordan," 231.

school), who includes among the baptismal gifts "regeneration and adoption and remission of sins and all the other blessings that came to us through baptism," which Christ prefigured in himself.[96] The same is stated by Hilary, who speaks of the anointing of heavenly glory and the adoption for God's children, the sacrament prefigured in Jesus's baptism.[97] An anonymous patristic author, pondering on Christ's immediate coming out of the water, perceives here the mysterious relationship to believers:

> [The] baptized in Christ immediately come up from the water in the sense that they advance in virtue and are raised up to heavenly dignity. Those who enter the water as carnal children of Adam the sinner immediately come up from the water as persons who have been made spiritual children of God.[98]

Ultimately, according to Chromatius, Jesus's fulfillment of all justice in Matthew 3:15 means in fact the fulfilment of "every sacrament of our salvation."[99]

The Fathers of the Church clearly perceive a connection between the Spirit, heavenly glory, and the sonship of Christ, understood as the gifts for the baptized. They are not the first ones to spot this connection. While much scholarship relating to the theme of baptism in Paul concentrates on Romans 6, the data of Romans 8 should not be lost. Paying attention to the latter, we can see that the analogy highlighted by the Fathers is also present in Paul.[100]

---

96. Reuss, ed., *Matthäus-Kommentare aus der griechischen Kirche*, 101. Cf. Simonetti, *Matthew 1–13*, 51. Theodore of Mopsuestia even speaks of us being baptized "in the same baptism as that in which Christ our Lord in the flesh was baptized." See Alphonse Mingana, ed., *Commentary of Theodore of Mopsuestia on the Lord's Prayer and on the Sacraments of Baptism and the Eucharist* (Cambridge: Heffer, 1935), 66. Cf. McDonnell, "Jesus' Baptism in the Jordan," 221.

97. Hilary of Poitiers, *In Matthaeum* (SC 254:110). Cf. Simonetti, *Matthew 1–13*, 53–54.

98. PG 56:658. Cf. Simonetti, *Matthew 1–13*, 53.

99. Chromatius of Aquileia, *Tractatus in Matthaeum* (CCL 9a:244–45). Cf. Simonetti, *Matthew 1–13*, 52.

100. Unfortunately, scholars often focus on Rom 6, missing the baptismal meaning of Rom 8. See e.g. Richard P. Carlson, "The Role of Baptism in Paul's Thought," *Interpretation* 47, no. 3 (1993): 255–66; Hartman, *Into the Name of the Lord Jesus*, 51–81 (cf. only modest, scattered references to baptism and the gift of sonship [55, 81]); Ferguson, *Baptism in the Early Church*, 146–65 (the author sees a connection between the gift of the Christian filiation and the baptism of Jesus [101], but does not elaborate on this theme in Paul); David Hellholm, "Vorgeformte Tauftraditionen und deren Benutzung in den Paulusbriefen," 415–95 in *Ablution, Initiation, and Baptism: Late Antiquity, Early Judaism, and Early Christianity*, ed. David Hellholm et al., BZNW 176 (Berlin: De Gruyter, 2011); Bert J. Lietaert Peerbolte, "Paul, Baptism, and Religious Experience," 181–204 in *Experientia*, vol. 2, *Linking Text and Experience*, ed. Colleen Shantz and Rodney A. Werline, EJL 35 (Atlanta: SBL Press, 2012), esp. 190–99. The only one who reflects on linking Rom 8 to the baptism of Jesus is Kvalbein, "The Baptism of Jesus as a Model

It is quite hard to overlook the numerous parallels running between the picture of new life in Romans 8 and Jesus's baptism in the Jordan. Let us list them systematically:

1) *The Spirit.* In the Gospel accounts, at the Jordan, the Spirit descends "into" Jesus (καταβαῖνον εἰς αὐτόν) (Mark 1:10), or "upon" him (ἐπ' αὐτόν) (Matt 3:16; Luke 3:22). The prepositions εἰς in Mark and ἐπί in Matthew and Luke suggest that the Spirit remains with Christ, which is also confirmed by John, speaking about the descent of the Spirit (καταβαίνω) and its remaining (μένω) on the Son (John 1:32).[101] What the evangelists write about coincides with Romans 8:9-11, where Paul, using the terms οἰκέω and ἐνοικέω, describes the permanent dwelling of the Spirit in a Christian.[102] The constant and dynamic presence of the Spirit in Christ and in believers, originating in baptism, connects the Jordan with the description of new life in Romans 8. Just as the Spirit rests upon Christ, filling him, anointing for his mission, and allowing its fulfilment, so, by coming to Christians, it helps them to fulfill God's saving plan for them (Rom 8:4). In Paul, as in Matthew 3:15, the presence of the Spirit is closely related to the fulfillment of God's righteousness. As in Christ filled with the Spirit the prophecies of Jeremiah 31:33 and Ezekiel 36:26-28 come to fruition (Matt 3:15), so they are fulfilled in the baptized, who thanks to the Spirit become the participants of the New Covenant, in which the Law becomes interiorized and written in their hearts (Rom 8:2-4).[103] Fulfilling

---

for Christian Baptism," 76-78. A reference to baptismal elements in Rom 8 also appears in: Norman R. Petersen, "Pauline Baptism and 'Secondary Burial,'" *Harvard Theological Review* 79, nos. 1-3 (1986): 217-26, esp. 218-20; Burrows, "Baptism in Mark and Luke," 114 (the author reflects on the tension between the life of Jesus and the life of a Christian: Luke 12:50 and Rom 8:23, reference to baptismal metaphor rather than event); Oda Wischmeyer, "Hermeneutische Aspekte der Taufe im Neuen Testament," 735-63 in *Ablution, Initiation, and Baptism: Late Antiquity, Early Judaism, and Early Christianity*, ed. David Hellholm et al., BZNW 176 (Berlin: De Gruyter, 2011), esp. 745: "Zugleich tritt die kommunitäre Qualität der Taufe in Erscheinung. Erst in Röm 6 findet Paulus zu einer thematisch eigenen Taufdeutung, und zwar im literarischen Zusammenhang seiner christologisch-soteriologischen Ausführungen in Röm 5-8. Hier liegen die hermeneutisch entscheidenden Deutungspotentiale der paulinischen Taufinterpretation."

101. France, *The Gospel of Mark*, 78: "It is indeed possible that Mark's choice of this preposition was more theologically determined: just as other NT writers will speak of the Spirit 'dwelling in' believers, so he comes to Jesus not just as a temporary equipment for a specific task, but as a permanent presence in his life."

102. On the verbs expressing the idea of the Spirit's permanent dwelling in a Christian, see LSJ, "οἰκέω," 1203; O. Michel, "οἰκέω," *TDNT* 5:135-36; BDAG, "ἐνοικέω," 338.

103. Stanislas Lyonnet, "Rom 8,2-4 a la lumiere de Jeremie 31 et d'Ezechiel 35-39," 231-41 in *Etudes sur l'Epître aux Romains*, ed. Stanislas Lyonnet, AnBib 120 (Rome: Pontifical Biblical Institute, 1990).

the righteous requirement of the Law in the life of believers in Romans 8:4 means living in accordance with the Spirit (Rom 8:4–5, 12–13), submitting to God's will expressed in his law (Rom 8:7) and pleasing God (Rom 8:8), which strongly connects the perspectives of Matthew and Paul. Finally, just as Christ experiences the guidance of the Spirit after his baptism in the Jordan (Matt 4:1; Luke 4:1), so do believers experience it after their baptism. The Spirit allows them to steer away from the former way of living according to the flesh (Rom 8:4–9) and to put to death the deeds of the body (Rom 8:13). Christian struggle brings to mind Jesus's struggle against Satan, which immediately follows Jesus's baptism (Matt 4:1; Mark 1:12–13; Luke 4:1–2).[104]

2) *Divine filiation and prayer.* The Spirit is closely related to Jesus's divine sonship. Immediately after the Spirit's descent upon the Messiah, the Father's voice is heard, announcing that Christ is his beloved Son, in whom he is well pleased (Mark 1:11; Matt 3:17; Luke 3:22). The Spirit, resting on Jesus, confirms his special relationship with the Father. Additionally, in Luke 3:21–22, the Spirit descends during Jesus's prayer. Likewise, in Romans 8:14, Paul describes the Spirit of adoption, by whose working Christians become the children of God. They are no longer slaves to fall back into fear, but they cry out to God: "Abba! Father!" (Rom 8:15). In Romans 8:15, the Spirit additionally accompanies Christian prayer which is modeled after Christ. Prayer, coupled with the Spirit, expresses, as in the case of Christ, their dignity as God's children.[105] The relationship between Romans 8:12–13 and 8:14 (γάρ) also suggests that the gift of divine filiation to believers remains an essential point of reference in their fight against sin.[106] In the same vein, Jesus's awareness of God's love and sonship pro-

---

104. David Wenham, *Paul: Follower of Jesus or Founder of Christianity?* (Grand Rapids, MI: Eerdmans, 1995), 348–50; John Coulson, "Jesus and the Spirit in Paul's Theology: The Earthly Jesus," *Catholic Biblical Quarterly* 79, no. 1 (2017): 77–96, esp. 86.

105. On the "Abba" prayer in Rom 8:15 and imitating Christ in his relationship with the Father, see Dunn, *Baptism in the Holy Spirit*, 22; C. E. B. Cranfield, *A Critical and Exegetical Commentary on the Epistle to the Romans: Introduction and Commentary on Romans I–VIII*, ICC (Edinburgh: T&T Clark, 1975), 400; Dunn, *Romans 1–8*, 453–54; Leon Morris, *The Epistle to the Romans*, PilNTC (Leicester, England; Grand Rapids, MI: Apollos; Eerdmans, 1988), 316; Brendan Byrne, *Romans*, SP 6 (Collegeville, MN: Liturgical Press, 1996), 253; Colin G. Kruse, *Paul's Letter to the Romans*, PilNTC (Cambridge, UK; Grand Rapids, MI: Eerdmans; Apollos, 2012), 337.

106. On the relationship between the identity of believers and their struggle against sin in Rom 8:12–13 and 14, see Dunn, *Romans 1–8*, 462; Trevor J. Burke, *Adopted into God's Family: Exploring a Pauline Metaphor*, NSBT 22 (Nottingham, England; Downers Grove, IL: Apollos; InterVarsity Press, 2006), 143–47; Volker Rabens, *The Holy Spirit and Ethics in Paul: Transformation and Empowering for Religious-Ethical Life*, WUNT II/283 (Tübingen: Mohr Siebeck,

vide him with the source of strength in his confrontation with Satan (Matt 3:17; 4:3; Mark 1:11; Luke 3:22; 4:3). There is obviously a fundamental difference between Christ as the Son of God and believers who are the *adopted* children of God (cf. υἱοθεσία in Rom 8:15).[107] In their case, the Spirit *makes them* part of God's family, introducing them into a community with the Father and the Son.

3) *Open heaven*. In the scene of Jesus's baptism, the Spirit descends from the open heaven, testifying to the identity of Christ as the Son to whom the Father's glory belongs. Likewise, in Romans 8, the Spirit, by introducing the baptized ever more deeply into the mystery of divine filiation, assures them of the heritage of glory, which they will share with Christ: "If children, then heirs, heirs of God and joint heirs with Christ—if, in fact, we suffer with him so that we may also be glorified with him" (Rom 8:17). The way to God's glory leads through immersion in the entirety of Jesus's life and following him in his attitudes, which is also assisted by the Spirit (Rom 8:5–6).[108] The process will culminate in the full conformation of believers to the Firstborn, which will be manifested in the final resurrection (Rom 8:29). The title of "the Firstborn" (πρωτότοκος), which Paul uses here, can be read as parallel to the "beloved one," (ἀγαπητός) which occurs in the Gospels (Matt 3:17; Mark 1:11; Luke 3:22).[109] The baptism of Jesus thus reveals not only his dignity but also the future communion with him which awaits the baptized. Christ will not become "the Firstborn among many brethren" until he gathers in his kingdom many brothers and sisters, who now follow him in their baptismal life.

In Romans 8, Paul presents a rich phenomenology of the Spirit, drawing on the experience of the Church and her baptismal liturgy. Considering how much Christology shapes Paul's thought at every level, an explanation for the phenomenon of the Spirit working in the baptized can also be sought in Christ's baptism. It could help in understanding the configuration of the three essential elements (Spirit, filiation, and heritage of glory) that we find in Romans 8:14–17, 23.[110] It is true that the apostle does not mention Jesus's bap-

---

2010), 213–15; Dirk J. Venter, "The Implicit Obligations of Brothers, Debtors and Sons (Romans 8:12–17)," *Neotestamentica* 48, no. 2 (2014): 283–302, esp. 294–98.

107. Beasley-Murray, *Baptism in the New Testament*, 65; France, *The Gospel of Mark*, 82.

108. Marcin Kowalski, "The Cognitive Spirit and the Novelty of Paul's Thought in Rom 8,5–6," *Biblica* 100, no. 1 (2020): 47–68, esp. 53–56.

109. Malina, *Chrzest Jezusa w czterech Ewangeliach*, 131n301.

110. On the aorist ἐλάβετε (Rom 8:15) and the first gifts of the Spirit (ἀπαρχή) (Rom 8:23), which may indicate baptism as a specific point at which Christians obtain the Spirit, see James M. Scott, *Adoption as Sons of God: An Exegetical Investigation into the Background of Huiothesia in the Pauline Corpus*, WUNT II/48 (Tübingen: Mohr Siebeck, 1992), 262–63; Thomas R.

tism explicitly, but the highlighted thematic links may constitute an allusion to it. It is also true that the account of Jesus's baptism, as recorded in the Gospels, is not a simple description of the Christian sacrament of initiation, and what the Lord experienced at the Jordan in many ways remains unique to him. However, on the basis of Romans 6 and 8, it can be argued that Jesus's baptism could have served as a reference point for the Christian understanding of believers' baptismal identity already in Paul's time.[111] To be sure, the interpretative lens through which Paul reads the baptism of Christ and a Christian's baptism is still the Lord's paschal mystery, a common approach for all the New Testament authors. We should not forget that the baptismal command was formulated by the risen Lord (Matt 28:19). Even if it reflects his pre-paschal experience and goes back to the Jordan, it is permeated with the light and understanding coming from resurrection.[112] No wonder then that for Paul Christ's paschal mystery will be the main point of reference to describe Christian baptism. At the same time, however, when introducing baptism in Corinth, the apostle had at his disposal the rich oral and written traditions about Jesus and the liturgical praxis of the Church.[113] It makes it at least probable that in Romans 8 Paul could have alluded to Jesus's baptism in the Jordan, establishing thus a connection, which, according to John Coulson, would have been comprehensible to his audience.[114]

Ultimately, as seen in Romans 6–8, the apostle, like the evangelists, reads the Savior's entire life, including his baptism, in the light of his death and resurrection. David Wenham spots in Romans 8:1–17 a connection between Gethsemane, Jesus's passion, death, resurrection, and his experience at the Jordan, which believers have access to through baptism.[115] In Romans 8:3, the apostle also links the paschal background to Christ's incarnation, in which the body of the Son becomes the place of defeating the cosmic power of sin. For Paul, the whole life of Jesus is a paschal life and a model for Christians, an approach discernible in texts such as 1 Thessalonians 1:6; Philippians 2:5–8; 1 Corinthians

---

Schreiner, *Romans*, BECNT 6 (Grand Rapids, MI: Baker, 1998), 423–24. The expression "to receive the Spirit" also appears in the context of baptism in Acts 2:38 and 10:47.

111. Kvalbein, "The Baptism of Jesus as a Model for Christian Baptism," 79.

112. Dunn, *Jesus and the Spirit*, 65.

113. Gerd Theissen, ""Evangelium" im Markusevangelium: Zum traditionsgeschichtlichen Ort des ältesten Evangeliums," 63–86 in *Mark and Paul: Comparative Essays Part II. For and Against Pauline Influence on Mark*, ed. Eve-Marie Becker, Troels Engberg-Pedersen, and Mogens Müller, BZNW 199 (Berlin: De Gruyter, 2014).

114. Coulson, "Jesus and the Spirit in Paul's Theology," 86.

115. Wenham, *Paul*, 275–80, 346–50. Similarly C. F. D. Moule, *The Holy Spirit*, MLT (London: Mowbrays, 1978), 33–34; Coulson, "Jesus and the Spirit in Paul's Theology," 86–87.

11:1, and Romans 8:12–17; 15:2–3, 7. In this perspective, the baptism of Christ can also become a point of reference for the description of Christian baptism, which introduces believers into the gift of the Spirit, divine filiation, and the fullness of glory in the Son (Rom 8:29).

Conclusions

To paraphrase the question posed by Tertullian, what do Antioch, symbolizing literal, historical-critical approach to the biblical text, and Alexandria, embodying theological-sacramental reading, have in common? Contemporary exegesis seems to distinguish and radically separate them, while leaning toward the Antiochian approach. Meyer postulates a creative combination of the two positions, taking into consideration the character of biblical texts. On the one hand, after all, the Scriptures are a product of their epoch, so it is necessary to place them in their proper historical and cultural context. On the other hand, they are marked by divine inspiration and truth, which call for the hermeneutics of faith and an approach that respects their universal and cross-cultural message. Examining carefully the pericopes describing Jesus's baptism in the Jordan, we saw how sterile and limited their reading can be, if we approach them from the radical historical-critical perspective. This approach postulates separating the event of Jesus's baptism from the theophany that followed it, treating the latter as a secondary, non-reliable, early Christian creation. In addition, according to the purely historical-critical school, there is no factual connection between the baptism of Jesus and the baptism of a Christian. The bond is again a product of the later tradition, projecting Christian rituals onto biblical texts.

The conclusions of the analyses conducted in the historical-critical spirit stand in stark contrast to the conclusions drawn from the Jordan pericopes by the Church Fathers, who can be considered representatives of the "Alexandrian" approach. For the Fathers, Jesus's baptism in Jordan is naturally and inextricably linked with theophany and foreshadows the baptism of a Christian. Although the Fathers do not essentially substantiate their intuitions exegetically, they can be defended on historical-literary grounds. The nature of ancient texts does not allow the separation of the historical event (the baptism of Jesus) from its interpretation (theophany), which are also closely connected with each other on the literary and thematic level. In Mark, this connection is provided by the topic of Jesus's sonship as a gift for sinners, who have no relationship with the Father; in Matthew it is the motif of the fulfillment of God's saving plan and his righteousness; in Luke it is the solidarity with humanity's seeking God's will.

In a holistic, historical-theological interpretation, in which baptism and theophany are interlocked, Jesus does not come to the Jordan to submit to a penitential rite, but to reveal his special relationship with the Father, being aware of his divinely appointed mission, and being accompanied by the Spirit. In these matters, a thorough reading of the Jordan pericopes is consistent with the interpretation of the Church Fathers. The latter also strongly emphasize the connection between the event that took place at the Jordan and the baptism of a Christian. The Fathers like to use the image of the Jordan waters sanctified by the Lord, and they speak of the baptismal garment he left us on the shore. The waters of the Jordan sanctified by the Spirit prefigure the waters of our baptism. Other elements that connect the baptism of Jesus and that of a Christian are the identity of God's children and the glory of heaven. Of course, the difference between the status of Christ as the Son of God and our adoption as God's children, as well as the uniqueness of the Lord's baptismal experience, must be emphasized, but this should not prevent us from looking for analogies between them. The Fathers were also deeply aware of the exceptionality of Jesus's baptism; however, they argued that he shared his experience with us. In the words of Philoxenus: Jesus's baptism is his and his baptism is ours.[116]

Paul himself encourages us to look for analogies between our and the Lord's baptism. Interestingly, the three elements that mark the baptismal experience of the Son (the Spirit, the dignity of God's child, and the heritage of glory) also appear in Romans 8, where the apostle describes our new life in Christ. Scholars usually do not associate this chapter with the baptism of believers, concentrating rather on Romans 6. Such an exclusive approach seems questionable when we take into consideration the argumentative links between chapter 6 and chapter 8, as well as the allusions to baptism in Romans 8:15, 23. In Romans 8, Paul not only describes the baptismal life of a Christian, but also seems to refer to the baptism of Christ. This may be indicated by the presence of the three aforementioned elements, the Spirit, the theme of sonship, and the glory of heaven, connecting the Jordan pericopes with the letter to the Romans. References to the baptism of Jesus in Romans 8 could result from the Pauline knowledge of Jesus traditions and the baptismal rites practiced by the apostle.

The primary perspective in which Paul reads the baptism of Christ and the baptism of a Christian is, of course, Christ's paschal mystery. Its light illumines the whole life of the Son, including the baptism in the Jordan, which is a model

---

116. Philoxenus, *Fragments of the Commentary on Matthew and Luke*, ed. J. W. Watt, CSCO 393 (Louvain: Corpusco, 1978), 13 (CSCO 393:16–17). Cf. McDonnell, "Jesus' Baptism in the Jordan," 220.

for believers. Here, Paul and the Fathers of the Church essentially agree. It also means that the Jesus tradition, at this very early stage of its formation (in the fifties of the first century AD, when Romans was written), assumes a theological and sacramental character, which modern exegesis should acknowledge. The theological-sacramental reading of the Jordan pericopes is not a secondary and dubious addition to the biblical narrative, but belongs to the very heart of the historical event of Jesus's baptism. By joining together Antioch and Alexandria we ultimately arrive at the full meaning of Jesus's baptism, which reveals the identity of the Son and of his followers. The inspired, ever real and sacramental character of the Jordan pericopes are the features that the New Testament authors would surely want us to discover.[117]

---

117. Meyer, *Critical Realism and the New Testament*, 33.

CHAPTER 8

Ancient and New: A Dialogue between Contemporary and Patristic Exegesis on the Scriptural Fulfillment Statements in the Johannine Farewell Discourse

Isacco Pagani

Introduction

The interpretation of Scripture is a fascinating topic, which has continually opened up vast and numerous horizons in the history of exegesis and theology, continuing to arouse "lively interest and significant debate."[1] As the Pontifical Biblical Commission (1993) pointed out, the issue is ancient, so it is not a modern phenomenon.[2] Its main motivation is linked to the very life of the Church, which draws from Scripture—and its interpretation, inevitably—for its life of prayer, faith, and proclamation, so "that the Word of God may become more and more the spiritual nourishment of the members of the people of God, the source for them of a life of faith, of hope and of love, and indeed a light for all humanity."[3]

The development of the debate leads to the acquisition of new tools of interpretation, using new exegetical methods and increasingly up-to-date knowledge. However, progress in interpretation should not devalue ancient interpretations. The diversity of tools and knowledge does not necessarily lead to a richer or a poorer set of results. As F. M. Young writes:

> We may not always find the conclusions of patristic exegesis satisfactory or plausible, but this is more often than not because of a different estimate of what seems problematic, or of what constitutes a valid cross-reference.

---

1. Pontifical Biblical Commission, *The Interpretation of the Bible in the Church* (Rome: Libreria Editrice Vaticana, 1993), Introduction.
2. Pontifical Biblical Commission, *The Interpretation of the Bible*, §A.
3. Pontifical Biblical Commission, *The Interpretation of the Bible*, §B.

From the Fathers' methods and their endeavors we might learn much. The fundamental exegetical question is: what does it mean? The answer may be obvious, or it may be arrived at by rational enquiry about word usage, about signification and metaphor, about syntax, about reference and about truth. There is no escape from that complexity.[4]

This contribution brings a case of contemporary exegesis into dialogue with the interpretations of some Fathers of the Church. Taking up Young's proposal, the purpose of this article is to test the actual benefit that an interpretation of our time derives from comparison with older exegesis. Four authors have been invited to the table of this dialogue, two from the Antiochene and two from the Alexandrian sphere,[5] in the hope that this will enrich the discussion with different nuances.

The case on the table is that of the fulfillment of Scripture statements in chapters 13–17 of the Fourth Gospel. The choice is based on various reasons. First, it is a well-defined part of the Gospel: the section develops between the washing of feet and the exit to the crossing of the Kidron Valley. The narrative dynamic is reduced to a minimum, since apart from Jesus's teaching the disciples, there is only the invitation to them to get up and leave (14:31), which however happens only in chapter 18, and the raising of Jesus's eyes to the Father (17:1), which does not exclude his disciples, but involves them indirectly in his prayer.

Secondly, the delimitation of the section makes it possible to work on a text that is internally coherent on at least two fronts: from a thematic point of view, unity is guaranteed by Jesus's last long speech to his own, the so-called Farewell Discourse;[6] from a narrative point of view, in all these chapters, the evangelist is almost completely silent,[7] while Jesus speaks about events that have already occurred or will happen. Thus, Jesus himself becomes a narrator in the narration, or rather a "second-degree narrator."[8]

---

4. Frances Young, *Biblical Exegesis and the Formation of Christian Culture* (Cambridge: Cambridge University Press, 1997), 4.

5. One of these, Origen, will only be asked to comment on John 13, as his commentary does not include chapters 15–17 of the Fourth Gospel.

6. Here, I do not use the singular form "Farewell Discourse" to take a position on the historical and literary composition of these chapters. In fact, the differences that emerge within these chapters do not contradict their thematic unity, related to the proximity of Jesus's arrest and his deliveries to the disciples. This is sufficient for what I am saying.

7. He only intervenes briefly in John 13:31, 36, 37, 38; 14:5, 6, 8, 9, 22, 23; 16:17, 18, 19, 29, 31.

8. See Gérard Genette, *Figures III : Discours du récit*, Collection Poétique (Paris: Seuil, 1972), 238–41.

Methodologically, the article has two parts. The first part is a proposal for an exegesis on the chosen case, in accordance with an approach based on contemporary methods. This section presents the results of a broader exegetical study[9] that succinctly answers two questions: *How does Jesus speak of the fulfillment of Scripture?* And, *what is the fulfillment of Scripture in the narrative context?* The second part of the article analyzes three areas of comparison between the exponents of Antiochene and Alexandrian exegesis—regarding the same statements about the fulfillment of Scripture and their contexts—with the intention of gaining some useful insights for our contemporary exegesis. In light of these gains, the conclusion of the article will propose an interpretation of the text that takes into account the ancient and the new in interpreting these statements about the fulfilled Scripture.

A Proposal of Contemporary Exegesis on the Statements of the Fulfillment of Scripture in the Farewell Discourse

How Jesus Speaks About the Fulfillment of the Scripture, or the Communicator

A comparison with the evangelist can be useful to describe how Jesus speaks about the fulfillment of the Scripture. First, if the evangelist is an observer who speaks about fulfillment, but he is not involved in the narration, Jesus is a character who speaks about the same theme, while *he is involved in the narrated events*. The comment of the evangelist after the piercing of Jesus with a spear helps us to understand the difference (John 19:35–37):[10]

> [35]An eyewitness (*ho eōrakōs*) has testified, and his (*autou*) testimony is true; he (*ekeinos*) knows that he is speaking the truth, so that you also may come to believe. [36]For this happened (*egeneto gar tauta*) so that the Scripture passage might be fulfilled: "Not a bone of it will be broken." [37]And again another passage says: "They will look upon him whom they have pierced."

The introduction in vv. 35–36—unique to the Fourth Gospel—explains the events personally viewed (*ho eōrakōs* / *autou* / *ekeinos*) as the fulfillment of Scripture (*egeneto gar tauta*): indeed, the conjunction *gar* has an explanatory force, which transfers the authenticity of eyewitness testimony to the double note of fulfillment. On the narrative level, the evangelist's intrusion has an

---

9. Isacco Pagani, *"Si compia la Scrittura": I rimandi al compimento della Scrittura pronunciati da Gesù in Gv 13–17*, AnBib Dissertationes 232 (Rome: G&B Press, 2021).

10. Scripture translations in this chapter are from the New American Bible.

Scriptural Fulfillment in the Johannine Farewell Discourse

extraordinary impact; but he is outside the narration, not involved in it. In fact, he speaks in third person (v. 35), addressing the reader directly.

Second, whereas the evangelist speaks about the fulfillment of the Scripture from a retrospective point of view (he rereads the events by interpreting them as a fulfillment), Jesus speaks about it *in a predictive way* (he anticipates the events by foretelling their fulfillment). The first time that the verb *plēroō* is used by the evangelist in relation to the Scripture is exemplary (John 12:37-38):

> [37] Although he had performed so many signs in their presence they did not believe (*episteuon*) in him, [38] in order that the word which Isaiah the prophet spoke might be fulfilled (*plērōthē*):
>
> "Lord, who has believed our preaching,
>
> to whom has the might of the Lord been revealed?"

The evangelist invites his reader to recognize the resistant disbelief toward Jesus—described by the imperfect *episteuon*—despite the signs done by him. Therefore, the next note of the fulfillment of the Scripture illustrates not a punctual and momentary reaction of the crowd (v. 34), but a persistent and growing attitude throughout Jesus's whole ministry.

On the other hand, John 13:18-19 is a clear example of the predictive modality of Jesus's speaking about the fulfillment of the Scripture:

> [18] I am not speaking of all of you. I know those whom I have chosen. But so that the Scripture might be fulfilled, "The one who ate my food has raised his heel against me." [19] From now on I am telling you before it happens (*pro tou genesthai*), so that when it happens (*hotan genētai*) you may believe that I AM.

Jesus openly declares that he speaks before the occurrence of the events (*pro tou genesthai*). However, he does not speak to describe how and when they will happen; in fact, he does not absolutely say what will happen, but he merely pronounces a generic claim: "When it happens" (*hotan genētai*). Thus, the utterance about the fulfillment of the Scripture anticipates his betrayal precisely to enable his listeners to recognize his own divine identity ("I AM").

In this way, Jesus's speaking alludes to the words of God in Isaiah 43:8-13:[11] similarly, he also anticipates events not to describe them, but to enable faith in him. Consequently, we must recognize a significant difference from how the evangelist speaks about the fulfillment of the Scripture, since the discourse of Jesus is similar to that of God, anticipating events to enable faith in him.

---

11. See Pagani, "*Si compia la Scrittura*," 79-94.

Third, if the evangelist informs the reader that the Scripture was fulfilled in the narrated events (sharing his own knowledge), Jesus uses *performative utterances about the fulfillment*. In this way, he sets a necessary condition for the disciples' faith after his resurrection. On the other hand, he even orders that the Scripture be fulfilled in future events (13:18; 15:25). An example of an informative function is the note in 19:24, in which the evangelist explains the decision of the soldiers not to divide the seamless tunic, and then points out the fulfillment of the Scripture.

> [24]So they said to one another, "Let's not tear it, but cast lots for it to see whose it will be," in order that the passage of Scripture might be fulfilled [that says]: "They divided my garments among them, and for my vesture they cast lots." This is what the soldiers did.

The cases of John 13:18 and 15:25 are different—normally, they are translated with a final nuance ("so that," "in order that")—nevertheless, an imperative translation is grammatically possible:[12] "But let the Scripture be fulfilled" (13:18); "But let the word written in their Law be fulfilled" (15:25). If this translation is acceptable, as I have tried to show in my doctoral research,[13] then the speaker's will takes *a performative force*: in these two passages, the expressions of the fulfillment of the Scripture coincide with its realization.

Eventually, particular attention must be paid to the note of the fulfillment of the Scripture in John 17. In v. 13, Jesus describes himself in a situation of movement: he is still in the world, but he is already moving toward the Father at the same time: "But *now I am coming to you*. I speak this *in the world* . . . "

We could say that this description illustrates a *Christ in transit*,[14] which has

---

12. See also: John 9:3; 14:31. For more information: Nigel Turner, *Grammatical Insights into the New Testament* (Edinburgh: T&T Clark, 1965), 147–48, quoted by William G. Morrice, "The Imperatival ἵνα," *Bible Translator* 23 (1972): 326–30, at 328. Daly-Danton also translates John 15:25 with an imperative: "Let what is written . . . be fulfilled." See Margaret Daly-Denton, "The Psalms in John's Gospel," 119–37 in *The Psalms in the New Testament*, ed. Steve Moyise and Maarten J. J. Menken, NTSI (London: T&T Clark, 2004), 131.

13. Pagani, *"Si compia la Scrittura,"* 26–27, 90, 109.

14. Jean Zumstein, "Die verklärte Vergangenheit: Geschichte *sub specie aeternitatis* nach Johannes 17," 207–17 in *Kreative Erinnerung: Relecture und Auslegung im Johannesevangelium*, ed. Jean Zumstein, *ATANT* 84 (Zürich: Theologischer Verlag, 2004), 210. See also: Takashi Onuki, *Gemeinde und Welt im Johannesevangelium: Ein Beitrag zur Frage nach der theologischen und pragmatischen Funktion des johanneischen "Dualismus"*, WMANT 56 (Neukirchen-Vluyn: Neukirchener, 1984), 167; Pagani, *"Si compia la Scrittura,"* 208–9, 221; Francis J. Moloney, *The Gospel of John*, SP 4 (Collegeville, MN: Liturgical Press, 1998), 468, 470; Klaus Wengst, *Das Johannesevangelium*, vol. 2, *Kapitel 11–21*, TKNT 4b (Stuttgart: Kohlhammer, 2001), 186, 197, 199.

a dynamic temporal position. The events are told by Jesus from points of view not always simultaneous with the narrative present time: sometimes it is retrospective and sometimes prospective.[15] On the contrary, the evangelist speaks about the fulfillment of the Scripture as a first-degree narrator, namely, only in reference to past events.

The nearest retrospective view of the note of the fulfillment of the Scripture is Jesus's reference to the safekeeping of his own, which took place throughout all the time he remained among them (*hote ēmēn met'autōn*). He does not mention specific actions or facts but recovers "the totality of the 'precedent' narrative."[16]

> [12]*When I was with them* I protected them (*etēroun autous*) in your name that you gave me, and I guarded them (*ephylaxa*), and none of them was lost (*oudeis ex autōn apōleto*) except the son of perdition, in order that the Scripture might be fulfilled.

Thus, Jesus speaks as if everything has already happened.[17] But in v. 13, immediately after the utterance of the fulfillment of the Scripture, Jesus returns to the narrative present and speaks with a future perspective: "But now I am coming to you. I speak this in the world so that *they may share my joy completely.*"

In conclusion, Jesus speaks about the fulfillment of Scripture as the Christ in transit, having the privilege of a "temporal mobility" with respect to the narrative present time. On the contrary, the evangelist does not have the same privilege.

What the Fulfillment of the Scripture Is in the Narrative Context, or What Is Communicated

When Jesus speaks about the fulfillment of the Scripture, he does not simply refer to individual biblical passages, as shown in his three notes of fulfillment. Two of them are quotations (John 13:18; 15:25), if "quotation" means a literal

---

15. See the study about "the order of the time of the story" in Genette, *Figures III*, 77–121. See also R. Alan Culpepper, *Anatomy of the Fourth Gospel: A Study in a Literary Design*, FoFaNT (Philadelphia: Fortress, 1983), 54–70.

16. See Genette, *Figures III*, 101–2.

17. The change of tense is interesting, because it moves from the durative/descriptive aspect of the action (imperfect *etēroun*) to the factual and resulting one (aorist *ephylaxa* and *apōleto*). Therefore, Jesus always speaks about the same safekeeping action, first emphasizing its entire duration (*hote ēmēn met'autōn*) and then claiming its complete realization (even while admitting parenthetically an exception with the locution *ei mē*). See Pagani, "Si compia la Scrittura," 181–86.

(or almost) duplication of a previous text with the addition of an introductory utterance,[18] whereas the third one has no quotation (John 17:12).

The case of John 13:18 is rather easy, because it is surely a quotation from Psalm 41:10. But the incomplete correspondence to both the MT and the LXX prevents identification of its proper textual source. Probably, the Johannine author translates from the MT, according to his own stylistic and thematic sensitivity.[19]

In John 15:25, the quotation is difficult to identify: the most reliable hypotheses support a reference either to Psalm 35:19 or to Psalm 69:5.[20] Both contain the expression *oi misountes me dōrean*, which is very close to the Johannine one: *emisēsan me dōrean*. Psalm 69 may have a slight advantage at most, because its overall context is similar to that of the Johannine discourse and because it is mentioned other times within the Fourth Gospel.[21] However, the Johannine author does not seem interested in making clear the exact source of his quotation; rather he focuses on the Law of those who reject Jesus in the fulfillment: "But in order that *the word written in their law* might be fulfilled . . ."

Consequently, we can deduce that *the response to the fulfillment of the Scripture in John 13–17 primarily concerns the scriptural entity of Israel as a whole.*[22]

---

18. See Richard B. Hays, *Echoes of Scripture in the Letters of in Paul* (New Haven: Yale University Press, 1989), 29–31; Dale C. Allison, *The New Moses: A Matthean Typology* (Edinburgh: T&T Clark, 1993), 19–22; Jean-Noël Aletti, *Le Messie souffrant, un défi pour Matthieu, Marc et Luc: Essai sur la typologie des évangiles synoptique*, LiRo 55 (Paris: Lessius, 2019), 25–35.

19. See Pagani, "*Si compia la Scrittura*," 72–79.

20. See e.g.: Edwin D. Freed, *Old Testament Quotations in the Gospel of John*, NTS 11 (Leiden: Brill, 1965), 94–95; Günter Reim, *Studien zum alttestamentliche Hintergrund des Johannesevangeliums*, SNTSMS 22 (Cambridge: Cambridge University Press, 1974), 42–45; Rudolf Schnackenburg, *Das Johannesevangelium*, vol. 3, *Kommentar zu Kap. 13–21*, HTKNT 4.3 (Freiburg: Herder, 1976), 30; Douglas J. Moo, *The Old Testament in the Gospel Passion Narratives* (Sheffield: The Almond Press, 1983), 243–44; Andreas Obermann, *Die christologische Erfüllung der Schrift im Johannesevangelium: Eine Untersuchung zur johanneischen Hermeneutik anhand der Schriftzitate*, WUNT 2.83 (Tübingen: Mohr Siebeck, 1996), 271–82; Maarten J. J. Menken, *Old Testament Quotations in the Fourth Gospel: Studies in Textual Form*, CBET 15 (Kampen: Kok Pharos, 1996), 139–45; Christian Dietzfelbinger, *Die Abschied des Kommenden: Eine Auslegung der johanneischen Abschiedsreden*, WUNT 95 (Tübingen: Mohr Siebeck 1997), 162–63; Margaret Daly-Denton, *David in the Fourth Gospel: The Johannine Reception of the Psalms*, AGJU 47 (Leiden: Brill, 2000), 203–8; Daly-Denton, "The Psalms," 130–32; Bruce G. Schuchard, *Scripture within Scripture: The Interrelationship of Form and Function in the Explicit Old Testament Citations in the Gospel of John*, SBLDS 133 (Atlanta: Scholars Press, 1992), 119–23.

21. See e.g.: Obermann, *Erfüllung*, 278–81.

22. Maurizio Marcheselli, "Davanti alla Scrittura di Israele: processo esegetico ed ermeneutica credente nel gruppo giovanneo," *Ricerche Storico Bibliche* 22 (2010): 175–95, at 178–79.

The contexts of these expressions of fulfillment provide a further clue: Jesus always declares *the purpose of his speaking*.[23]

	SPEAKING STATEMENT	PURPOSE
13:19	I am telling you before it happens	*so that when it happens you may believe that I AM*
16:1	I have told you this	*so that you may not fall away*
16:4	I have told you this	*so that when their hour comes you may remember that I told you*
17:13	I speak this in the world	*so that they may have my joy made complete in themselves*

Although the purpose of the discourse is always made explicit in these contexts, the declared purposes are different from time to time: to believe (John 13), to remember without being scandalized (John 15–16), and to share fully in Jesus's joy (John 17). In all instances, Jesus does not give instructions to have faith, or to remember, or to obtain the fullness of his joy. Simply, he says that his speech—and then also the utterance of the fulfillment of the Scripture—gives his disciples the conditions to believe, to remember, and to have his full joy in the future. Therefore, the content of these expressions of Jesus primarily consists *in starting a dynamism*, rather than in communicating information: with these words, Jesus begins and enables his disciples to follow a path of faith and memory toward the fullness of his joy.

Moreover, in the same contexts there is always a reference to a *critical situation*. And again, the analogy highlights some differences. In John 13:18, the utterance of the fulfillment of the Scripture is directly connected to the critical situation of the betrayal, which occurs despite the conscious election by Jesus ("I know those whom I have chosen") and which is described as an exception to the previous beatitude: "If you understand this, blessed are you if you do it. I am not speaking of all of you" (John 13:17–18a).

Even in John 15:25, the critical situation is clear, since the world's hatred is directly connected to the scriptural quotation: "They hated me without cause."

---

23. John 16:2 seems far from the utterance about the fulfillment of Scripture. However, the expression "I have told you this . . ." includes what Jesus said at least from 15:18. See Eugen Ruckstuhl and Peter Dschulnigg, *Stilkritik und Vervasserfrage im Johannesevangelium: Die johanneischen Sprachmerkmale auf dem Hintergrund des Neuen Testaments und des zeitgenössischen hellenistischen Schrifttums*, NTOA 17 (Göttingen: Universitätsverlag, 1991), 113. For a *status quaestionis* see Konrad Haldimann, *Rekonstruktion und Entfaltung: Exegetische Untersuchungen zu John 15 und John 16*, BZNW 104 (Berlin: De Gruyter, 2000), 230–37.

The context expands the range of the problem, shifting the attention from the hatred against Jesus to that against his own:

> If the world hates you, realize that it hated me first. If you belonged to the world, the world would love its own; but because you do not belong to the world, and I have chosen you out of the world, the world hates you (15:8).

> They will expel you from the synagogues; in fact, the hour is coming when everyone who kills you will think he is offering worship to God (16:2).

The hatred against the disciples is described in the form of violent persecution, as foretold in John 16:2.[24] Furthermore, Jesus explains that he is the cause of this hatred. Or more precisely, his election of the disciples out of the world is the reason of this hatred, because they no longer belong to it (15:19). It is remarkable that the foretelling of the world's hatred is linked to the word spoken by Jesus in 13:16, namely, in the context of the previous note of the fulfillment of the Scripture:

> Remember the word I spoke to you, "No slave is greater than his master." If they persecuted me, they will also persecute you. If they kept my word, they will also keep yours (15:20).

> Amen, amen, *I say to you, no slave is greater than his master* nor any messenger greater than the one who sent him (13:16).

Jesus appeals to the memory of the disciples so that they will remember his previous words in a new context. However, he adapts the teaching already given to a new situation, without merely repeating it: Jesus applies the slave-master relationship in reference to the persecution by the world and no longer in reference to his example in washing their feet (as it was in 13:16).

In John 17, the critical situation requires more attention to be understood. Normally, the expression "in order that the Scripture might be fulfilled" (*hina hē graphē plērōthē*) is directly subordinated to the previous reference to "the son of perdition" (*ho hyios tes apōleias*).[25] In most cases, it is interpreted as an allusion to John 13:18. However, some scholars have recently questioned this allusion, suggesting various alternative hypotheses.[26] I consider the first reason

---

24. For more information about *aposynagōgos*, see Pagani, "*Si compia la Scrittura*," 132–34.

25. For a synthesis, see Pagani, "*Si compia la Scrittura*," 228–31.

26. Wendy E. Sproston, "'The Scripture' in John 17:12," 24–36 in *Scripture: Meaning and Method. Essay Presented to Anthony Tyrrell Hanson for His Seventieth Birthday*, ed. Barry P. Thompson (Hull: University Press, 1987); Urban C. von Wahlde, "Judas, the Son of Perdition, and the Fulfillment of Scripture in John 17:12," 167–81 in *The New Testament and Early Christian Literature in Greco-Roman Context. Studies in Honor of David E. Aune*, ed. John Fotopoulos,

to be syntactic: the locution *ei mē* has an excluding value ("except"), which limits what is before, interrupting or delaying the normal course of the sentence.[27] If so, the subordination of the note of the fulfillment of Scripture to a parenthetical phrase would be at least anomalous for the Johannine style. But it will be more compliant, if it is referred to the statement "none of them was lost" (with an exception). On the one hand, this means that the utterance about the fulfillment of Scripture remains connected to the theme of betrayal, but not in a direct and exclusive way. On the other hand, this interpretation also admits a connection of this utterance to the themes of the world's hatred (John 17:14a) and of the non-belonging of the disciples to the world (John 17:14a, 16). As a result, the context of the note of fulfillment in 17:12 does not have a new critical situation but refers to the previous two.

Basically, these utterances of Jesus communicate *three specific aspects*: first, the fulfillment regarding Scripture as the overall and authoritative reality of Israel's faith; second, it serves to begin the post-Easter path of the disciples, which is characterized by a dynamic faith, memory, and fullness of the joy of the Risen One; and eventually, it always provides a response within a critical situation.

A Comparison between Antiochene and Alexandrian Exegesis: Three Areas of Comparison

The results of the exegetical study just proposed encounter three areas of dialogue with the commentaries of the four ancient authors chosen as our interlocutors. A first area concerns the relationship between the fulfillment of Scripture and the knowledge of Jesus; a second concerns the relationship between the fulfillment of Scripture and the human freedom of the disciples; and a third concerns the relationship between Jesus's statements of fulfillment and the anticipation of the disciples' life after Easter.

The Relationship between the Fulfillment of Scripture and the Knowledge of Jesus

Both the Antiochene and the Alexandrian authors interpret the three statements of fulfillment under consideration as a way of Jesus's expression of his

---

NTS 122 (Leiden: Brill, 2006).

27. See Friedrich Blass, Albert Debrunner, and Friedrich Rehkopf, *Grammatik des neuentestamentlichen Griechisch*, 14th ed. (Göttingen: Vandenhoeck & Ruprecht, 1976), §465; Edwin A. Abbott, *Johannine Grammar* (London: Adam & Charles Black, 1906), §2164.

predictive knowledge. The different sensibilities of the Antiochenes and the Alexandrians are evident in the arguments by which this knowledge is understood and interpreted exegetically.

John Chrysostom is careful to point out that in John 13:18 Jesus does not intend to denounce the betrayer, but to be of help to all listeners (including Judas).[28] Indeed, he wants to gently rebuke the one who is about to betray him, in order to convert him, and at the same time to propose an example to the other disciples should they find themselves in similar circumstances.

> What patience indeed! Even now he does not denounce the traitor, but hides him, giving him a chance to repent. He rebukes him and does not rebuke him with these words: "He who eats my bread has lifted up his heel against me." It seems to me that the words "There is no servant greater than his master," are said so that if one receives any wrong from his servants or other people of inferior rank, he should not be upset.... "He who was fed by me, who sat at my table," he says. He expressed himself in this way to teach the disciples to help even those who did them wrong, even when there was no hope of correcting them.[29]

The point of these statements of Jesus, Chrysostom continues, commenting on John 15:25, is also to show how his own knowledge is rooted in the prophetic tradition, which had already predicted hatred without cause:

> And this explanation [vv. 18–24] was not enough for him, but he also quoted the prophet, showing that he had long predicted these events with the words, "They hated me without reason." ... Since many were astonished that the Jews did not believe, he [Jesus] quoted to them the prophets who had long predicted this and had the reasons for their unbelief.[30]

Thus, the relationship between the fulfillment of Scripture and Jesus's knowledge in the exegesis of John 13–17 is understood by the Antiochenes

---

28. The other Antiochene, Theodore of Mopsuestia, seems to pay less interest to this topic. His main position on the subject is derived from certain paraphrases of Johannine expressions, as is the case, for example, with regard to the pronouncement of the fulfillment of Scripture in John 17:12, which he interprets, "Already for a long time it was known that it would happen." In other words, it seems that for this author the pronouncements about the fulfillment of Scripture are a way in which Jesus expresses knowledge already known to him. Theodore of Mopsuestia, *Commentarius in Evangelium Iohannis Apostoli*, trans. and ed. J.-M. Vosté, CSCO (Louven: Ex Officina Orientali, 1940), 210.

29. Chrysostom, *Commentarius in sanctum Joannem Apostulum et Evangelistam* (PG 59:385–90, at 387β). Unless otherwise noted, all subsequent translations of patristic texts are the author's.

30. Chrysostom, *Commentarius in sanctum Joannem Apostulum et Evangelistam* (PG 59:413–20, at 417β).

both in relation to the events within the narrative (intradiegetic) and to what happens beyond the narrative itself (extradiegetic). In speaking of fulfillment, Jesus reveals his knowledge of what is happening in the narrative present as well as what will happen in the disciples' historical future.

On the Alexandrian side, the sensibility seems to be different. It is interesting to note that the authors focus much more on the part before the statement about the fulfillment of Scripture in the commentaries on John 13:18: "I know those whom I have chosen." Origen, in particular, dwells on the meaning of the verb "to know" (*oida*): referring especially to other Gospel passages (Luke 13:26; Matt 7:22), he limits the value of Jesus's statements to the narrative moment in which he speaks. Jesus knew Judas when he chose him, but his submission to sin withdrew him from Jesus's knowledge, since he removed himself by betrayal from the group of those chosen by Jesus.[31]

With the same sensitivity, Cyril addresses the question of the relationship between Jesus's knowledge and the fulfillment of Scripture in his commentary on John 17:12: not only does he rule out the presence of a specific Old Testament quotation, but he also denies that there is any direct causality between the fulfillment of Scripture and Judas's betrayal. Rather, on this occasion he calls for a careful study of the value of these statements of Jesus, which otherwise run the risk of being misunderstood, with serious theological and soteriological consequences.

> Which passages of Scripture does he want to talk about? The ones that contain many predictions about him. But Judas was not lost that the Scripture might be fulfilled. . . . This is a typical way of quoting Scripture, where its words seem to be the cause of events. Therefore, we must carefully examine everything, both the sayings, the themes, and the rules of Scripture, in order to avoid coming to absurd conclusions.[32]

---

31. Cyril of Alexandria offers the same interpretation in his commentary on John 13:18. He too dwells on the first part of v. 18 and presents two possible keys to reading it: the first is that Jesus wants to point to the traitor, while the second is that he wants to specify the identity of the true disciple. While dwelling on the figure of Judas, Cyril also addresses the question of Jesus's knowledge: "If we believe that Christ knows everything, why did he choose Judas, and why did he include him among the other disciples, knowing that he would betray him, being entangled in the laces of avarice?," in Cyril, *Commentariorum in Joannem* (PG 74:106–282, at 128C–D). Through an excursion within the Scriptures, passing through the figures of Adam and Saul, Cyril arrives at a conclusion similar to Origen's: the logic of Jesus's choice of Judas is not one of cause and effect, that is, Jesus did not choose Judas so that he would betray him. There is a culpable responsibility in the one who wasted that choice by his own rejection.

32. Chrysostom, *Commentarius in sanctum Joannem Apostulum et Evangelistam* (PG 59:437–42, at 440β).

For the bishop of Alexandria, therefore, a distinction must be made: by proclaiming the fulfillment of Scripture, Jesus does not take away Judas's freedom of choice, but reveals his own (Jesus's) divine knowledge of the human heart.

> Scripture, which cannot lie, foretold that this betrayal would take place. For Scripture is the Word of God, who knows all things and who knows the conduct and the life that everyone will lead from the beginning to the end. That is why the Psalmist, who attributes to God the knowledge of all things, past and future, addresses Him at one point: "You know all my thoughts from afar; you search my path and my resting place; all my ways are known to you" (Ps 139:2–3).[33]

The Alexandrian authors, therefore, seem to be more concerned with developing the relationship between the statements about the fulfillment of Scripture and Jesus's knowledge at the intradiegetic level than at the extradiegetic level. The motive is Christological and soteriological: by speaking of the fulfillment of the Scriptures, Jesus manifests prior knowledge of facts and people, including Judas and his betrayal; how does this square with the freedom of the disciples?

The Relationship between the Fulfillment of Scripture and the Human Freedom of the Disciples

Indeed, the relationship between Jesus's statements about the fulfillment of the Scripture and human freedom is a second area of synthesis.

Although the subject is treated less explicitly and thoroughly than in the Alexandrian authors, some interest in this area can also be found in the Antiochene authors. The focus is less on the character of Judas and his betrayal and more on the ethical dimension that emerges from these texts for the life of the disciples after Easter. This confirms the specificity of extradiegetic and not just intradiegetic attention, as exemplified in Chrysostom's commentary on John 13:18–19.[34] Without excluding consideration for Judas and his freedom, the bishop of Constantinople also emphasizes the implications of Jesus's words and actions for all the disciples: he will be an example for them in the time after Easter.

> All these things were written, so that we might not be angry with those who do wrong to us, but that we might exhort them and have compassion on

---

33. Cyril, *Commentariorum in Joannem* (PG 74:447–608, at 522C).
34. Chrysostom, *Commentarius in sanctum Joannem Apostulum et Evangelistam* (PG 59:387β–388γ).

them.... Therefore Christ benefited the one who was about to betray him, washed his feet, rebuked him in secret, admonished him with moderation, and did not disdain to serve him, to admit him to his table, and to be kissed by him. Nevertheless, he did not repent, and Christ continued to do him good as far as it was in his power.[35]

As we have already shown, the Alexandrian side shows a quantitatively greater sensitivity on this issue, although it focuses much more on the intradiegetic level, not only with regard to Judas's freedom, but also with regard to the opposition of the Jews.

Commenting on the quotation in John 13:18, Origen focuses on the words of the psalm quotation, which he interprets as a periphrasis (*parapephrastai*) of Psalm 40, as he reads it in the Greek version of the LXX. The Johannine author would have interpreted the expression "exalt (*megalynō*) the heel" as "lift up" (*epairō*), understanding Judas's gesture as a willingness to "trample on the Son of God" (*ton hyion tou theou katapatōn*). Continuing his commentary, Origen arrives at a tropological explanation of the heel, and thus of the fulfillment of the Scripture: just as the heel is the last extremity of the body, so Judas becomes the last of the apostles, grasping (*kykleō*) Jesus with his iniquity (*anomia*).[36]

In the same way, Cyril of Alexandria problematizes the question of the fulfillment of the Scripture, considering the objection that "if [out of avarice, Judas] raised his heel against Christ, as he himself says, he should not be held guilty, since he was compelled by the necessity of the fulfillment of Scripture."[37] The bishop of Alexandria rules out the possibility that the fulfillment of the Scripture consists in the execution of a destiny already foretold in previous prophecies: if this were the case, he concludes, there would be the risk that Scripture and the Holy Spirit themselves were a source of sin; instead, it is the freedom of Judas that shuns Jesus's choice.

> [Jesus] chose Judas and counted him among his holy disciples, for at first he was a good disciple. But after he was gradually tempted by Satan and, ensnared by the passion for gain, fell into that vice, and once he became such, he rejected him. Therefore, he who chose him is not to blame. It was indeed up to him [Judas] not to fall, if he wished to follow the best, and to devote his whole person to the sincere following of Christ.[38]

---

35. Chrysostom, *Commentarius in sanctum Joannem Apostulum et Evangelistam* (PG 59: 387–388y).
36. Origen, *Commentariorum in Evangelium secundum Joannem* (PG 14:739–830, at 776D–77C).
37. Cyril, *Commentariorum in Joannem* (PG 74:128D).
38. Cyril, *Commentariorum in Joannem* (PG 74:129D–132A).

Cyril then reiterates the value of Judas's human freedom in the face of knowing Jesus and the fulfillment of the Scripture in his commentary on John 17:12, where he reiterates that Jesus's insistence on the fulfillment of Scripture regarding betrayal was a moment of possibility for Judas to change, an opportunity that Judas voluntarily rejected.

> The Word of God, who knows everything in advance, and sees the future as well as the present; in addition to the rest he said about Christ, also foretold this, that the traitor disciple would perish. But it was not God's will and command to know and tell the future, and much less did this prediction compel him to commit this crime and weave these snares against the Savior; rather, it was to divert him. In fact, having known it, it would have been possible for him, if he had wanted to, to avoid this betrayal and not to do it, since it was within his will to go in the desired direction. . . . I think we have left no room for doubt.[39]

Regarding his commentary on John 15:25, Cyril seems to add an additional passage to his interpretation of the relationship between the statement of the fulfillment of the Scripture and human freedom. The fact that Jesus quotes Scripture to show that it predicted unreasonable hatred of him is not meant to bind the freedom of the Jews (as if they could not choose otherwise). In fact, he is proclaiming the fulfillment of Scripture to convert them and to demonstrate God's deliberate mercy toward the Jews, in spite of their wickedness.

> In the book of Psalms it is written, as if referring to the words of Christ rebuking the folly of the Jews, "They hate me with violent hatred." . . . At this point, the Lord usefully demonstrates that he did not ignore the wickedness of the Jews and shows that he foretold and knew what was to come, but that he nevertheless exercised generosity and mercy that was convenient to God.[40]

The Relationship between Jesus's Statements of Fulfillment and the Anticipation of the Disciples' Life after Easter

A final major issue of particular interest to the exegesis of these ancient authors regarding the fulfillment statements in the Johannine Farewell Discourse is how they relate to the post-Easter life of the disciples. Indeed, on both sides (Antiochene and Alexandrian) there is great insistence on the connection between Jesus's anticipation and the disciples' faith in the time after Easter.

In his commentary on John 13:18, Theodore of Mopsuestia explains that

---

39. Cyril, *Commentariorum in Joannem* (PG 74:521C, 526C).
40. Cyril, *Commentariorum in Joannem* (PG 74:283–444, at 416B, D).

Jesus speaks of the fulfillment of the Scripture so that the disciples will recognize Jesus's knowledge when the events occur. He is not anticipating information about events but preparing their post-Easter Christological faith.

> His testimony was not about the traitor because it was said in the prophecy, but because of the events themselves. "For what reason I have foretold this, I now make manifest (v. 19). Even now I tell you before it happens, so that when it happens, you may believe that I am. Certainly he says—I could not reveal what is going to happen; but lest you believe that I do not even know the thoughts of those who follow me, and without knowing anything about it I am afflicted with shame at what is happening to me, behold I am foretelling the events before they take place, so that—when they take place—you may know who I am."[41]

In the same vein, the bishop of Mopsuestia comments on Jesus's manner of speaking in John 15:18–16:4a. He emphasizes that the speech is intended to prepare the disciples for steadfastness, even if they cannot understand what he is saying at that moment:

> [Jesus] openly declares the reason why he preaches these things to them [the disciples], namely, wanting to make them more steadfast in view of the tribulations that are to be endured (v 4).... But it is probable that when he himself said these things with some hint, they did not even understand the words, for they could not yet bear the harshness of such speech.[42]

Chrysostom also mentions this theme when commenting on the prayer form of chapter 17, especially v. 15. The fact that Jesus is praying gives the disciples a special perspective that prepares them to understand how they will be kept in the time after Easter:

> At the end [Jesus] speaks to the Father, and shows his love for them; it is as if he is saying, "Since you are calling me to you, keep them safe. For I am coming to you." What are you saying? You can protect them, can't you? Of course, I can. Then why are you saying this? "That they may have in themselves the fullness of my joy," that is, so that they would not be troubled, imperfect as they are. With these words he shows that he said all these things for their serenity and for their joy, otherwise his words would seem contradictory.[43]

---

41. Theodore of Mopsuestia, *Commentarius in Evangelium Iohannis Apostoli*, 184.
42. Theodore of Mopsuestia, *Commentarius in Evangelium Iohannis Apostoli*, 207.
43. Chrysostom, *Commentarius in sanctum Joannem Apostulum et Evangelistam* (PG 59:439–440β).

On the Alexandrian side, it is Cyril who is most insistent on this point. In his commentary on John 13:19, the bishop of Alexandria points out that Jesus's anticipation is not intended to inform the disciples in advance of what will happen; rather, his intention is to enable them, at the appropriate time, to recognize the consistency between his word and the events that will take place in the future. So, the statement about the fulfillment of the Scripture does not determine the facts in advance, as if it could not be otherwise, but prepares the disciples to know how to understand the meaning of what will happen and thus to believe.

> "Therefore, from this moment on, I am telling you what is now at the gates, but I am not yet communicating to you the knowledge of the facts, so that when they come to pass, by comparing the result of the facts with my predictions, you will believe that I am indeed the one of whom the divine Scripture has foretold such things." . . . Indeed, as we have said before, whoever compares what has been foretold by the sacred Scriptures concerning the crime of the traitor will, I believe, come to a most manifest and easiest true understanding of him.[44]

Later, in the commentary on John 15:18–16:4a, Cyril further clarifies the value of this anticipatory mode of Jesus's speech, pointing out a twofold advantage for the disciples: the first is the advantage of a test of faith, because the disciples will be able to remember that Jesus spoke to them in advance of the tribulations they would encounter; the second advantage is that the memory of these words orients and strengthens the disciple, enabling him to pass through the test with solidity.

> "I did not foretell these things to you, he says, in order to weaken the strength of your soul, nor even to instill in you a premature terror of the evils to come, but rather to give you advance knowledge of them, so that by this you might gain a double advantage. First, because, remembering that I had foretold these things to you, and being astonished that I knew them, you would have had a certain proof of faith at the same time as the danger. . . . Secondly, those who are already prepared and know that something will happen to them, will be seized with less fear and will easily overcome everything that may seem difficult, and will maintain an intrepid spirit in those same difficult hours."[45]

With regard to this last aspect, it is interesting to note that both lines of interpretation (Antiochene and Alexandrian) point out that the anticipations

---

44. Cyril, *Commentariorum in Joannem* (PG 74:132C–D).
45. Cyril, *Commentariorum in Joannem* (PG 74:428A).

present in Jesus's speeches are not intended to inform the disciples, but to prepare them for a dynamic of memory, so that in the face of new events they can remember what he said, and by remembering they can believe in him.

In this regard, the presence in all the commentaries on John 17:11–19 of a mention of the role of the Holy Spirit in this dynamic of memory deserves final consideration. No real treatment of the subject is found in these commentaries, but the detail seems worthy of attention.

Commenting on Jesus's prayer as a form of preparation of the disciples for the coming post-Easter period, Theodore points out that Jesus's speech will be effective in due time through the action of the Holy Spirit, who will enable them to remember what was said.

> Just as in the form of prayer he [Jesus] has said what would happen to him and what would later happen to his disciples, so in the form of a prayer he comforts them for their tribulations and teaches them not to lose heart because of the things that will happen to them.... These things, too, he said in the form of a prayer that they might happen to them. But it happened to them because of the Spirit, when they rejoiced to suffer for him, the very ones who had previously forsaken their master for small things.[46]

In the same way, the bishop of Constantinople connects the keeping of the disciples with the empowerment to persevere through the action of the Spirit. Differently from Theodore, however, the connection is made to the call to sanctification in truth (John 17:17).

> By saying "keep them," he was not only asking the Father to protect them from danger, but also that they would persevere in the faith. That is why he added: "Sanctify them in the truth." That is: make them sanctified through the gift of the Spirit and through true faith. Just as he said, "You are already pruned because of the word I spoke to you" (John 15:3), he now repeats the same concept, that is, "Educate them, teach them the truth." He says, however, that this will be the work of the Spirit.[47]

> But by saying here, "Keep them in the truth," he openly indicates that they will be led to the knowledge of the truth by the light of the truth. Knowledge of the truth cannot be attained without spiritual enlightenment (*pneumatos phōtismou*).[48]

---

46. Theodore of Mopsuestia, *Commentarius in Evangelium Iohannis Apostoli*, 227.
47. Chrysostom, *Commentarius in sanctum Joannem Apostulum et Evangelistam*, (PG 59:441–48, at 442–443a.
48. Cyril, *Commentariorum in Joannem* (PG 74:538A).

This search of the patristic commentaries has revealed some interesting elements useful for a dialogue with contemporary exegesis on Jesus's statements about the fulfillment of the Scripture in John. The first element is the twofold attention that the ancient authors pay to the relationship between these statements, the knowledge of Jesus, and human freedom. Although with varying attention to the intradiegetic and extradiegetic levels, all the authors are careful not only to distinguish but also to relate three realities: the fulfillment of the Scripture, the speaking of Jesus, and the listening of the disciples.

Alongside this element is a second, namely, the impact of these sayings on the faith of the disciples. All the authors agree that the effect of the reference to the fulfilled Scripture and Jesus's words in the narrative context is not immediate. A dynamic of memory is initiated and left open in the story: the disciples are empowered to remember what Jesus said after Easter, including the fact that Scripture is fulfilled. Even if they did not understand or gather specific information, it is important that they heard it.

Finally, all the authors allude to the action of the Holy Spirit in this dynamic of memory. Although this theme is not fully developed, all of them make the connection between the disciples' ability to remember and the action of the Spirit.

Conclusion

An interesting point of comparison that emerges from this analysis of Jesus's statements on the fulfillment of the Scriptures in the Fourth Gospel concerns the strong dynamic dimension that emerges from these Johannine chapters, both at the level of the communicator (the "Christ in transit") and at the level of what is communicated (the beginning of the path of faith-memory-joy, in relation to various critical situations).

This point also offers a significant field of comparison between the patristic exegesis on the Antiochene and Alexandrian sides: in fact, despite the different sensitivities that have emerged, all the authors considered converge substantially on the function of Jesus's way of speaking in relation to the faith of the disciples.

The exegesis of the Fathers has pointed out that Jesus's speech does not have an informational purpose, and that the predictive (or anticipatory) aspect of his speech does not come to a definitive resolution within the narrative (at least for the disciples who remained with Jesus). Moreover, all the ancient authors have emphasized the importance of deepening the relationships between the fulfilled Scripture, the speaking of Jesus, and the listening of the disciples. In different ways and with different sensitivities, the comparison between Antiochenes and Alexandrians also highlighted the importance of distinguishing the interactions between the function of these three subjects at the intradiegetic and extradiegetic levels. In this way, the patristic exegesis envisages a believing understanding that goes beyond the narrative: these observations of the Fathers show that the narrative remains open, even if at some point "the book" was closed (see John 20:30). Somehow, the ancient authors grasp that the text refers to the life of the Johannine community and to the activity of the believing readers.

How, then, are we to understand this way of interpreting the narrative? An answer to this question could be worked out with the help of the relecture model, proposed by Prof. J. Zumstein.[49] He developed a study of the Johannine text which interprets it in a non-static way: the Gospel is the written result of a historical journey of "creative memory,"[50] which develops a peculiar argumentative strategy and a theological coherence. An advantage of this approach is that it does not put an alternative between the stratification of its formation (closer to the Antiochene sensibility) and the unitary perspective of its theological message (more congruous with the Alexandrian sensibility).

Apropos of the expressions about the fulfillment of Scripture in John 13–17, the critical situations progressively illustrated can help us to reconstruct the historical sequence of the formation of the text. In a context of a still vivid perception of the events and of Jesus's absence, the question of his betrayal despite the election of the disciples could have been prevalent (John 13). Then, when the Johannine community began to experience persecutions and hostilities, the critical argument became the rejection of both Jesus and his own (John 15–16). Later, the context of fulfillment in John 17 does not describe a new critical situation but offers a summary of the previous two: the Johannine community developed an awareness of having to remain in the world for a long time, in ongoing critical conditions like perdition and hatred of the world.

---

49. See Jean Zumstein, "Ein gewachsenes Evangelium: Der Relecture-Prozess bei Johannes," 9–37 in *Johannesevangelium – Mitte oder Rand des Kanons? Neue Standortbestimmungen*, ed. Thomas Söding, QD 203 (Freiburg: Herder, 2003), 17n21. See also: Jean Zumstein, "Der Prozess der Relecture in der johanneischen Literatur," 15–30 in *Kreative Erinnerung: Relecture und Auslegung im Johannesevangelium*, ed. Jean Zumstein, ATANT 84 (Zürich: Theologischer Verlag 2004); Andreas Dettwiler, *Die Gegenwart des Erhöten: Eine exegetische Studie zu den johanneischen Abschiedsreden (John 13,31–16,33) unter besonderer Berücksichtigung ihres Relecture-Charakters*, FRLANT 169 (Göttingen: Vandenhoeck & Ruprech, 1995), 44–52.

50. Zumstein, "Ein gewachsenes Evangelium," 30–32.

Thus, the consciousness of being on the path grows in *the believing understanding of the progression within these historical phases* (see table below): gradually, the Johannine community realizes that its own dynamic of faith consists in a journey of witness memory (see 15:26–27), while they experience being kept safe and unified over time within the world by the Father and the Son.

STEPS	POST-EASTER CONSCIOUSNESS	TEXT
first	dynamic of faith	*You may believe that I AM* (13:19)
second	journey of witness memory	*When their hour comes you may remember that I told you* (16:4)
third	safekeeping by Father and Son over time in the world	*Holy Father, keep them in your name that you have given me, so that they may be one just as we are. When I was with them I protected them in your name that you gave me* (17:11–12)

Adopting this model of interpretation also allows us to grasp the insight that the Fathers offer regarding the action of the Spirit in this dynamic of memory. The history of the Johannine community as a journey of witness and memory is accompanied by *the awareness of a pneumatological experience*: the Paraclete is the one who will first testify to Jesus (15:26–27) and the one who will teach the disciples everything, reminding them of all that Jesus told them (14:26).[51] As the awareness of an itinerary of memory matures, the Johannine community progressively develops a theological reflection on its own experience, recognizing the action of the Holy Spirit in its historical events.

Consequently, in these Johannine passages, the notes of the fulfillment of Scripture guarantee a continuity, without creating a rigid repetition. Thus, on the one hand they foster the historical development of responsiveness to the theme of the definitive fulfillment; and on the other hand, they provide a valid criterion for interpreting the entire believing experience of the Johannine community.

Concretely, these notes highlight *the importance of memory*, both for the formation of the text and for the development of a theological concept. In our case, this "creative memory" presents at least four elements: first, the memory of the original event, namely the experience of Jesus; second, the memory

---

51. See e.g.: Jean Zumstein, "La dynamique du souvenir: À propos de la conception johannique du temps," 485–98 in *La mémoire revisitée: Études johanniques*, ed. Jean Zumstein, MoBi 71 (Geneva: Labor et Fides, 2017), 490–94.

that updates the previous notes of the fulfillment of the Scripture, within (new) critical situations; third, the memory that interprets the whole Scripture of Israel, as a common point of reference between Jesus, the Johannine author, and the reader; and fourth, the memory as a dynamism that involves a historical process and a pneumatological action.

The insight suggested by patristic exegesis also allows us to understand the value of the relationship between the narrative (or discourse) of the text and the life of the Johannine community, defining even better the meaning of creative memory: in the text, Jesus empowers his own to an act of memory that goes beyond the boundaries of the book. Through the words of Jesus and with the help of the Spirit, the believing community is enabled to remember past actions and words and to understand them in the context of the post-Easter time. It is this memory that enables the community to hold together the historical events and their narrative in a faithful and always current way.

This corresponds to what Ricoeur also observes more generally about memory, understood as a mediation between lived time and narrative:

> In fact, I believe that the problem of memory poses a neglected question to philosophers, starting with myself: because I put the time and the story in direct relationship, neglecting the mediation of memory between the lived time and the narrative configurations.[52]

But this final reflection on memory also allows us to posit that while interpretation is an ongoing process that develops and shifts in focus, ancient exegesis, Antiochene and Alexandrian, and contemporary exegesis participate in the same processes of interpretation and need to consult each other on a regular basis. Ancients and moderns engage in this same mediation between lived time and narrative and share the goal of understanding and engaging this definitive note of fulfillment enacted in the person of Jesus. This ongoing conversation, ancient and new, among Antioch, Alexandria, and current biblical scholarship, must be the basis for beginning to grasp the transcendent mystery of God's Word, an ongoing task this side of eternity.

---

52. Paul Ricoeur, *Das Rätsel der Vergangenheit: Erinnern—Vergessen—Verzeihen*, EKV 2 (Göttingen: Wallstein, 1998), 49. See also Giuseppe Segalla, "La memoria storica di Gesù in Giovanni 6: fra storia e teologia," *Annali di Scienze Religiose* 9 (2004): 213–24, at 213–15.

Bibliography

Abbott, Edwin A. *Johannine Grammar*. London: Adam & Charles Black, 1906.
Aland, Kurt. *Neutestamentliche Entwürfe*. Theologische Bücherei 63. Munich: Kaiser, 1979.
Aletti, Jean-Noël. *Le Messie souffrant, un défi pour Matthieu, Marc et Luc: Essai sur la typologie des évangiles synoptique*. Le livre et le rouleau 55. Paris: Lessius, 2019.
Alexander, Philip S. "'Homer the Prophet of All' and 'Moses Our Teacher': Late Antique Exegesis of the Homeric Epics and the Torah of Moses." In *The Use of Sacred Books in the Ancient World*, edited by Tjitze Baarda, Aire van der Kooij, and Adam S. van der Woude, 127–42. Leuven: Peeters, 1998.
Alexopoulos, Stefanos. *The Presanctified Liturgy in the Byzantine Rite: A Comparative Analysis of its Origins, Evolution, and Structural Components*. Leuven: Peeters, 2009.
Allison, Dale C. *The New Moses: A Matthean Typology*. Edinburgh: T&T Clark, 1993.
Alter, Robert. *The Art of Biblical Narrative*. Revised edition. New York: Basic, 2011.
———. "How Convention Helps Us Read: The Case of the Bible's Annunciation Type-Scene." *Prooftexts* 3, no. 2 (1983): 115–30.
Amit, Yairah. *Reading Biblical Narratives*. Minneapolis: Fortress, 2001.
Anderson, Gary A. "King David and the Psalms of Imprecation." In *The Harp of Prophecy: Early Christian Interpretation of the Psalms*, edited by Brian E. Daley and Paul R. Kolbet, 29–45. Notre Dame, IN: University of Notre Dame Press, 2015.

Ashby, G. W. *Theodoret of Cyrrhus as Exegete of the Old Testament*. Grahamstown: Rhodes University, 1972.
Augustine. *Enarrationes in Psalmos*. Edited by Eligius Dekkers and Johannes Fraipont. Corpus Christianorum, Series Latina 38–39. Turnhout: Brepols, 1956.
———. *Enarrationes in Psalmos*. Edited by A. Cleveland Coxe. NPNF 1/8.
Auslander, Shalom. "In This Time of War, I Propose We Give Up God." *New York Times*. April 15, 2022. https://www.nytimes.com/2022/04/15/opinion/passover-giving-up-god.html.
Auwers, Jean-Marie. "L'organisation du psautier chez les Pères grecs." In *Le Psautier chez les Pères*, 37–54. Strasbourg: Centre d'Analyse et de Documentation Patristiques, 1994.
Backhaus, Knut. *Die "Jüngerkreise" des Täufers Johannes*. Paderborner Theologische Studien 19. Paderborn: Schöningh, 1991.
Bandt, Cordula, Franz X. Risch, and Barbara Villani, eds. *Die Prologtexte zu den Psalmen von Origenes und Eusebius*. Texte und Untersuchungen zur Geschichte der altchristlichen Literatur 183. Berlin: De Gruyter, 2018.
Barr, James. "The Image of God in the Book of Genesis: A Study of Terminology." *Bulletin of the John Rylands Library* 51 (1968): 11–26.
Barth, Karl. *Church Dogmatics*, vol. III/1. Translated by Harold Knight, G. W. Bromiley, J. K. S. Reid, and R. H. Fuller. Edinburgh: T&T Clark, 1960.
Bauckham, Richard. *Jesus and the Eyewitnesses: The Gospels as Eyewitness Testimony*. 2nd ed. Grand Rapids, MI: Eerdmans, 2017.
Beasley-Murray, George Raymond. *Baptism in the New Testament*. London, New York: Macmillan; St Martin's Press, 1962.
Benedict XVI. Post-Synodal Apostolic Exhortation On the Word of God in the Life and Mission of the Church *Verbum Domini*. September 30, 2010. Rome: Libreria Editrice Vaticana, 2010.
———. *What Is Christianity?: The Last Writings*. Edited by Elio Guerriero and Georg Gänswein. Translated by Michael J. Miller. San Francisco: Ignatius, 2023.
Benoit, André, and Charles Munier. *Die Taufe in der Alten Kirche (1.-3. Jahrhundert)*. Traditio Christiana 9. Bern: Peter Lang, 1994.
Berthelot, Katell. "Les titres des livres bibliques: Le témoignage de la Bibliothèque de Qumrân." In *Flores Florentino: Dead Sea Scrolls and Other Early Jewish Studies in Honour of Florentino García Martínez*, edited by Anthony Hilhorst, Émile Puech, and Eibert Tigchelaar, 127–40. Leiden: Brill, 2007.
Betz, Hans Dieter. "Jesus' Baptism and the Origins of the Christian Ritual." In *Ablution, Initiation, and Baptism: Late Antiquity, Early Judaism, and Early*

Christianity, edited by David Hellholm, Tor Vegge, Øyvind Norderval, and Christer Hellholm, 377-96. Beihefte zur Zeitschrift für die neutestamentliche Wissenschaft und die Kunde der älteren Kirche 176. Berlin: De Gruyter, 2011.

Bird, Phyllis. "'Male and Female He Created Them': Gen 1:27b in the Context of the Priestly Account of Creation." *Harvard Theological Review* 74 (1981): 129-59.

Blass, Friedrich, Albert Debrunner, and Friedrich Rehkopf. *Grammatik des neuentestamentlichen Griechisch*. 14th edition. Göttingen: Vandenhoeck & Ruprecht, 1976.

Boersma, Hans. "The Church Fathers' Spiritual Interpretation of the Psalms." In *Living Waters from Ancient Springs: Essays in Honor of Cornelis Van Dam*, edited by Jason van Vliet, 41-55. Eugene, OR: Wipf & Stock, 2011.

Bock, Darrell L. *Luke: 1:1–9:50*. Baker Exegetical Commentary on the New Testament. Grand Rapids, MI: Baker Academic, 1994.

Boring, M. Eugene. *Mark: A Commentary*. New Testament Library. Louisville: Westminster John Knox, 2012.

Bornkamm, Günther. *Jesus of Nazareth*. New York: Harper & Row, 1960.

Boyarin, Daniel. *Border Lines. The Partition of Judaeo-Christianity*. Philadelphia: University of Pennsylvania Press, 2004.

Breck, John. "Theoria and Orthodox Hermeneutics." *Saint Vladimir's Theological Quarterly* 20, no. 4 (1976): 195-219.

Brey, Gerald. *Biblical Interpretation: Past and Present*. Downers Grove, IL: InterVarsity Press, 1996.

Briody, Joseph. "The Rejection of Saul in First Samuel 13:7b-15 and 15:1–35: Synchrony, Diachrony, Theology." STD diss., Boston College, 2020. ProQuest Dissertations and Theses.

Brueggemann, Walter. *Theology of the Old Testament*. Minneapolis: Fortress, 1997.

Bultmann, Rudolf. *Die Geschichte der synoptischen Tradition*. With the assistance of Gerd Theißen. 5th edition. Göttingen: Vandenhoeck und Ruprecht, 1979.

———. *Jesus and the Word*. London: Collins, 1934.

Burke, Trevor J. *Adopted into God's Family: Exploring a Pauline Metaphor*. New Studies in Biblical Theology 22. Nottingham, England; Downers Grove, IL: Apollos; InterVarsity Press, 2006.

Burrows, Edward W. "Baptism in Mark and Luke." In *Baptism, the New Testament and the Church: Historical and Contemporary Studies in Honour of R.E.O. White*, edited by Stanley E. Porter and Reginald E. O. White,

99–115. Journal for the Study of the New Testament Supplement Series 171. Sheffield: Sheffield Academic, 1999.

Byrne, Brendan. *Romans*. Sacra Pagina 6. Collegeville, MN: Liturgical Press, 1996.

Cadiou, René. *Commentaires inédits des Psaumes: Etude sur le textes d'Origène contenus dans le manuscrit Vindobonensis 8*. Paris: Les Belles Lettres, 1936.

Campbell, Antony F. *1 Samuel*. Forms of the Old Testament Literature 7. Grand Rapids, MI: Eerdmans, 2003.

Carlson, Richard Paul. "The Role of Baptism in Paul's Thought." *Interpretation* 47, no. 3 (1993): 255–66.

Caruso, Ada. "Ipotesi di ragionamento sulla localizzazione del 'Mouseion' di Alessandria." *Archeologia Classica* 62, no. 1 (2011): 77–126.

Cassuto, Umberto Moshe David. *A Commentary on the Book of Exodus*. Translated by I. Abrahams. Skoie, IL: Varda.

Catechism of the Catholic Church. 2nd edition, in accordance with the official Latin text promulgated by Pope John Paul II. Vatican City: Libreria Editrice Vaticana, 2019; distributed by: Washington, DC: United States Conference of Catholic Bishops, 2019.

Chapa, Juan. "La materialidad de la Palabra: manuscritos que hablan." *Estudios Bíblicos* 69 (2011): 9–37.

Childs, Brevard S. *Biblical Theology of the Old and New Testaments: Theological Reflection on the Christian Bible*. Minneapolis: Fortress, 1993.

———. *The Book of Exodus: A Critical, Theological Commentary*. Philadelphia: Westminster, 1974.

———. "Psalm 8 in the Context of the Christian Canon." *Interpretation* 23 (1969): 20–31.

Chilton, Bruce. "John the Baptist: His Immersion and His Death." In *Dimensions of Baptism: Biblical and Theological Studies*, edited by Stanley E. Porter and Anthony R. Cross, 25–44. Journal for the Study of the New Testament Supplement Series 234. London: Sheffield Academic, 2002.

Chromatius of Aquileia. *Tractatus in Matthaeum*. In *Chromatii Aquileiensis Opera*, edited by R. Étaix and J. Lemarié, 185–498. Corpus Christianorum, Series Latina 9a. Turnhout, Belgium: Typographi Brepols Editores Pontificii, 1974.

Clement of Alexandria. *Stromateis*. Translated by John Ferguson. Fathers of the Church 85. Washington, DC: Catholic University of America Press, 1991.

Collins, John J. *Encounters with Biblical Theology*. Minneapolis: Fortress, 2005.

Congregation for the Clergy. *The Priest and The Third Christian Millennium:*

Teacher of the Word, Minister of the Sacraments, and Leader of the Community. Vatican City: Libreria Editrice Vaticana, 1999.

Conzelmann, Hans. *Jesus*. Philadelphia: Fortress, 1973.

Cortese, Enzo. "Sulle redazioni finali del Salterio." *Revue Biblique* 106, no. 1 (1999): 66–100.

Coulson, John. "Jesus and the Spirit in Paul's Theology: The Earthly Jesus." *Catholic Biblical Quarterly* 79, no. 1 (2017): 77–96.

Cranfield, Charles Ernest Burland. *A Critical and Exegetical Commentary on the Epistle to the Romans*. 2 vols. International Critical Commentary. Edinburgh: T&T Clark, 2004.

Crawford, Matthew R. *The Eusebian Canon Tables*. Oxford: Oxford University Press, 2019.

Cullman, Oscar "Die Neuen Arbeiten zur Geschichte der Evangelientradition." In *Vorträge und Aufsätze: 1925 – 1962*, edited by Oscar Cullman, 41–90. Tübingen: Mohr Siebeck, 1966.

Culpepper, R. Alan. *Anatomy of the Fourth Gospel: A Study in a Literary Design*. Foundation and Facets, New Testament. Philadelphia: Fortress, 1983.

Cyril of Alexandria. *Commentariorum in Joannem*. PG 74:9–756.

———. *Glaphyra on the Pentateuch*. Translated by Nicholas P. Lunn. Fathers of the Church 138. Washington, DC: Catholic University of America Press, 2019.

Daley, Brian E. "Finding the Right Key: The Aims and Strategies of Early Christian Interpretation of the Psalms." In *The Harp of Prophecy: Early Christian Interpretation of the Psalms*, edited by Brian E. Daley and Paul R. Kolbet, 11–28. Notre Dame, IN: University of Notre Dame Press, 2015.

Daly-Denton, Margaret. *David in the Fourth Gospel: The Johannine Reception of the Psalms*. Arbeiten zur Geschichte des antiken Judentums und des Urchristentums 47. Leiden: Brill, 2000.

———. "The Psalms in John's Gospel." In *The Psalms in the New Testament*, edited by Steve Moyise and Maarten J. J. Menken, 119–37. New Testament and the Scriptures of Israel. London: T&T Clark, 2004.

Davies, W. D., and Dale C. Allison. *A Critical and Exegetical Commentary on the Gospel According to Saint Matthew*. International Critical Commentary on the Holy Scriptures. Edinburgh: T&T Clark, 1988.

DeCock, Miriam. *Interpreting the Gospel of John in Antioch and Alexandria*. Writings from the Greco-Roman World Supplement Series 17. Atlanta: SBL Press, 2020).

Dell, Katherine. "Psalms." In *The Oxford Handbook of the Reception History of the Bible*, ed. Michael Lieb, Emma Mason, and Jonathan Roberts, 37–51. Oxford: Oxford University Press, 2011.

BIBLIOGRAPHY

Dettwiler, Andreas. *Die Gegenwart des Erhöten: Eine exegetische Studie zu den johanneischen Abschiedsreden (John 13,31–16,33) unter besonderer Berücksichtigung ihres Relecture-Charakters.* Forschungen zur Religion und Literatur des Alten und Neuen Testaments 169. Göttingen: Vandenhoeck & Ruprech, 1995.

Devreesse, Robert. *Les anciens commentateurs grecs des Psaumes.* Vatican City: Biblioteca Apostolica Vaticana, 1970.

———. "Chaînes exégétiques grecques." In *Dictionnaire de la Bible: Supplément*, vol. 1, 1084–1233. Paris: Letouzey et Ané, 1926.

Didymus the Blind. *Lezioni sui Salmi. Il Commento ai Salmi scoperto a Tura.* With introduction, translation, and annotation by Emanuela Prinzivalli. Milan: Paoline, 2005.

Dietrich, Walter. "The Layer Model of the Deuteronomistic History and the Book of Samuel." In *Is Samuel among the Deuteronomists?: Current Views on the Place of Samuel in a Deuteronomistic History*, 39–65. Edited by Cynthia Edenburg and Juha Pakkala. Atlanta: SBL Press, 2013.

Dietzfelbinger, Christian. *Die Abschied des Kommenden. Eine Auslegung der johanneischen Abschiedsreden.* Wissenschaftliche Untersuchungen zum Neuen Testament 95. Tübingen: Mohr Siebeck, 1997.

Diodorus of Tarsus. *Commentary on the Psalms 1–51.* Translated by Robert C. Hill. Atlanta: SBL Press, 2005.

———. *Diodori Tarsensis Commentarii in Psalmos: I. Commentarii in Psalmos I–L.* Edited by Jean-Marie Olivier. Turnhout: Brepols, 1980. French translation: Louis Mariès, "Extraits du commentaire de Diodore de Tarse sur les Psaumes," *Recherches de Science Religieuse* 9, no. 1 (1919): 79–101.

Dodd, Charles H. *According to the Scriptures: The Substructure of New Testament Theology.* London: Nisbet & Co., 1952.

———. *The Founder of Christianity.* New York: Macmillan, 1970.

Donahue, John R., and Daniel J. Harrington. *The Gospel of Mark.* Sacra Pagina 2. Collegeville, MN: Liturgical Press, 2002.

Dorival, Gilles. "Les titres des psaumes en hébreu et en grec: les écarts quantitatifs." in *L'écrit et l'esprit: études d'histoire du texte et de théologie biblique en hommage à Adrian Schenker*, ed. Dieter Böhler, Innocent Himbaza, and Philippe Hugo, 58–70. Göttingen: Vandenhoeck & Ruprecht, 2005.

Driver, S. R. *Notes on the Hebrew Text and the Topography of the Books of Samuel.* Oxford: Clarendon, 1913.

Dupont, Anthony. "The *Enarrationes in Psalmos* by Augustine of Hippo: The Psalms as the Voice(s) of the Church and Christ." In *David, Messianism, and Eschatology: Ambiguity in the Reception History of the Book of Psalms in Judaism and Christianity*, edited by Erkki Koskenniemi and David Willgren Davage, 319–36. Turku, Finland: Åbo Akademi University, 2020.

Dunn, James D. G. *Baptism in the Holy Spirit: A Re-Examination of the New Testament Teaching on the Gift of the Spirit in Relation to Pentecostalism Today.* Philadelphia: Westminster, 1970.

———. *Beginning from Jerusalem.* Christianity in the Making 2. Grand Rapids, MI: Eerdmans, 2009.

———. *Jesus Remembered.* Christianity in the Making 1. Grand Rapids, MI: Eerdmans, 2003.

———. *Jesus and the Spirit: A Study of the Religious and Charismatic Experience of Jesus and the First Christians as Reflected in the New Testament.* London: SCM, 1975.

———. *The Parting of the Ways: Between Christianity and Judaism and Their Significance for the Character of Christianity.* 2nd edition. London: SCM Press, 2006.

———. *Romans 1–8.* Word Biblical Commentary 38A. Dallas: Word, 1988.

Eaton, John H. *The Psalms: A Historical and Spiritual Commentary with an Introduction and New Testament.* London: T&T Clark, 2003.

Eck, Ernest van. "The Baptism of Jesus in Mark: A Status Transformation Ritual." *Neotestamentica* 30, no. 1 (1996): 187–215.

Edwards, James R. "The Baptism of Jesus According to the Gospel of Mark." *Journal of the Evangelical Theological Society* 34, no. 1 (1991): 43–57.

Enslin, Morton Scott. "John and Jesus." *Die Zeitschrift für die Neutestamentliche Wissenschaft und die Kunde der älteren Kirche* 66, nos. 1–2 (1975): 1–18.

Ephrem the Syrian. *Commentary on the Diatessaron.* Edited by Louis Leloir. Sources Chrétiennes 121. Paris: Cerf, 1966.

———. *Hymns on Epiphany.* In *Des Heiligen Ephraem des Syrers Hymnen de Nativitate (Epiphania)*, edited by Edmund Beck, 131–77. Corpus Scriptorum Christianorum Orientalium 187. Louvain: Corpus Scriptorum Christianorum Orientalium, 1959.

Epiphanius. *Panarion.* In Epiphanius, *Panarion, Haer. 34–64*, edited by Karl Holl, 403–524. Griechischen christlichen Schriftsteller der ersten drei Jahrhunderte 31. Leipzig: J.C. Hinrichs'sche Buchhandlung, 1922.

Eusebius of Caesarea. *Commentaria in Psalmos.* PG 23.

Evans, Craig A. "The Baptism of John in a Typological Context." In *Dimensions of Baptism: Biblical and Theological Studies*, edited by Stanley E. Porter and Anthony R. Cross, 45–71. Journal for the Study of the New Testament Supplement Series 234. London: Sheffield Academic, 2002.

Ferda, Tucker S. "The Historicity of Confusion: Jesus, John the Baptist, and the Construction of Public Identity." *Journal of Biblical Literature* 139, no. 4 (2020): 747–67.

Ferguson, Everett. "Athanasius' *Epistula ad Marcellinum* in interpretationem Psalmorum." In *Studia Patristica* 16, part 2, edited by Elisabeth A. Livingstone, 295–308. Texte und Untersuchungen zur Geschichte der altchristlichen Literatur 129. Berlin: Akademie Verlag, 1985.

———. *Baptism in the Early Church: History, Theology, and Liturgy in the First Five Centuries*. Grand Rapids, MI: Eerdmans, 2009.

Fiedrowicz, Michael. *Psalmus vox totius Christi: Studien zu Augustinus "Ennarrationes in Psalmos"*. Freiburg: Herder, 1997.

Fischer, Balthasar. "Le Christ dans les Psaumes: La dévotion aux Psaumes dans l'Église des martyrs." *La Maison-Dieu* 27, no. 1 (1951): 86–113.

Flint, Peter W. "Five Surprises in the Qumran Psalms Scrolls." In *Flores Florentino: Dead Sea Scrolls and Other Early Jewish Studies in Honour of Florentino García Martínez*, edited by Anthony Hilhorst, Émile Puech, and Eibert Tigchelaar, 183–95. Leiden: Brill, 2007.

———. "The Prophet David at Qumran." In *Biblical Interpretation at Qumran*, edited by Matthias Henze, 158–67. Grand Rapids, MI: Eerdmans, 2005.

Forcellini, Egidio, Giuseppe Furlanetto, Francesco Corradini, and Josephus Perin, eds. *Lexicon Totius Latinitatis*. Patavii: Gregoriana, 1965.

Fraine, Jean de. *Adam et son lignage: Études sur la notion de "personnalité corporative" dans la Bible*. Museum Lessianum - Section Biblique 2. Bruges: Desclée de Brouwer, 1959.

France, R. T. *The Gospel of Mark: A Commentary on the Greek Text*. New International Greek Testament Commentary. Grand Rapids, MI; Carlisle: Eerdmans; Paternoster, 2002.

———. *The Gospel of Matthew*. New International Commentary on the New Testament. Grand Rapids, MI: Eerdmans, 2007.

Freed, Edwin D. *Old Testament Quotations in the Gospel of John*. New Testament Studies 11. Leiden: Brill, 1965.

Froehlich, Karlfried. *Biblical Interpretation in the Early Church*. Sources of Early Christian Thoughts. Philadelphia: Fortress, 1984.

Fuchs, Ernst. *Zur Frage nach dem historischen Jesus*. Gesammelte Aufsätze 2. Tübingen: Mohr Siebeck, 1965.

Fusco, Vittorio. "Gesù e le Scritture di Israele." In *La Bibbia nell'antichità cristiana*, vol. 1, *Da Gesù a Origene*, edited by Enrico Norelli, 35–63. Bologna: Edizioni Dehoniane Bologna, 1993.

García Martínez, Florentino, ed. *The Dead Sea Scrolls Translated: The Qumran Texts in English*. Leiden: Brill, 1994.

García Martínez, Florentino, and Eibert J. C. Tigchelaar, eds. *The Dead Sea Scrolls Study Edition (Translations)*. Leiden: Brill, 1997.

Gargano, Guido I. *Clemente e Origene nella Chiesa cristiana alessandrina: Estraneità, dialogo o inculturazione*. Cinisello Balsamo (MI): Edizioni San Paolo, 2011.

Genette, Gérard. *Figures III: Discours du récit*. Collection Poétique. Paris: Seuil, 1972.

Giambrone, Anthony. "Prosopological Exegesis and Christological Anagnorisis in Jesus's Reading of Psalm 110." *Nova et Vetera* 18, no. 4 (2020): 1267–1284.

Gibbs, Jeffrey A. "Israel Standing with Israel: The Baptism of Jesus in Matthew's Gospel (Matt 3:13–17)." *Catholic Biblical Quarterly* 64, no. 3 (2002): 511–26.

Gillingham, Susan. "From Liturgy to Prophecy: The Use of Psalmody in Second Temple Judaism." *Catholic Biblical Quarterly* 64, no. 3 (2002): 470–89.

———. "The Messiah in the Psalms: A Question of Reception History and the Psalter." In *King and Messiah in Israel and the Ancient Near East: Proceedings of the Oxford Old Testament Seminar*, edited by John Day, 209–37. Sheffield: Sheffield Academic, 1998.

———. "Studies of the Psalms: Retrospect and Prospect." *The Expository Times* 119, no. 5 (2007): 209–16.

Gillmayr-Bucher, Susanne. "The Psalm Headings: A Canonical Relecture of the Psalms." In *The Biblical Canons*, edited by Jean-Marie Auwers and Henk Jan De Jonge, 247–54. Leuven: Leuven University Press, 2003.

Girolami, Maurizio. *La recezione del Salmo 21 (LXX) agli inizi dell'era Cristiana: Cristologia ed ermeneutica biblica in costruzione*. Rome: Istituto Patristico Augustinianum, 2011.

Gögel, Rolf. *Zur Theologie des biblischen Wortes bei Origenes*. Dusseldorf: Patmos-Verlag, 1963.

Grappone, Antonio. "Omelie tradotte e/o tradite?" In *L'Oriente in Occidente: l'opera di Rufino di Concordia*, edited by Maurizio Girolami, 59–115. Brescia: Morcelliana, 2014.

Grech, Prosper. "L'interpretazione patristica dei Salmi." *Augustinianum* 48, no. 1 (2008): 221–35.

Green, Joel B. "Scripture and Theology: Uniting the Two So Long Divided." In *Between Two Horizons: Spanning New Testament Studies and Systematic Theology*, edited by Joel B. Green and Max Turner, 23–43. Grand Rapids, MI: Eerdmans, 2000.

Greer, Rowan A. "The Rise of the Christian Bible." In James L. Kugel and Rowan A. Greer, *Early Biblical Interpretation*, 107–203. Philadelphia: Westminster, 1986.

Gregory of Nyssa. *Prologus in Canticum Canticorum*. In *Gregorii Nysseni Opera*, vol. 4, edited by Hermannus Langerbeck, 3-13. Leiden: Brill, 1960.

Gruber, Winfried. *Die peneumatische Exegese bei den Alexandrimen: Ein Beitrag zur Noematik der heiligen Schrift*. Schriften und Vorträge im Rahmen der Theologischen Fakultät in Graz, Reihe D, Heft 3/4. Graz: Akademische Druck und Verlagsanstalt, 1957.

Guelich, Robert A. *Mark 1-8:26*. Word Biblical Commentary 34A. Dallas: Word, 1989.

Guinan, Michael D. *The Pentateuch*. Message of Biblical Spirituality 1. Collegeville, MN: Liturgical Press, 1990.

Haenchen, Ernst. *Der Weg Jesu: Eine Erklärung des Markus-Evangeliums und der Kanonischen Parallelen*. De Gruyter Lehrbuch. Berlin: De Gruyter, 1968.

Hägerland, Tobias. "The Future of Criteria in Historical Jesus Research." *Journal for the Study of the Historical Jesus* 13, no. 1 (2015): 43-65.

Hagner, Donald A. *Matthew 1-13*. Word Biblical Commentary 33A. Dallas: Word, 1993.

Haldimann, Konrad. *Rekonstruktion und Entfaltung: Exegetische Untersuchungen zu John 15 und John 16*. Beihefte zur Zeitschrift für die neutestametliche Wissenschaft 104. Berlin: De Gruyter, 2000.

Hall, Christopher A. *Reading Scripture with the Church Fathers*. Downers Grove, IL: InterVarsity Press, 1998.

Hamilton, Victor P. *Exodus: An Exegetical Commentary*. Grand Rapids, MI: Baker Academic, 2011.

Hanson, Paul D. *Isaiah 40-66*. Interpretation: A Bible Commentary for Teaching and Preaching. Louisville: John Knox, 1995.

Hanson, R. P. C. *Allegory and Event: A Study of the Sources and Significance of Origen's Interpretation of Scripture*. Louisville: Westminster John Knox, 2002.

Harkins, Franklin T. "Christ and the Eternal Extent of Divine Providence in the *Expositio Super Iob ad Litteram* of Thomas Aquinas." *Viator* 47 (2015): 123-52.

Harl, Marguerite. *La chaîne palestinienne sur le psaume 118 (Origène, Eusèbe, Didyme, Apollinaire, Athanase, Théodoret)*, vol. 1. Paris: Cerf, 1972.

Harnack, Adolf von. *Marcion: Das Evangelium vom Fremden Gott. Eine Monographie zur Geschichte der Grundlegung der Katholischen Kirche*. 2nd edition. Texte und Untersuchungen zur Geschichte der altchristlichen Literatur 45. Leipzig: J. C. Hinrichs'sche Buchhandlung, 1924.

Harrington, Daniel J. *The Gospel of Matthew*. Sacra Pagina 1. Collegeville, MN: Liturgical Press, 2007.

Hartman, Lars. *Into the Name of the Lord Jesus: Baptism in the Early Church*. Studies of the New Testament and Its World. Edinburgh: T&T Clark, 1997.

Hays, Richard B. *Echoes of Scripture in the Letters of in Paul*. New Haven: Yale University Press, 1989.

Heine, Ronald E. "Restringing Origen's Broken Harp: Some Suggestions Concerning the Prologue to the Caesarean Commentary on the Psalms." In *The Harp of Prophecy: Early Christian Interpretation of the Psalms*, edited by Brian E. Daley and Paul R. Kolbet, 47–74. Notre Dame, IN: University of Notre Dame Press, 2015.

Hellholm, David. "Vorgeformte Tauftraditionen und deren Benutzung in den Paulusbriefen." In *Ablution, Initiation, and Baptism: Late Antiquity, Early Judaism, and Early Christianity*, edited by David Hellholm, Tor Vegge, Øyvind Norderval, and Christer Hellholm, 415–95. Beihefte zur Zeitschrift für die neutestamentliche Wissenschaft und die Kunde der älteren Kirche 176. Berlin: De Gruyter, 2011.

Hernández Carracedo, José Manuel. *La caracterización de Jesús en las notas del narrador del evangelio de Juan: Una guía de la lectura para el relato*. Monografías Bíblicas 78. Estella, Navarra: Verbo Divino, 2020.

Hilary of Poitiers. *Instructio Psalmorum*. In Sources Chrétiennes 515, edited by Jean Doignon and Patrick Descourtieux, 126–67. Paris: Cerf, 2008.

———. *In Matthaeum*. Edited by Jean Doignon. Sources Chrétiennes 254. Paris: Cerf, 1978.

Hill, Robert C. "Introduction." In Theodoret of Cyrus, *Commentary on the Psalms, 1–72*, translated by Robert C. Hill, 1–36. Fathers of the Church 101. Washington, DC: Catholic University of America Press, 2000.

———. *Of Prophets and Poets: Antioch Fathers on the Bible*. Brookline, MA: Holy Cross Orthodox Press, 2007.

Hippolytus. *Elenchos*. 134–89 in *Hippolytus Werke*, vol. 3, *Refutatio Omnium Haeresium*. Edited by Paul Wendland. Griechischen christlichen Schriftsteller der ersten drei Jahrhunderte 26. Leipzig: J.C. Hinrichs'sche Buchhandlung, 1916.

Holladay, Carl R. "Baptism in the New Testament and Its Cultural Milieu: A Response to Everett Ferguson, Baptism in the Early Church." *Journal of Early Christian Studies* 20, no. 3 (2012): 343–69.

Hollenbach, Paul. "The Conversion of Jesus: Jesus the Baptizer to Jesus to Healer." In Aufstieg und Niedergang der römischen Welt 25.1, edited by Wolfgang Haase, 196–219. Berlin: De Gruyter, 1982.

Jacob of Serugh. *Homiliae Selectae Mar-Jacobi Sarugensis*. 5 vols. Edited by P. Bedjan. Leipzig: Harrassowitz, 1905-1910.

Jerome. *Commentariorum in Matthaeum Libri IV*. Edited by D. Hurst and M. Adriaen, *In Sancti Hieronymi Presbyteri Opera: Pars 1.7*. Corpus Christianorum, Series Latina 77. Turnhout, Belgium: Typographi Brepols Editores Pontificii, 1969.

———. *Commentarioli in Psalmos*. In *S. Hieronymi Presbyteri Opera*, Pars 1, Opera Exegetica 1, edited by Germanus Morin, 163–245. Corpus Christianorum, Series Latina 72. Turnholt: Brepols, 1959.

———. *Contra Rufinum*. In *Saint Jérôme: Apologie contre Rufin*, edited by Pierre Lardet, 242–51. Sources Chrétiennes 303. Paris: Cerf, 1983.

———. *Tractatus sive Homiliae in Psalmos*. In *S. Hieronymi Presbyteri Opera*, Pars 2, *Opera Homiletica*, 3–447. Corpus Christianorum, Series Latina 78. Turnholt: Brepols, 1958.

John Chrysostom. *Commentarius in sanctum Joannem Apostulum et Evangelistam*. PG 59:23–482.

———. *Homilies on 2 Corinthians*. Edited and translated by Talbot W. Chambers. NPNF 1/12:271–420.

———. *Homilies on Hebrews*. Edited by Philip Schaff. Translated by Frederic Gardiner. NPNF 1/14: 333–522.

———. *Homilies on Matthew*. PG 57. Translated by George Prevost, edited by M. B. Riddle, NPNF 1/10.

Johnson, Luke Timothy. *The Gospel of Luke*. Sacra Pagina 3. Collegeville, MN: Liturgical Press, 1991.

Jónsson, Gunnlauger A. *The Image of God: Genesis 1:26–28 in a Century of Old Testament Research*. Translated by Lorraine Svendsen. *Coniectanea biblica: Old Testament Series* 26. Lund: Almqvist & Wiksell International, 1988.

Joseph, Alison L. *Portrait of the Kings: The Davidic Prototype in Deuteronomistic Poetics*. Minneapolis: Fortress, 2015.

Juel, Donald H. *Mark*. Augsburg Commentary on the New Testament. Minneapolis: Augsburg, 1990.

Kaiser, Walter C., Jr. "Psalm 72: An Historical and Messianic Current Example of Antiochene Hermeneutical Theoria." *Journal of the Evangelical Theological Society* 52, no. 2 (2009): 257–70.

Kannengiesser, Charles. *Handbook of Patristic Exegesis*. The Bible in Ancient Christianity 1. Leiden: Brill, 2006.

Kantor, Benjamin Paul. "The Second Column (Secunda) of Origen's Hexapla in Light of Greek Pronunciation." PhD diss., University of Texas, Austin, 2017.

Käsemann, Ernst. "On the Subject of Primitive Christian Apocalyptic." In *New

Testament Questions of Today, edited by Ernst Käsemann, 108–37. New Testament Library. London: SCM Press, 1969.

Keener, Craig S. *The Gospel of Matthew: A Socio-Rhetorical Commentary*. Grand Rapids, MI: Eerdmans, 2009.

Keith, Chris. "The Narratives of the Gospels and the Historical Jesus: Current Debates, Prior Debates and the Goal of Historical Jesus Research." *Journal for the Study of the New Testament* 38, no. 4 (2016): 426–55.

Kowalski, Marcin. "Baptism – the Revelation of the Filial Relationship of Christ and the Christian." *The Biblical Annals* 11, no. 3 (2021): 459–95.

———. "Meditatio of Lectio Divina Following Upon Exegesis-Informed Lectio: The Test Case of Romans 7:7–25." In *Piercing the Clouds: Lectio Divina and Preparation for Ministry*, edited by Kevin Zilverberg and Scott Carl, 82–97. Catholic Theological Formation Series. Saint Paul, MN: Saint Paul Seminary Press, 2021.

———. "The Cognitive Spirit and the Novelty of Paul's Thought in Rom 8,5–6." *Biblica* 100, no. 1 (2020): 47–68.

Kruse, Colin G. *Paul's Letter to the Romans*. Pillar New Testament Commentary. Cambridge; Grand Rapids, MI: Eerdmans; Apollos, 2012.

Kugel, James L. "Topics in the History of the Spirituality of the Psalms." In *Jewish Spirituality: From the Bible through the Middle Ages*, edited by Arthur Green, 113–44. New York: Crossroad, 1986.

Kugel, James L. and Rowan A. Greer. *Early Biblical Interpretation*. Philadelphia: Westminster, 1986.

Kvalbein, Hans. "The Baptism of Jesus as a Model for Christian Baptism: Can the Idea Be Traced Back to New Testament Times?" *Studia Theologica* 50, no. 1 (1996): 67–83.

Labahn, Michael. "Kreative Erinnerung als Nachösterliche Nachschöpfung: Der Ursprung der Christlichen Taufe." In *Ablution, Initiation, and Baptism: Late Antiquity, Early Judaism, and Early Christianity*, edited by David Hellholm, Tor Vegge, Øyvind Norderval, and Christer Hellholm, 337–76. Beihefte zur Zeitschrift für die neutestamentliche Wissenschaft und die Kunde der älteren Kirche 176. Berlin: De Gruyter, 2011.

Lane, William L. *The Gospel of Mark*. New International Commentary on the New Testament. Grand Rapids, MI: Eerdmans, 1974.

Lauchert, Friedrich, ed. *Die Kanones der wichtigsten altkirchlichen Concilien nebst den apostolischen Kanones*. Freiburg: Mohr Siebeck, 1896.

Levenson, John Douglas. *The Hebrew Bible, the Old Testament, and Historical Criticism: Jews and Christians in Biblical Studies*. 1st edition. Louisville: Westminster John Knox, 1993.

———. "The Last Four Verses in Kings." *Journal of Biblical Literature* 103, no. 3 (1984): 353–61.
Lewis, C. S. *Reflections on the Psalms*. Boston: Mariner, 1958, 2012.
Lienhard, Joseph T., ed. *Exodus, Leviticus, Numbers, Deuteronomy*. Ancient Christian Commentary on Scripture, Old Testament 9. Downers Grove, IL: InterVarsity Press, 2001.
———. "Origen as Homilist." In *Preaching in the Patristic Age: Studies in Honor of Walter J. Burghardt, S.J.*, edited by David G. Hunter, 36–72. New York: Paulist, 1989.
Lietzmann, Hans, ed. *Das Muratorische Fragment und Die Monarchianischen Prologe zu den Evangelien*. Bonn: Marcus & Weber, 1921.
Lietaert Peerbolte, Bert Jan. "Paul, Baptism, and Religious Experience." In *Experientia*, vol. 2, *Linking Text and Experience*, edited by Colleen Shantz and Rodney A. Werline, 181–204. Early Judaism and Its Literature 35. Atlanta: SBL Press, 2012.
Lohfink, Gerhard. *Studien zum Neuen Testament*. Stuttgarter Biblische Aufsatzbände 5. Stuttgart: Katholisches Bibelwerk, 1989.
Lonergan, Bernard. *Insight: A Study of Human Understanding*. New York: Philosophical Library, 1970.
———. *Method in Theology*. New York: Herder and Herder, 1972.
Löning, Karl. "Die Funktion des Psalters im Neuen Testament." In *Der Psalter in Judentum und Christentum*, edited by Erich Zenger, 269–95. Freiburg im Breisgau: Herder, 1998.
Lubac, Henri de. *History and Spirit: The Understanding of Scripture According to Origen*. Translated by Anne Englund Nash. San Francisco: Ignatius, 2007.
Luz, Ulrich. *Matthew 1–7: A Commentary on Matthew 1–7*. Hermeneia. Minneapolis: Fortress, 2007.
Lyonnet, Stanislas. "Rom 8,2–4 a la lumiere de Jeremie 31 et d'Ezechiel 35–39." In *Etudes sur L'epître aux Romains*, edited by Stanislas Lyonnet, 231–41. Analecta Biblica 120. Rome: Pontifical Biblical Institute, 1990.
Maier, John. "Zur Verwendung der Psalmen in der synagogalen Liturgie (Wochentag und Sabbat)." In *Liturgie und Dichtung: Ein interdisziplinäres Kompendium II*, edited by Hansjakob Becker and Reiner Kaczynski, 55–90. St. Ottilien: Eos Verlag Erzabtei St. Ottilien, 1983.
Malina, Artur. *Chrzest Jezusa w czterech Ewangeliach: Studium narracji i teologii*. Studia i Materiały Wydziału Teologicznego Uniwersytetu Śląskiego w Katowicach 34. Katowice: Ksiegarnia sw. Jacka; Wydział Teologiczny Uniwersytetu Slaskiego, 2007.

Marafioti, Domenico. "Sant'Ilario e il libro dei Salmi." *Rassegna di Teologia* 48, no. 3 (2007): 455–66.

Marasco, Gabriele. "Alessandria nascita e morte di una Biblioteca." *Studi sull'Oriente Cristiano* 15, no. 2 (2011): 5–16.

Marcheselli, Maurizio. "Davanti alla Scrittura di Israele: processo esegetico ed ermeneutica credente nel gruppo giovanneo." *Ricerche Storico Bibliche* 22 (2010): 175–95.

Marcos, Natalio Fernández. "David the Adolescent: On Psalm 151." In *The Old Greek Psalter*, edited by Robert J. V. Hiebert, Claude E. Cox, and Peter J. Gentry, 205–17. Sheffield: Sheffield Academic, 2001.

Marcus, Joel. "Jesus' Baptismal Vision." *New Testament Studies* 41, no. 4 (1995): 512–21.

———. *John the Baptist in History and Theology*, Studies on Personalities of the New Testament (Columbia, SC: University of South Carolina Press, 2018.

———. *Mark 1–8: A New Translation with Introduction and Commentary*. Anchor Bible. New Haven: Yale University Press, 2008.

Margerie, Bertrand de. *Introduction a l'histoire de l'exégèse*, vol. 1. Paris: Cerf, 1980.

Marshall, I. Howard. *The Gospel of Luke: Commentary on the Greek Text*. New International Greek Testament Commentary. Exeter: Paternoster, 1978.

Martens, John W. "Catholic Hermeneutics of the New Testament." *St. Vladimir's Theological Quarterly* 63, no. 2 (2019): 213–35.

Martens, Peter W. *Origen and Scripture: The Contours of the Exegetical Life*. Oxford: Oxford University Press, 2012.

———. "Revisiting the Allegory/Typology Distinction: The Case of Origen." *Journal of Early Christian Studies* 16 (2008): 283–317.

Mays, James L. "The David of the Psalms," *Interpretation* 40, no. 2 (1986): 143–55.

McDonnell, Kilian. "Jesus' Baptism in the Jordan." *Theological Studies* 56, no. 2 (1995): 209–36.

McGinn, Bernard, and Susan E. Schreiner. "According to the Scriptures: Biblical Interpretation Prior to 1600." Pages 1891–1922 in *The Jerome Biblical Commentary for the Twenty-First Century*. Edited by John J. Collins, Gina Hens-Piazza, Barbara Reid, and Donald Senior. London: T&T Clark, 2022.

McGuckin, John A. "Moses and the 'Mystery of Christ' in St. Cyril of Alexandria's Exegesis – Part 1." *Coptic Church Review* 21, no. 1 (2000): 24–32.

———. "Origen's Use of the Psalms in the Treatise on First Principles." In *Meditations of the Heart: The Psalms in Early Christian Thought and Practice, Essays in Honour of Andrew Louth*, 97–118. Turnhout: Brepols, 2011.

———. *The Westminster Handbook to Origen*. Louisville: Westminster John Knox, 2004.

Meier, John P. *A Marginal Jew: Rethinking the Historical Jesus*, vol. 2, *Mentor, Message, and Miracles*. New Haven: Yale University Press, 1994.

Meiser, Martin. "David and Psalms in Ancient Christian Exegesis." In *David, Messianism, and Eschatology: Ambiguity in the Reception History of the Book of Psalms in Judaism and Christianity*, edited by Erkki Koskenniemi and David Willgren Davage, 282–318. Turku, Finland: Åbo Akademi University, 2020.

Menken, Maarten J. J. *Old Testament Quotations in the Fourth Gospel: Studies in Textual Form*. Contributions to Biblical Exegesis and Theology 15. Kampen: Kok Pharos, 1996.

Metzger, Bruce and Roland Murphy, eds. *New Oxford Annotated Bible with the Apocryphal/Deuterocanonical Books*. New York: Oxford University Press, 1991.

Meyer, Ben F. *The Aims of Jesus*. London: SCM Press, 1979. Reprint: *The Aims of Jesus*, with an Introduction by N. T. Wright, Princeton Theological Monograph Series 48. Eugene, OR: Pickwick, 2002.

———. *Critical Realism and the New Testament*, Princeton Theological Monograph Series 17 (Allison Park, PA: Pickwick, 1989), 45–49.

———. "Jesus Christ." Pages 773–96 in *The Anchor Bible Dictionary*, vol. 1. Edited by David Noel Freedman, Gary A. Herion, David F. Graf, John David Pleins, and Astrid B. Beck. New York: Doubleday, 1992.

———. *Reality and Illusion in New Testament Scholarship*. Collegeville, MN: Michael Glazier, 1994. Reprint: Eugene, OR: Pickwick, 2016.

Moberly, R. W. L. *The God of the Old Testament*. Grand Rapids: Baker, 2020.

Moloney, Francis J. *The Gospel of John*. Sacra Pagina 4. Collegeville, MN: Liturgical Press, 1998.

Moo, Douglas J. *The Old Testament in the Gospel Passion Narratives*. Sheffield: Almond Press, 1983.

Morrice, William G. "The Imperatival ἵνα." *Bible Translator* 23 (1972): 326–30.

Morris, Leon. *The Epistle to the Romans*. Pillar New Testament Commentary. Leicester; Grand Rapids, MI: Apollos; Eerdmans, 1988.

Moule, C. F. D. *The Holy Spirit*. Mowbrays Library of Theology. London: Mowbrays, 1978.

Nardi, Carlo. "Laodicea (concili)." In *Nuovo Dizionario Patristico e di Antichità Cristiane*, edited by Angelo Di Berardino, 2735–2736. Rome: Marietti, 2008.

Nassif, Bradley. "Antiochene Θεωρία in John Chrysostom's Exegesis." In

Exegesis and Hermeneutics in the Churches of the East, edited by Vahan S. Hovhanessian, 51–66. New York: Peter Lang, 2009.

———. "Antiochene Theoria and Theological Interpretation of Scripture." In *The Oxford Handbook of the Bible in Orthodox Christianity*, edited by Eugen J. Pentiuc, 347–62. Oxford: Oxford University Press, 2022.

Nautin, Pierre. *Origène: sa œuvre et sa vie*. Paris: Beauchesne, 1977.

Niskanen, Paul. "The Poetics of Adam: The Creation of *Adam* in the Image of *Elohim*." *Journal of Biblical Literature* 128 (Fall 2009): 417–36.

Nolland, John. *Luke 1:1–9:20*. Word Biblical Commentary 35A. Dallas: Word, 1989.

———. "'In such a manner it is fitting for us to fulfil all righteousness': Reflections on the Place of Baptism in the Gospel of Matthew." In *Baptism, the New Testament and the Church: Historical and Contemporary Studies in Honour of R.E.O. White*, edited by Stanley E. Porter and Reginald E. O. White, 63–80. Journal for the Study of the New Testament Supplement Series 171. Sheffield: Sheffield Academic, 1999.

Norelli, Enrico. "Introduzione: La Bibbia come problema alle origini del cristianesimo." In *La Bibbia nell'antichità cristiana*, vol. 1, *Da Gesù a Origene*, edited by Enrico Norelli, 9–33, 199–233. Bologna: Edizioni Dehoniane Bologna, 1993.

Noth, Martin. *The Deuteronomistic History*. 2nd ed. Journal for the Study of the Old Testament Supplement Series 15. Translated by Jane Doull, John Barton, Michael D. Rutter, D. R. Ap-Thomas, and David J. A. Clines. Sheffield: JSOT Press, 1991. Originally published as part of *Überlieferungsgeschichtliche Studien*, vol. 1, *Die sammelnden und bearbeitenden Geschichtswerke im Alten Testament*, 2. unveränderte Auflage. Tübingen: M. Niemeyer, 1943, 1957.

Obermann, Andreas. *Die christologische Erfüllung der Schrift im Johannesevangelium: Eine Untersuchung zur johanneischen Hermeneutik anhand der Schriftzitate*. Wissenschaftliche Untersuchungen zum Neuen Testament 2.83. Tübingen: Mohr Siebeck, 1996.

Oestreich, Bernhard. "Die Taufe als Symbol für das eschatologische Gericht." In *Die Taufe: Theologie und Praxis*, edited by Roberto Badenas, 31–55. Studien zur Adventistischen Ekklesiologie 3. Lüneburg: Advent-Verlag, 2002.

Onuki, Takashi. *Gemeinde und Welt im Johannesevangelium: Ein Beitrag zur Frage nach der theologischen und pragmatischen Funktion des johanneischen "Dualismus."* Wissenschaftliche Monographien zum Alten und Neuen Testament 56. Neukirchen-Vluyn: Neukirchener, 1984.

Origen. *Commentariorum in Evangelium secundum Joannem*. PG 14:22–830.

———. *Contra Celsum*. In *Gegen Celsus Buch V–VIII*, edited by Paul Koetschau, 153–220. Griechischen christlichen Schriftsteller der ersten drei Jahrhunderte 3. J. C. Hinrichs'sche Buchhandlung, 1899.

———. *Contra Celsum*. Edited and translated by Henry Chadwick. Cambridge: Cambridge University Press, 1980.

———. *Homélies sur les psaumes 36 à 38*. Edited by Emanuela Prinzivalli, Henri Crouzel, and Luc Brésard. Sources Chrétiennes 411. Paris: Cerf, 1995.

———. *Homilies on Genesis and Exodus*. Translated by Ronald E. Heine. Fathers of the Church 71. Washington, DC: Catholic University of America Press, 1982.

———. *Homilies on the Psalms: Codex Monacensis Graecus 314*. Translated by Joseph W. Trigg. Fathers of the Church 9. Washington, DC: Catholic University of America Press, 2020.

———. *Die neuen Psalmenhomilien: eine kritische Edition des Codex Monacensis Graecus 314*. Edited by Lorenzo Perrone, Marina Molin Pradel, Emanuela Prinzivalli, and Antonio Cacciari. Griechischen christlichen Schriftsteller der ersten drei Jahrhunderte 19. *Origenes Werke* 13. Munich: De Gruyter, 2015.

———. *Philocalie, 1–20. Sur les Écritures; La Lettre à Africanus sur l'histoire de Suzanne*. Edited by Marguerite Harl. Sources Chrétiennes 302. Paris: Cerf, 1983.

———. *Philocalie, 21–27: Sur le libre arbitre*. Edited by Éric Junod. Sources Chrétiennes 226. Paris: Cerf, 2006.

———. *De principiis*. Translated by G. W. Butterworth, *On First Principles*. Notre Dame, IN: Ave Maria Press, 2013.

———. *De principiis*. Edited and translated by John Behr, *On First Principles: A Reader's Edition*. Oxford: Oxford University Press, 2019.

Origen. "Fragmenta." In *Origenes Werke*. Edited by Erich Klostermann. Griechischen christlichen Schriftsteller der ersten drei Jahrhunderte 41.1. Leipzig: J. C. Hinrichs, 1941.

Osborn, Eric. *Tertullian, First Theologian of the West*. Cambridge: Cambridge University Press, 2001.

Pagani, Isacco, *"Si compia la Scrittura": I rimandi al compimento della Scrittura pronunciati da Gesù in Gv 13–17*. Analecta Biblica Dissertationes 232. Rome: G&B Press, 2021.

Perdue, Leo G. *Reconstructing Old Testament Theology: After the Collapse of History*. Overtures to Biblical Theology. Minneapolis: Fortress, 2005.

Perhai, Richard J. *Antiochene Theoria in the Writings of Theodore of Mopsuestia and Theodoret of Cyrus*. Minneapolis: Fortress, 2015.

Petersen, Norman R. "Pauline Baptism and 'Secondary Burial'." *Harvard Theological Review* 79, nos. 1–3 (1986): 217–26.
Philo of Alexandria. *De plantatione.* Translated by F. H. Colson and G. H. Whitaker. Loeb Classical Library 247. Cambridge, MA: Harvard University Press, 1930.
Philoxenus. *Fragments of the Commentary on Matthew and Luke.* Edited and translated by J. W. Watt. Corpus Scriptorum Christianorum Orientalium 393. Louvain: Corpusco, 1978.
Pidel, Aaron. "*Christi Opera Proficiunt:* Ratzinger's Neo-Bonaventurian Model of Social Inspiration." *Nova et Vetera English Edition* 13 (2015): 693–711.
———. *The Inspiration and Truth of Scripture: Testing the Ratzinger Paradigm.* Verbum Domini 4. Washington, DC: Catholic University of America Press, 2023.
Pius XII, Pope. Encyclical On Promoting Biblical Studies *Divino afflante Spiritu.* September 30, 1943. Washington, DC: National Catholic Welfare Conference, 1943.
Pliny the Younger. *Lettres. Livre X. Panégyrique de Trajan.* Edited by Marcel Durry. Paris: Les Belles Lettres, 1959.
Pontifical Biblical Commission. *The Interpretation of the Bible in the Church.* April 15, 1993. Rome: Libreria Editrice Vaticana, 1993.
Porter, Stanley E., and Reginald E. O. White, eds. *Baptism, the New Testament and the Church: Historical and Contemporary Studies in Honour of R.E.O. White.* Journal for the Study of the New Testament Supplement Series 171. Sheffield: Sheffield Academic, 1999.
Priotto, Michelangelo, *Esodo: nuova versione, introduzione e commento.* I libri biblici, Primo Testamento 2. Milan: Paoline, 2014.
Quinn, Jerome D., and William C. Wacker. *The First and Second Letters to Timothy.* Eerdmans Critical Commentary. Grand Rapids, MI: Eerdmans, 2000.
Rabens, Volker. *The Holy Spirit and Ethics in Paul: Transformation and Empowering for Religious-Ethical Life.* Wissenschaftliche Untersuchungen zum Neuen Testament 283. Tübingen: Mohr Siebeck, 2010.
Ratzinger, Joseph / Pope Benedict XVI. *From the Baptism in the Jordan to the Transfiguration.* Vol. 2 of *Jesus of Nazareth.* New York: Doubleday, 2007.
Ratzinger, Joseph. "Die Bedeutung der Väter für die Gegenwärtige Theologie." *Tübinger Theologische Quartalschrift* 148 (1968): 257–82.
———. *Behold the Pierced One: An Approach to a Spiritual Christology.* San Francisco: Ignatius, 1986.

———. "The Question of the Concept of Tradition: A Provisional Response." 41–89 in *God's Word: Scripture, Tradition, Office*. Edited by Peter Hünermann and Thomas Söding. Translated by Henry Taylor. San Francisco: Ignatius, 2008.

———. *Introduction to Christianity*. Translated by J. R. Foster. 2nd edition. San Francisco: Ignatius, 2004.

———. *Milestones: Memoirs 1927–1977*. Translated by Erasmo Leiva-Merikakis. San Francisco: Ignatius, 1998.

———. *Principles of Catholic Theology: Building Stones for a Fundamental Theology*. San Francisco: Ignatius, 1987.

———. *Truth and Tolerance: Christian Belief and World Religions*. San Francisco: Ignatius, 2004.

Reim, Günter. *Studien zum alttestamentliche Hintergrund des Johannesevangeliums*. Society for New Testament Studies Monograph Series 22. Cambridge: Cambridge University Press, 1974.

Reuss, Joseph, ed. *Matthäus-Kommentare aus der griechischen Kirche*. Berlin: Akademie-Verlag, 1957.

Ricoeur, Paul. *Das Rätsel der Vergangenheit: Erinnern—Vergessen—Verzeihen*. Essener Kulturwissenschaftliche Vorträge 2. Göttingen: Wallstein, 1998.

Risch, Franz X. "Das Handbuch des Origenes zu den Psalmen: Zur Bedeutung der zweiten Randkatene im Codex Vindobonensis theologicus graecus 8." *Adamantius* 20 (2014): 36–48.

Robbins, Vernon K. "Divine Dialogue and the Lord's Prayer: Socio-Rhetorical Interpretation of Sacred Texts." *Dialogue* 28, no. 3 (1995): 117–46.

Robinson, Henry Wheeler. *Corporate Personality in Ancient Israel*. 2nd edition. Edinburgh: T. & T. Clark, 1981 [original publication: 1936].

Robinson, James M. *A New Quest for the Historical Jesus*. Studies in Biblical Theology 43. London: SCM Press, 1959.

Romeny, R. B. ter Haar. "Early Antiochene Commentaries on Exodus." In *Studia Patristica* 30, edited by Elizabeth A. Livingstone, 114–15. Peeters: Leuven, 1997.

Römer, Thomas. *The So-called Deuteronomistic History: A Sociological, Historical, and Literary Introduction*. London: T&T Clark, 2007.

Römer, Thomas, and Albert de Pury. "Deuteronomistic Historiography: History of Research and Related Issues." In *Israel Constructs Its History: Deuteronomistic Historiography in Recent Research*, 24–139. English Language edition. Journal for the Study of the Old Testament Supplement Series 306. Edited by Albert de Pury, Thomas Römer, and Jean-Daniel Macchi. Sheffield: Sheffield Academic, 2000.

Rondeau, Marie-Josèphe. *Les commentaires patristiques du Psautier (IIIe-Ve siècles)*. 2 vols. Rome: Pontificium Istitutum Studiorum Orientalium, 1985.

———. "Exégèse du Psautier et anabase spirituelle chez Grégorie de Nysse." In *Epektasis: Mélanges patristiques offerts au Cardinal Jean Daniélou*, edited by Jacques Fontaine and Charles Kannengiesser, 517–31. Paris: Beauchesne, 1972.

———. "D'où vient la technique exégétique utilisée par Grégoire de Nysse dans son traité 'Sur les titres des Psaumes'?." In *Mélanges d'histoire des religions offerts à Henri-Charles Puech*, 263–87. Paris: Presses Universitaire de France, 1974.

Rose, Martin. "Deuteronomistic Ideology and Theology of the Old Testament." In *Israel Constructs Its History: Deuteronomistic Historiography in Recent Research*, 424–55. Journal for the Study of the Old Testament Supplement Series 306. Edited by Albert De Pury, Thomas Römer, and Jean-Daniel Macchi. Sheffield: Sheffield Academic, 2000.

Rowley, H. H. *The Servant of the Lord: and Other Essays on the Old Testament*. 2nd edition, revised. Oxford: Blackwell, 1965.

Ruckstuhl, Eugen, and Peter Dschulnigg. *Stilkritik und Vervasserfrage im Johannesevangelium. Die johanneischen Sprachmerkmale auf dem Hintergrund des Neuen Testaments und des zeitgenössischen hellenistischen Schrifttums*. Novum Testamentum et Orbis Antiquus 17. Göttingen: Universitätsverlag, 1991.

Runesson, Anna. *Exegesis in the Making: Postcolonialism and New Testament Studies*. Leiden: Brill, 2011.

Runia, David T. "Philo's Reading of the Psalms." In *The Studia Philonica Annual: Studies in Hellenistic Judaism. Volume XIII 2001*, edited by David T. Runia and Gregory E. Sterling, 102–21. Providence, RI: Brown Judaic Studies, 2001.

Salkin, Jeffrey. "Hey, New York Times—Leave My God Alone!" religionnews.com, Religion News Service. April 18, 2022. https://religionnews.com/2022/04/18/times-auslander-god/.

Sánchez-Navarro, Luis. "The Ecclesial Reading of Scripture." 72–86 in *In the School of the Word: Biblical Interpretation from the New to the Old Testament*. By Carlos Granados and Luis Sánchez-Navarro. Translated by Kristin Towle. With an introduction to the English edition by Kevin Zilverberg. Catholic Theological Formation Series. Saint Paul, MN: Saint Paul Seminary Press, 2021.

———. "The Inspiration and Truth of Scripture: Do They Still Matter?" 7–21 in *The Word of Truth, Sealed by the Spirit*. Edited by Matthew C. Genung and Kevin Zilverberg. Catholic Theological Formation Series. St. Paul, MN: Saint Paul Seminary Press, 2022.

———. "The Testimonial Character of Sacred Scripture." 17–31 in *In the School of the Word: Biblical Interpretation from the New to the Old Testament*. By Carlos Granados and Luis Sánchez-Navarro. Translated by Kristin Towle. With an introduction to the English edition by Kevin Zilverberg. Catholic Theological Formation Series. Saint Paul, MN: Saint Paul Seminary Press, 2021.

———. *Un cuerpo pleno: Cristo y la personalidad corporativa en la Escritura*. Studia Bíblica Matritensia 4. Madrid: Universidad San Dámaso, 2021.

Sanders, Ed P. *Jesus and Judaism*. London: SCM Press, 1985.

Sargent, Benjamin. "'Interpreting Homer from Homer': Aristarchus of Samothrace and the Notion of Scriptural Authorship in the New Testament." *Tyndale Bulletin* 65, no. 1 (2014): 125–39.

Schenke, Ludger. *Die Urgemeinde: Geschichtliche und theologische Entwicklung*. Stuttgart: Kohlhammer, 1990.

Schmid, Josef. *Studien zur Geschichte des griechischen Apokalypse-Textes*. München: Karl Zink, 1955–1956.

Schmid, Konrad. *Is There Theology in the Hebrew Bible?* Critical Studies in the Hebrew Bible 4. Translated by Peter Altmann. Winona Lake, IN: Eisenbrauns, 2015.

Schmid, Konrad, and Jens Schröter. *The Making of the Bible: From the First Fragments to Sacred Scripture*. Translated by Peter Lewis. Cambridge, MA: Belknap Press of Harvard University Press, 2021.

Schnackenburg, Rudolf. *Das Johannesevangelium*, vol. 3, *Kommentar zu Kap. 13–21*. Herders theologischer Kommentar zum Neuen Testament 4.3. Freiburg: Herder, 1976.

Schreiner, Thomas R. *Romans*. Baker Exegetical Commentary on the New Testament 6. Grand Rapids, MI: Baker, 1998.

Schuchard, Bruce G. *Scripture within Scripture: The Interrelationship of Form and Function in the Explicit Old Testament Citations in the Gospel of John*. Society of Biblical Literature Dissertation Series 133. Atlanta: Scholars Press, 1992.

Scott, James M. *Adoption as Sons of God: An Exegetical Investigation into the Background of Huiothesia in the Pauline Corpus*. Wissenschaftliche Untersuchungen zum Neuen Testament 48. Tübingen: Mohr Siebeck, 1992.

Seewald, Peter. *Benedict XVI: A Life*. Vol. 1, *Youth in Nazi Germany to the Second Vatican Council 1927–1965*. Translated by Dinah Livingstone. London: Bloomsbury, 2020.

Segalla, Giuseppe. "La memoria storica di Gesù in Giovanni 6: fra storia e teologia." *Annali di Scienze Religiose* 9 (2004): 213–24.

Segovia, Fernando F. *Decolonizing Biblical Studies: A View from the Margins.* Maryknoll, NY: Orbis, 2000.

Seisdedos, Francisco A. "La 'teōria' antioquena." *Estudios Bíblicos* 11 (1952): 31–67.

Silva, Moisés. "The Greek Psalter in Paul's Letters: A Textual Study." In *The Old Greek Psalter*, edited by Robert J. V. Hiebert, Claude E. Cox, and Peter J. Gentry, 277–88. Sheffield: Sheffield Academic, 2001.

Simonetti, Manlio. *Biblical Interpretation in the Early Church: An Historical Introduction to Patristic Exegesis.* Translated by John A. Hughes. Edited by Anders Bergquist and Markus Bockmuehl. Edinburgh: T&T Clark, 1994.

———. "Exegesis, Patristic." Pages 897–903 in *Encyclopedia of Ancient Christianity*, vol. 1. Edited by Angelo Di Berardino. Downers Grove, IL: IVP Academic, 2014.

———. *Matthew 1–13*. Ancient Christian Commentary on Scripture. Downers Grove, IL: InterVarsity Press, 2001.

———. "I 'Salmi' nel Nuovo Testamento." *Orpheus* 9, no. 1 (1988): 1–20.

Slade, Darren M. "Patristic Exegesis: The Myth of the Alexandrian-Antiochene Schools of Interpretation." *Socio-Historical Examination of Religioun and Ministry* 1, no. 2 (2019): 155–76.

Soggin, J. Alberto. *Introduction to the Old Testament: From Its Origins to the Closing of the Alexandrian Canon.* Revised edition. Translated by John Bowden. Old Testament Library. Philadelphia: Westminster, 1980.

Sonnet, Jean-Pierre. "God's Repentance and 'False Starts' in Biblical History (Genesis 6–9; Exodus 32–34; 1 Samuel 15 and 2 Samuel 70)." *Vetus Testamentum Supplements* 133 (2010): 469–94.

Sproston, Wendy E. "'The Scripture' in John 17:12." In *Scripture: Meaning and Method. Essay Presented to Anthony Tyrrell Hanson for his Seventieth Birthday*, edited by Barry P. Thompson, 24–36. Hull: University Press, 1987.

Stein, Robert H. *Mark.* Baker Exegetical Commentary on the New Testament. Grand Rapids, MI: Baker Academic, 2008.

Taylor, Joan E. *The Immerser: John the Baptist Within Second Temple Judaism.* Studying the Historical Jesus. Grand Rapids, MI: Eerdmans, 1997.

Ternant, Paul. "La 'theōria' d'Antioche dans le cadre des sens de l'Écriture [Part I]." *Biblica* 34 (1953): 135–58.

———. "La 'theōria' d'Antioche dans le cadre des sens de l'Écriture [Part II]." *Biblica* 34 (1953): 354–83

———. "La 'theōria' d'Antioche dans le cadre des sens de l'Écriture [Part III]." *Biblica* 34 (1953): 456–86.

BIBLIOGRAPHY

Tertullian. *Adversus Praxean*. In *Quinti Septimi Florentis Tertulliani Opera*, Pars 2, edited by Aemilius Kroymann and Ernest Evans, 1159–1205. Corpus Christianorum, Series Latina 2. Turnholt: Brepols, 1954.

———. *De anima*. In *Quinti Septimi Florentis Tertulliani Opera*, Pars 2, edited by Jan. H. Waszink, 779–869. Corpus Christianorum, Series Latina 2. Turnholt: Brepols, 1954.

———. *De carne Christi*. In *Quinti Septimi Florentis Tertulliani Opera*, Pars 2, edited by Aemilius Kroymann, 871–917. Corpus Christianorum, Series Latina 2. Turnholt: Brepols, 1954.

———. *De oratione*. In *Quinti Septimi Florentis Tertulliani Opera*, Pars 1, edited by Gerardus F. Diercks, 255–74. Corpus Christianorum, Series Latina 1. Turnholt: Brepols, 1954.

Theissen, Gerd. "'Evangelium' im Markusevangelium: Zum Traditionsgeschichtlichen Ort des Ältesten Evangeliums." In *Mark and Paul: Comparative Essays Part II. For and Against Pauline Influence on Mark*, edited by Eve-Marie Becker, Troels Engberg-Pedersen, and Mogens Müller, 63–86. Beihefte zur Zeitschrift für die neutestamentliche Wissenschaft und die Kunde der älteren Kirche 199. Berlin: De Gruyter, 2014.

Theodore of Mopsuestia. *Commentarius in Evangelium Iohannis Apostoli*. Translated and edited by J.-M. Vosté. Corpus Scriptorum Christianorum Orientalium. Louven: Ex Officina Orientali, 1940.

———. *Commentary of Theodore of Mopsuestia on the Lord's Prayer and on the Sacraments of Baptism and the Eucharist*. Edited by Alphonse Mingana. Cambridge: Heffer, 1935.

———. *In Jobum*. PG 66:697–98.

Theodoret of Cyrus. *Commentary on the Psalms, 1–72*. Translated by Robert C. Hill. Fathers of the Church 101. Washington, DC: Catholic University of America Press, 2000.

———. *Commentary on the Psalms, 73–150*, translated by Robert C. Hill, 18–21. Fathers of the Church 101. Washington, DC: Catholic University of America Press, 2001.

———. *The Questions on the Octateuch*, vol. 1, *On Genesis and Exodus*. Translated by Robert C. Hill. Library of Early Christianity 1. Washington, DC: Catholic University of America Press, 2007.

Thomas Aquinas. *The Literal Exposition on Job*. Translated by Anthony Damico. Atlanta: Scholars Press, 1989.

Torjesen, Karen Jo. *Hermeneutical Procedure and Theological Method in Origen's Exegesis*. Berlin: De Gruyter, 1985.

Trigg, Joseph W. *Biblical Interpretation*. Message of the Fathers of the Church 9. Wilmington, DE: Michael Glazier, 1988.

---. "Introduction." In *Homilies on the Psalms: Codex Monacensis Graecus 314*, translated by Joseph W. Trigg, 3–33. Fathers of the Church 9. Washington, DC: Catholic University of America Press, 2020

Turner, David L. *Matthew*. Baker Exegetical Commentary on the New Testament. Grand Rapids, MI: Baker Academic, 2008.

Turner, Nigel. *Grammatical Insights into the New Testament*. Edinburgh: T&T Clark, 1965.

Vanhoye, Albert Cardinal. "The Reception in the Church of the Dogmatic Constitution 'Dei Verbum'." In *Opening up the Scriptures: Joseph Ratzinger and the Foundations of Biblical Interpretation*, edited by José Granados, Carlos Granados and Luis Sánchez-Navarro, 104–25. Grand Rapids, MI: Eerdmans, 2008.

Veijola, Timo. *Das Königtum in der Beurteilung der deuteronomistischen Historiographie: eine redaktionsgeschichtliche Untersuchung*. Annales Academiae Scientiarum Fennicae B 198. Helsinki: Suomalainen Tiedeakatemia, 1977.

Venter, Dirk J. "The Implicit Obligations of Brothers, Debtors and Sons (Romans 8:12–17)." *Neotestamentica* 48, no. 2 (2014): 283–302.

Vermes, Geza. *The Dead Sea Scrolls in English*. 4th edition. Sheffield: Sheffield Academic, 1995.

Von Rad, Gerhard. *Old Testament Theology*, vol. 1, *The Theology of Israel's Historical Traditions*. Translated by D. M. G. Stalker. New York: Harper and Row, 1962.

Wahlde, Urban C. von. "Judas, the Son of Perdition, and the Fulfillment of Scripture in John 17:12." In *The New Testament and Early Christian Literature in Greco-Roman Context. Studies in Honor of David E. Aune*, edited by John Fotopoulos, 167–81. New Testament Studies 122. Leiden: Brill, 2006.

Waltke, Bruce K., and James M. Houston. *The Psalms as Christian Worship: A Historical Commentary*. Grand Rapids, MI: Eerdmans, 2010.

Webb, Robert L. "Jesus' Baptism: Its Historicity and Implications." *Bulletin for Biblical Research* 10, no. 2 (2000): 261–309.

---. *John the Baptizer and Prophet: A Socio-Historical Study*. Journal for the Study of the New Testament Supplement Series 62. Sheffield: JSOT Press, 1991.

Weinfeld, Moshe. *Deuteronomy and the Deuteronomic School*. Winona Lake, IN: Eisenbrauns, 1992.

Wengst, Klaus. *Das Johannesevangelium*, vol. 2, *Kapitel 11–21*. Theologischer Kommentar zum Neuen Testament 4b. Stuttgart: Kohlhammer, 2001.

Wenham, David. *Paul: Follower of Jesus or Founder of Christianity?* Grand Rapids, MI: Eerdmans, 1995.

White, Thomas Joseph. *Exodus*. Brazos Theological Commentary on the Bible. Grand Rapids, MI: Brazos, 2016.

Wilken, Robert L. "Cyril of Alexandria as Interpreter of the Old Testament." In *Theology of Cyril of Alexandria: A Critical Appreciation*, edited by Thomas G. Weinandy and Daniel A. Keating, 1–21. London: T&T Clark, 2003.

Williamson, Peter S. *Catholic Principles for Interpreting Scripture: A Study of the Pontifical Biblical Commission's* The Interpretation of the Bible in the Church. Rome: Pontifical Biblical Institute, 2001.

Wischmeyer, Oda. "Hermeneutische Aspekte der Taufe im Neuen Testament." In *Ablution, Initiation, and Baptism: Late Antiquity, Early Judaism, and Early Christianity*, edited by David Hellholm, Tor Vegge, Øyvind Norderval, and Christer Hellholm, 735–63. Beihefte zur Zeitschrift für die neutestamentliche Wissenschaft und die Kunde der älteren Kirche 176. Berlin: De Gruyter, 2011.

Young, Frances M. "Alexandrian and Antiochene Exegesis." In *A History of Biblical Interpretation*, vol. 1, *The Ancient Period*, edited by Alan J. Hauser and Duance F. Watson, 334–54. Grand Rapids, MI: Eerdmans, 2003.

———. *Biblical Exegesis and the Formation of Christian Culture*. Cambridge: Cambridge University Press, 1997.

and wanted to Zilverberg, Kevin. "Daniel Reinterprets Jeremiah's 'Seventy Years': A Biblical Interpretive Trajectory up to the Present Day." Archbishop Ireland Memorial Library Lecture, University of St. Thomas, St. Paul, MN. April 25, 2022.

Zumstein, Jean. "La dynamique du souvenir: À propos de la conception johannique du temps." In *La mémoire revisitée: Études johanniques*, edited by Jean Zumstein, 485–98. Monde de la bible (Paris) 71. Geneva: Labor et Fides, 2017.

———. "Ein gewachsenes Evangelium: Der Relecture-Prozess bei Johannes." In *Johannesevangelium – Mitte oder Rand des Kanons? Neue Standortbestimmungen*, edited by Thomas Söding, 9–37. Quaestiones Disputatae 203. Freiburg: Herder, 2003.

———. "Der Prozess der Relecture in der johanneischen Literatur." In *Kreative Erinnerung. Relecture und Auslegung im Johannesevangelium*, edited by Jean Zumstein, 15–30. Abhandlungen zur Theologie des Alten und Neuen Testaments 84. Zürich: Theologischer Verlag 2004.

———. "Die verklärte Vergangenheit: Geschichte *sub specie aeternitatis* nach Johannes 17." In *Kreative Erinnerung: Relecture und Auslegung im Johannesevangelium*, edited by Jean Zumstein, 207–17. *Abhandlungen zur Theologie des Alten und Neuen Testaments* 84. Zürich: Theologischer Verlag, 2004.

Contributors

JOSEPH BRIODY is a priest of the Diocese of Raphoe (Donegal, Ireland). Ordained in 1995, his further studies include the STL (Saint Patrick's College, Maynooth), the SSL (Pontifical Biblical Institute, Rome), and the STD (Boston College, School of Theology and Ministry). In 2013, after years of pastoral ministry in parishes and schools in Donegal, he joined the faculty of Saint John's Seminary, Brighton, Massachusetts. He served as seminary Director of Sacred Liturgy and formation advisor. He collaborated in various ways in the work of liturgical translation, as assistant to the Vox Clara Committee (English language) and the Sapienti Committee (Irish language). He currently serves as Director of Spiritual Formation and Professor of Sacred Scripture at Saint John's Seminary.

MAURIZIO GIROLAMI is a Catholic priest of the Diocese of Concordia-Pordenone and professor of New Testament Exegesis and Patrology at the Theological Faculty of Triveneto, where he is Vice Dean and Director of the Library. Since 2023 he has been Vice President of the Italian Biblical Association. He is also a visiting professor at the Studium Biblicum Franciscanum in Jerusalem and at the Ecumenical Institute in Venice. His publications include *La ricezione del Salmo 21 (LXX) nei primi secoli dell'era cristiana: Cristologia ed ermeneutica biblica in costruzione* (Rome, 2011); the edited presentation of the Pastoral Epistles in the volume, with A. Martin and C. Broccardo, *Edificare sul fondamento: Introduzione alle lettere deuteropaoline e alle lettere cattoliche non giovannee* (Turin, 2015); *Le prime vie per seguire Gesù: Introduzione alla patrologia (I-III secolo)* (Padua, 2021); and *Il giorno degli inizi: Un percorso biblico e storico per riscoprire la domenica* (Milan, 2022).

FR. MARCIN KOWALSKI is a member of the Pontifical Biblical Commission. He studied at the Pontifical Biblical Institute in Rome (SSL and SSD), receiving a *doctor habilitatus* in theology. He is a director of the Abraham Joshua Heschel

Center for Catholic–Jewish Relations and assisting professor at the John Paul II Catholic University of Lublin (KUL). He is also a Lecturer at the Institute of Biblical Studies KUL, visiting professor at the Pontifical Urbaniana University, and the New Testament Editor of the biblical quarterly *The Biblical Annals*. His scientific interests comprise the letters of Paul, ancient rhetoric, socio-rhetorical approach, sociology and anthropology of culture, and the Bible in culture. He is the author of *Transforming Boasting of Self into Boasting in the Lord* (Lanham, MD: University Press of America, 2013), *2 Corinthians: A Commentary* (Katowice: Jacek, 2018), *Tomorrow is Sunday: Years A–B–C* and *Tomorrow Is a Feast* (Krakow: Stacja7, 2019–2022), and *The Spirit in Romans 8: Paul, the Stoics, and Jewish Authors in Dialog* (Göttingen: Vandenhoeck & Ruprecht, 2023).

Hryhoriy Lozinskyy, SSD, is a priest of the Eparchy of Mukacevo (Ukraine) and Adjunct Professor of Sacred Scripture at the Byzantine Catholic Seminary of Saints Cyril and Methodius, Pittsburgh, Pennsylvania. He is author of *The Feasts of the Calendar in the Book of Numbers: Num 28:16–30:1 in the Light of Related Biblical Texts and Some Ancient Sources of 200 BCE–100 CE* (Tübingen: Mohr Siebeck, 2022) and other publications on the Pentateuch.

Juana L. Manzo is Associate Professor of Scripture and Coordinator of the Spanish Master of Arts in Pastoral Ministry Collaborative Program between Mexican American Catholic College and University of Incarnate Word in San Antonio since 2023. She is authoring the book of Ben Sira for the Wisdom Commentary Series. She has published "Feeding the Poor in Isaiah 58:1–9a: A Call to Justice, Mercy and True Worship" and "The Memory of Mary's Mission According to Guadalupan Sermons." She was Professor of Scripture for twelve years at the St. Mary's Seminary in Houston. She earned a PhD from the Catholic University of America, an STL and STB from the Gregorian University, and an MA and BA from the University of St. Thomas in Houston.

John W. Martens, PhD, is professor of theology and director of the Centre for Christian Engagement at St. Mark's College, the affiliated Catholic College at the University of British Columbia, in Vancouver, British Columbia. He has written extensively on children in early Christianity and Judaism, including *"Let the Little Children Come to Me": Childhood and Children in Early Christianity* (CUA Press, 2009) with Cornelia Horn, and *Children and Methods: Listening To and Learning From Children in the Biblical World* (Brill, 2020) with Kristine Henriksen Garroway. He is a general editor of the newly published *Liturgy and Life Study Bible* (Collegeville: Liturgical Press, 2023).

PAUL V. NISKANEN, PhD, is Professor of Theology at the University of St. Thomas in St. Paul, Minnesota. He is the author of *Isaiah 56–66* in the Berit Olam series (Collegeville: Liturgical Press, 2014) and co-author of the forthcoming volume on Isaiah in the Catholic Commentary on Sacred Scripture series (Baker Academic).

ISACCO PAGANI is a priest of the Archdiocese of Milan (Italy) and holds a doctorate in Sacred Scripture from the Pontifical Biblical Institute in Rome. He is currently Assistant Professor of Biblical Greek and New Testament (Gospel and Johannine Literature) at the Diocesan Seminary and the Theological Faculty of Northern Italy. He is also Rector of Philosophy at the Diocesan Seminary of Milan and a member of the Italian Biblical Association (ABI), the Italian Biblical Society (SBI), and the Lorenzo Valla Foundation. In addition to scientific and informative articles, he has published his doctoral thesis *"Si compia la Scrittura": I rimandi al compimento della Scrittura pronunciati da Gesù in Gv 13–17* (Rome: G&B Press, 2021), and he is one of the reviewers of the Italian Revised Ecumenical Literary Translation (TLER) of the New Testament.

FR. LUIS SÁNCHEZ-NAVARRO holds an SSD from the Pontifical Biblical Institute (Rome) and also a doctorate in Greek philology from Complutense University (Madrid, Spain). He is Professor of New Testament at the Ecclesiastical University of San Dámaso (Madrid). Among his other publications, in Spanish, but also in English and Italian, he was co-editor of *Opening Up the Scriptures: Joseph Ratzinger and the Foundations of Biblical Interpretation* (Eerdmans, 2008), and has recently co-authored with Carlos Granados *In the School of the Word: Biblical Interpretation from the New to the Old Testament* (St. Paul Seminary Press, 2021). He is also the author of *A Light for the Nations: The Scriptures on the Universal Mission of Israel and the Church* (CUA Press: forthcoming).

Index of Names and Subjects

Abraham, 43n27, 60, 121
Adam, 41, 88, 130, 131n79, 155n31
Alexandria, school of. *See* Antioch and Alexandria
allegory/allegorical sense. *See also* typology
   in Alexandrian exegesis, 25–28, 40–42, 63, 65, 115
   in Antiochene exegesis, 14, 115n4
   distinct from typology, 55n4
   in Origen's exegesis, 14, 26–27, 40–41, 57, 101–3, 105
   in patristic exegesis of Exod 2:11–22, 63, 65
   in patristic exegesis of the Pentateuch, 54–55, 68
Alleluia psalms, 84, 89n57
Alpha and Omega, 16
Ambrose, 83
Annunciation, 48
Antioch and Alexandria
   SCHOOL OF ALEXANDRIA
      Antioch reacted against, 28–29, 41, 107–8
      better known than Antioch, 69
      exegesis of Exodus 2:11–22, 62–66
      exegesis of John 13–17, 153–65
      exegesis of the Pentateuch, 54–55, 62–66, 68–70
      exegetical principles of, 25–28, 40–42, 63, 65, 100, 113, 115, 115n4
      in historical context of city of Alexandria, 66
   SCHOOL OF ANTIOCH
      exegesis of Exodus 2:11–22, 59–62
      exegesis of John 13–17, 153–65
      exegesis of the Pentateuch, 54–55, 59–62, 68–70
      exegetical principles of, 14, 29–31, 57, 100, 107–8, 113, 115n4
      less well known than Alexandria, 69
      major representatives of, 14
      parallels with modern historical criticism, 1, 30, 115–16, 141
      reacted against Alexandria, 28–29, 41, 107–8
      theoria, 30, 60, 60n23, 69, 108
   SYNTHESIS OF
      challenges to sharp distinction between, 57
      in exegesis of Jesus's baptism, 115–16, 141–43
      in exegesis of John 13–17, 153–65
      Meyer on, 1–2, 3, 5, 7, 55, 56, 114–15, 141
      and polyvalence of the literal sense, 24–25, 31–37
Antiochus IV (king), 27
Apollinaris of Laodicea, 83
Aquinas, 3, 24–25, 32, 33, 35n29
Aristarchus of Samothrace, 80
Arius/Arianism, 17n14, 66

INDEX OF NAMES AND SUBJECTS

Asaph, psalms attributed to, 84, 87, 89n57
Asterious of Scythopolis, 83
Athanasius, 17n14, 84, 90–91, 92n65, 96, 97
Augustine, 80n32, 92, 93–94, 95n68, 97–98

Bandt, Cordula, 85, 88
baptism of Jesus
   historical-critical interpretation of, 116–25, 126, 132, 141
   historical-theological interpretation of, 125–32, 142
   patristic exegesis of, 122, 126–28, 129, 130, 135–36, 141–42
   Paul on the relation between Jesus's baptism and Christian baptism, 132–41, 142–43
   and synthesis of Antioch and Alexandria, 115–16, 141–43
   unjustifiably separated from the theophany, 123–25
Bardaisan, 82
Basil, 94, 96
Beasley-Murray, George R., 126, 133–35, 139n107
Benedict XVI (pope) (Joseph Ratzinger), 17–18, 19, 21, 39n5, 52, 114n3
Biblical Theology movement, 42–44
Brueggemann, Walter, 38–39
Bultmann, Rudolf, 43, 117, 132
Byzantine liturgy, 56, 66–67

canonical criticism, 96, 116, 125n50
catenae, 83
Childs, Brevard
   and canonical criticism, 96
   contemporaries of, 53
   division of Exod 2:11–22, 58n16
   on the task of the Christian interpreter, 43–44
   on typology, 41, 50, 51, 52
Christ. *See* Jesus Christ

Chromatius of Aquileia, 126–27, 136
Chrysostom. *See* John Chrysostom
Church
   ecclesial/communal dimension of inspiration and interpretation, 17–22
   in exegesis of Ps 75[74], 104, 105, 112
   Scripture witnesses to, 19–20
   Zipporah as type of, 62, 65
Clement of Alexandria, 56, 62–63, 88, 92n65
Codex Alexandrinus, 84
continuity *vs.* discontinuity, hermeneutics of, 10
covenant, 45, 46, 47, 137
Cyril of Alexandria
   on baptism, 127, 135n92
   exegesis of Exod 2:11–22, 56, 63–66, 67, 68
   exegesis of John 13–17, 155n31, 155–56, 157–58, 160

David
   idealized in Deuteronomistic History, 39, 48, 49–53
   psalms attributed to, 75–76, 78, 79, 84, 87, 89nn57–58, 95, 96, 98
Dead Sea Scrolls, 74–75
Demetrius III (Seleucid king), 27
Deuteronomistic History, 39–40, 44–53
Didymus the Blind, 72n4, 83, 90n61
Diodorus of Tarsus, 14, 95, 108
Divino afflante Spiritu. *See* Pius XII (pope)
Duhm, Bernhard, 42n21, 47
Dunn, James D. G., 119, 121–23, 125n50, 126n52, 130, 131n79, 132–34, 138n105, 140n112

Enlightenment, 4, 6, 10, 25, 29, 41
Ephrem the Syrian, 128, 131, 135
Epiphanius of Salamis, 85, 85n49, 101
Eusebius of Caesarea

Index of Names and Subjects

on Origen's works, 72, 85
on the psalms, 75n18, 82–85, 88–90, 91n62, 92n65, 93, 95, 96, 99
Eusebius of Emesa, 59n21, 68
Eusebius of Vercelli, 83
Eustathius of Antioch, 95n68, 107
Evagrius of Pontus, 94
Exodus 2:11–22
  Alexandrian interpretation of, 62–66
  Antiochene interpretation of, 59–62
  in the Byzantine liturgical tradition, 66–67
  context in the biblical text, 57–59
Ezra, 87, 90, 119

Father, 118, 119, 122, 124, 127–32, 138–39, 141–42. *See also* Trinity
filiation. *See* sonship, divine
Former Prophets, 46, 50
Formgeschichte, 116, 123
fulfillment of Scripture in John 13–17
  anticipates the disciples' post-Easter life, 151–53, 158–65
  in Antiochene and Alexandrian exegesis, 153–65
  and the disciples' human freedom, 156–58
  Jesus's manner of speaking about, in contrast to the narrator's, 146–49, 162
  Jesus's predictive knowledge of, 153–56
  Jesus's statements of, 149–53, 162
  suitability as case study, 145–46

Garden of Eden, 26, 27, 30
Genesis, book of. *See also* Index of Scripture References
  in Byzantine liturgical cycle, 67
  literal sense of Garden of Eden, 26, 27, 30
  literal sense of the "image of God," 31–33

patristic authors interpreted without reference to surrounding cultures, 42n19
Gershom, 58n18, 59, 65
glory, 116, 128, 136, 139, 141–42
Gnosticism, 14, 82
Gögel, Rolf, 102
Good Samaritan, 27, 35
goodwill, 2, 5, 6
Gregory of Nyssa, 91–93, 94, 95, 96, 97
Gruber, Winfried, 102

Hades, 64, 67
Harnack, Adolf von, 27
Hexapla, 72, 85
Hezekiah (king), 49
Hilary of Poitiers, 83, 87n50, 88n54, 88n55, 92, 92n64, 93n66, 94, 97, 135, 136
Hippolytus, 83
historical criticism. *See also* Antioch and Alexandria; literal sense
  and Biblical Theology movement, 43
  historical maximalism of contemporary conservative commentators, 29n8
  historical-critical interpretation of Jesus's baptism, 116–25, 126, 132, 141
  historical-theological interpretation of Jesus's baptism, 125–32, 142
  Meyer's critique of, 114
  not sufficient to deal with questions of faith, 2
  parallels between school of Antioch and modern criticism, 1, 30, 115–16, 141
  and patristic interpretations of the psalms, 96
Holy Saturday, 64
Holy Spirit. *See also* Trinity
  and baptism of Christians, 134, 135–39, 142

199

INDEX OF NAMES AND SUBJECTS

and baptism of Jesus, 118, 121, 122, 124, 125, 127–39, 142
in patristic exegesis of John 13–17, 161, 162, 164, 165
role in Origen's exegesis, 102
Holy Week, 66–67
Homer, commentaries on, 71, 80, 83n38, 96

image of God (Gen 1:27), 31–33
inspiration
"bipartite" and "tripartite" models of, 21–22
ecclesial/communal dimension of, 17–22
intended sense. *See also* literal sense
and Antiochene *theoria*, 30
Meyer on, 3, 4, 24, 26, 30
polyvalence of, in the Old Testament, 25–37
similarity to Aquinas's definition of the literal sense, 24–25, 35n29
interpretation
"bipartite" and "tripartite" models of, 21–22
ecclesial/communal dimension of, 17–22
interdependence of "letter" and "spirit" in, 13–17, 21–22, 39
objectivity and subjectivity in, 3–8
The Interpretation of the Bible in the Church (Pontifical Biblical Commission), 30n11, 41n13, 50, 51n66, 53n76, 114n3, 144
Irenaeus, 14

Jacob of Serugh, 130, 131, 135
Jeroboam, 48
Jerome, 14, 42, 83, 84–85, 88n55, 92, 93, 94, 135
Jesus Christ. *See also* baptism of Jesus; fulfillment of Scripture in John 13–17

as Alpha and Omega, 16
in Byzantine liturgical interpretation of Exod 2:21–22, 67
in Christological readings of the Pentateuch, 54–55, 61–66, 68–70
in Christological readings of the psalms, 79, 81, 90, 94–98, 100
fulfills the Servant of YHWH prophecies, 36
on the Old Testament, 16, 69–70
in Origen's allegorical interpretation of the Good Samaritan, 27
in Origen's Christocentric exegesis, 79n28, 96, 102–7, 110, 111, 112–13
psalms quoted by, 78–80, 94, 97, 98, 150, 157
as typological fulfillment of David, 39–40, 41, 50–53
Jethro/Reuel, 58n15, 58n18, 64, 65
Jews and Judaism
Alexandrian converts from Judaism, 66
anti-Jewish readings of the Psalms, 109n38, 112, 113
common ground between Jewish and Christian interpreters, 42, 43
in patristic exegesis of Ps 75[74], 105–6, 110–11, 112, 113
psalms in the Jewish Scriptures, 73–76
Job, book of, 47, 67. *See also* Index of Scripture References
John Chrysostom
emblematic of Antioch, 14
exegesis of Exod 2:11–22, 56, 59–61, 65
exegesis of Jesus's baptism, 126, 128, 130
exegesis of John 13–17, 154, 156–57, 159
homilies on Genesis, 68
John the Baptist, 117, 118, 120, 121, 124, 125, 126, 128, 130, 133
Jonah, 80n30

Index of Names and Subjects

Jordan River. *See* baptism of Jesus
Josiah, 49
Judas, 154, 155, 156–58
Justin Martyr, 72, 83, 122

kingship, 39–40, 47–53

Laodicea, Council of, 82
Lent, 67
Lewis, C. S., 46n45, 53
literal sense. *See also* intended sense
  in Alexandrian exegesis, 40, 115n4
  in Antiochene exegesis, 14, 29–31, 57, 107–8
  Aquinas's concept of, 3, 24–25, 35n29
  grammatical analysis of, 101n5
  in Origen's exegesis, 31, 57, 90, 101–3, 104, 112
  in patristic exegesis of Exod 2:11–22, 59, 61, 63, 66, 68–69
  polyvalence of, 25–37
  of the psalms, 94–96
  relation to Antiochene *theoria*, 30
  relation to typology, 41
  as starting point for allegory, 40, 57
  in Theodoret's exegesis of Ps 75[74], 110, 111, 113
Liturgy of the Presanctified Gifts, 66–67
Lonergan, Bernard, 2, 5, 7

Manasseh (king), 48
Marcion, 82
Meier, John, 117, 118–21, 123n38
Melchizedek, 62
Meyer, Ben F.
  on alienation from the biblical text, 5–6, 9–11
  on Christological reading of the Old Testament, 68–69
  on the "intended sense," 3, 4, 24, 26, 30
  on interpretation and the interpreter, 3–8
  on necessity of conversion, 6–7
  project of, 2–3
  on synthesis of Athens and Alexandria, 1–2, 3, 5, 7, 55, 56, 114–15, 141
  on theologically responsible biblical hermeneutics, 55–56, 59, 66
Midian, flight to. *See* Exodus 2:11–22
monarchy. *See* kingship
monasticism, 94, 109
Mosaic Law, 47, 50, 91, 105–6
Moses
  in exegesis of Exod 2:11–22, 57–66
  psalms attributed to, 84, 87, 89n57, 96
Muratorian fragment, 82

name of God (Exod 3:14), 33–34
Newman, John Henry, 115
Nicaea, Council of, 90, 107
Noth, Martin, 44–45, 49, 53

Old Testament
  anti-Jewish readings of, 109n38, 112, 113
  Christological readings of, 41–42, 49–53, 54–55, 61–66, 68–70
  typological interpretation of, 38–40, 41, 52
  undervalued by Gnosticism, 14
Origen
  approach to allegorical sense, 14, 26–27, 40–41, 57, 101–3, 105
  approach to literal sense, 31, 57, 90, 101–3, 104, 112
  Christocentric interpretation of all of Scripture, 79n28, 96, 102–7, 110, 111, 112–13
  composed the Hexapla, 72, 85
  emblematic of Alexandria, 13
  emphasis on spiritual life of the individual, 102, 110, 111, 112–13
  exegesis of Jesus's baptism, 130, 135n92

201

INDEX OF NAMES AND SUBJECTS

exegesis of John 13, 145n5, 155, 157
exegesis of the forty-two stopping places in Numbers, 55
exegesis of the Garden of Eden, 27, 30
exegesis of the Good Samaritan, 27, 35
exegesis of the psalms, 83, 84–88, 95, 97, 100, 103–7
homilies on the Pentateuch, 62n28, 68

Pamphilus, 85, 89
Passover, 38
patristic exegesis
    Christological reading of the Pentateuch, 54–55, 61–66, 68–70
    complementarity of spirit and letter in, 14–15, 16, 53
    complements contemporary methods, 144–45, 165
    of Jesus's baptism, 122, 126–28, 129, 130, 135–36, 141–42
    of John 13–17, 153–65
    of the psalms, 71–72, 83–98, 103–11
Paul
    applies Isa 49:6 to himself and Barnabas, 36
    believed Adam really existed, 88
    interpretations of the psalms, 77–78
    on letter and Spirit, 16
    on relation between Jesus's baptism and Christian baptism, 132–41, 142–43
    typological interpretation of David, 51
Pentateuch. *See also* Exodus 2:11–22
    in Byzantine liturgical cycle, 66–67
    Christological reading of, 54–55, 61–66, 68–70
    scarcity of patristic commentaries on, 68
pesharim, 27–28
Philo of Alexandria, 25–26, 31, 41, 62, 88

Philoxenus, 142
Pius XII (pope), 38n1, 42, 42n17–20, 44, 50, 52, 53
Plato, 71
Pliny the Younger, 81
Pontifical Biblical Commission, 29n8, 30n11, 41n13, 50, 51n66, 53n76, 114n3, 144
postmodern interpretation, 4, 6
preaching, 112
Procopius of Gaza, 83
prosopological interpretation, 78, 80, 84, 87, 94, 101n5, 104, 110
Protestant Reformation, 25
Psalm of Ethan, 84, 89n57
Psalm of Moses, 84, 89n57
psalm/Psalter, meaning of, 73–74
Psalms, book of
    compared to classical anthologies, 71
    formation of canon of, 81–83
    Jerome's translations of, 42n19
    in the Jewish Scriptures, 73–76
    in the New Testament, 77–80, 94
    patristic exegesis of, 71–72, 83–98, 103–11
    prosopological interpretation of, 78, 80, 84, 87, 94, 104, 110
    quoted by Jesus, 78–80, 94, 97, 98, 150, 157
    titles and headings of psalms, 74, 75, 76, 85, 91–93, 95, 104, 110

Qumran, 27–28, 74–75, 75n14, 94, 98

Ratzinger, Joseph. *See* Benedict XVI (pope) (Joseph Ratzinger)
religionswissenschaft and *religionsgeschichte*, 4
revelation, models of, 21–22
Risch, Franz Xaver, 85, 88
"robe of glory," 116, 142

Index of Names and Subjects

Sancta Mater Ecclesia (1964), 29n8
Satan, 61, 64, 67, 138
Saul (king), 39, 48, 49, 51, 155n31
sensus plenior, 42
Septuagint, 72
Servant of YWHW, 34–36, 121
Solomon, psalms attributed to, 76, 84, 87, 89n57, 97
sons of Korah, psalms attributed to, 84, 87, 89n57
sonship, divine, 121, 122, 125, 129, 131, 132n80, 134, 136, 138–39, 141–42
suspicion, hermeneutic of, 3, 5

Teaching of St. Gregory, 128, 130n74
Tertullian, 80n31, 81n35, 114, 141
Theodore of Mopsuestia
    exegesis of Jesus's baptism, 135–36
    exegesis of John 13–17, 154n28, 158–59, 161
    on literal sense of Genesis, 30
    as a major representative of Antioch, 14
    polemic against allegorical interpreters, 30
    rejected non-historical biblical books, 29
Theodoret of Cyrus
    exegesis of Exod 2:11–22, 56, 61–62, 65, 68
    exegesis of Ps 75[74], 100, 108–13
    exegetical principles, 109
    wrote about Council of Laodicea, 82n37
Theodorus of Heraclea, 83
theoria (θεωρία), 30, 60, 60n23, 69, 108
Tolkien, J. R. R., 26
Torjesen, Karen Jo, 101–3
Trinity, 65, 80, 88, 92
Trypho, 72
typology
    of Athens and Alexandria, 41–42
    in the Deuteronomistic History, 39–40, 44–53
    in patristic exegesis of the Pentateuch, 55, 59, 61–62, 64, 68
    relation to allegory, 55n4
    relation to literal sense, 41

Valentinus, 82
Varro, 84
Villani, Barbara, 85, 88

Wort/Antwort, 21

Zipporah, 62, 64, 65
Zumstein, Jean, 163

Index of Scripture References

Genesis	
1	16
1:27	31–33
1:28	32
2–3	26
4:10	41n13
4:21	73n5
14:17–24	62
22	121
24:11–27	58
29:1–14	58

Exodus	
1–2	58
1:1–20	67
1:15–2:10	62n28
2:1–22	59
2:2–10	58
2:2a	59
2:5–10	67
2:11	58, 58n15
2:11–15	58, 64
2:11–22	57–70
2:13	58
2:14	60, 61, 63, 64
2:15	58
2:15a	61
2:16–22	58, 58n15
2:21	62
2:21–22	59
2:22	58n18, 59
2:22a	59
2:23–25	58
3:1	58n15
3:1–12	57, 59
3:12	33
3:14	33–34
4–5	62n28
4:20	58n18
4:24–26	58n18
5:1	60
7–14	58
12	55
15:22–27	56n8
18:4	58n18
33:11–23	56n8

Numbers	
33	55
35:6	76n16

Deuteronomy	
6:5	49
17:14–20	49
38:43	106

Judges	
9:7–15	25
12:6	76n16

1 Samuel	
8:7–9	49
13:7b–15	48n50
13:14	49, 51, 52
15:1–35	48n50
15:28	49, 51
16:1	49, 51
16:7	49
16:12–13	49
16:16–23	76
16:18	73
28	85n44

2 Samuel	
6–20	50
7	48, 49, 50
7:11–17	50
7:13–16	50
7:14	78, 98
7:26–29	50
23:1	76

1 Kings	
1–2	50
9:4	49
11:4	50
11:6	50
11:38	50
14:8	50

2 Kings	
2:24	76n16
10:14	76n16
17:7–41	46
25:27–30	49

INDEX OF SCRIPTURE REFERENCES

2 Chronicles
29:30	76n16

Ezra
9:6–15	119

Nehemiah
9:6–37	119
12:27	73n5

Judith
16:1	73

2 Maccabees
2:13	76

3 Maccabees
6:35	73

Job
21:1	73
21:12	73n5
30:31	73

Psalms
1	86, 92
1:5–9	92
2	92
2:7	121
4:1	73
4:7	86
5:13	125n48
17:51	75n12
21:2	79
30:6	79
31:1–2	77
32	88
32:2	73n5
35:19	150
36	85n44
37	85n44, 103
38	85n44
39	89n58
41:10	150
48:5	73n5
50	86
50:21	125n48
51:2	75n12
53:2	75n12
56:9	73n5
58	90
62	89
68:23–24	77
69:5	150
69:26	74
71:20	75n12
72	74n9, 76, 92
72:20	76
75	100–113
75:1	104, 110
75:1–2	111
75:2	104, 110
75:2–3	106
75:2–10	104
75:3a	104
75:3a–b	110
75:3b	105
75:3c	110
75:3c–4	110
75:4	105, 110
75:4–6	111
75:4b	105
75:4c	105
75:5–6	106
75:7	111
75:8	111
75:8a	106
75:8b	106
75:9	106, 111
75:10a	107
75:11	107, 111
75:11a	107
75:11b	107
77:70	75n12
80:3	73n5
88:4	75n12
88:21	75n12
88:36	75n12
88:50	75n12
89	48, 92
89:25–27	98
89:34–38	50
90	74
91:4	73n5
93	76
97	76
106	92
107:3	73n5
108	74
109:1	74, 78
109:8	74
110	74
110:1	50
111	74
115:4	106
117	74
117:25–26	79
121:5	75n12
123	75
131:10–11	75n12
131:17	75n12
132:11–12	50
134:4	110
139:2–3	156
142	76
143:9	73n5
143:10	75n12
144:1	75n12
145	75
149:3	73n5
150:3	73n5
151	74, 76
151:1	75n12
151:2	73n5

Wisdom
19:18	73n5

Sirach
prol. 1	79n29
prol. 8–10	79n29
9:12	125n48
40:21	73n5
47:8	76

Isaiah
5:12	73n5
6:6	131
7:14	42
11:2	121, 129
38:20	73n5
41:8	34n25
42:1	121, 129
42:1–4	34n25
43:8–13	147
49:1–7	34n25, 35
49:3	35
49:5	35
49:6	36
50:4–11	34n25
52:13–53:12	34n25
53	80n30
61:1	121, 129
63:19	121
64:1	129
66:20 LXX	73n6

Jeremiah
25:15–16	106
25:15–28	111
31:33	137

Lamentations
3:14	73
5:14	73

Ezekiel
1:1	121
26:13	73n5
33:32	73n5
36–37	129
36:26–28	137

Daniel
3:5	73n5
3:7	73n5
3:10	73n5
3:15	73n5
3:29	119
9	35
9:5	119
9:15	119

Joel
3:1	129

Amos
5:23	73

Nahum
2:11	27

Habbakuk
2:4	125n48

Zechariah
6:14 LXX	73n6

Malachi
2:17 LXX	125n48

Odes
7:20	73n5

Matthew
1–2	128n66
1:23	42
3:13	127
3:15	124, 129, 130, 137
3:16	124, 127, 128, 137
3:16–17	125
3:17	124, 128, 129, 138, 139
4:1	131, 138
4:3	139
4:18–45	105
5:18	16
7:22	155
8:17	36
11:29	130
12:17–21	36
12:28	131
12:31–32	131
22:41	78
26:67	36
28:18–20	132
28:19	135, 140

Mark
1:5	124
1:9	127
1:10	124, 128, 137
1:10–11	125
1:11	124, 128, 138, 139
1:12	131
1:12–13	138
3:29	131
9:7	128n64
10:32–33	130
12:35	78
15:38	128

Luke
1:1–4	22, 36n31
1:31–35	128
1:32–33	50
1:69	48
2:32	36
3:21	125, 127, 128, 129
3:21–22	124, 138

INDEX OF SCRIPTURE REFERENCES

3:22	125, 128, 137, 138, 139
4:1	131, 138
4:1–2	138
4:3	139
4:18–19	131
7:41–42	88
10:21–22	131
10:27–29	27
12:10–12	131
12:50	136n100
13:26	155
20:39	78
20:42	74, 80
22:37	80n30
24:36–49	69
24:44	70, 79

John

1:1	79
1:29	125, 126
1:30	125
1:31	125
1:32	137
1:32–33	125
1:34	125
3:5–8	131
3:34	131
4:23–24	131
6:63	131
7:37–39	131
9:3	148n12
11:45	109n38
12:37–38	147
13	151, 163
13:16	152
13:17–18a	151
13:18	148, 149, 150, 151, 152, 154, 155, 155n31, 157, 158
13:18–19	147, 156
13:19	151, 159, 160, 164
13:31	145n7
13:36	145n7
13:37	145n7
13:38	145n7
14:5	145n7
14:6	145n7
14:8	145n7
14:9	145n7
14:10	17n14
14:17	131
14:22	145n7
14:23	145n7
14:26	131, 164
14:31	145, 148n12
15–16	151, 163
15:3	161
15:8	152
15:18	151n23
15:18–16:4a	159, 160
15:18–24	154
15:19	152
15:20	152
15:25	148, 149, 150, 151, 154, 158
15:26–27	131, 164
16:1	151
16:2	151n23, 152
16:4	151, 159, 164
16:13–15	131
16:17	145n7
16:18	145n7
16:19	145n7
16:29	145n7
16:31	145n7
17	151, 152, 163
17:1	145
17:11–12	164
17:11–19	161
17:12	149, 150, 153, 154n28, 155, 158
17:13	148, 149, 151
17:14	65
17:14a	153
17:15	159
17:16	153
17:17	161
19:24	148
19:34	147
19:35	147
19:35–36	146
19:35–37	146
20:30	163

Acts of the Apostles

1:1–20	36n31
1:20	74, 87
2:38	139n110
8:34	78n24
10:47	139n110
13:21–23	51
13:22–23	48
13:47	36

Romans

1:3	77
1:3–4	132n82
2:27–29	16
3:4	77n21
3:19	77n22
3:20	77n21
4:3	77n22
4:6	77
5:12	88
5:14	14n4
6	133, 136, 140, 142
6:1	133
6:3–4	133
6:5	133
6:6–7	133
6:8–9	133
6:14	133
7:6	16
7:22	106
8	136, 139, 140, 142

Index of Scripture References

8:1–17	140	15:3	77n21	**1 Timothy**	
8:2–4	137	15:7	141	3:15	105
8:3	140	15:9	77n21	4:1	77n22
8:4	137, 138	15:10	77n22	5:18	77n22
8:4–5	138	15:12	77n22	6:20	11
8:4–9	138				
8:5–6	139	**1 Corinthians**		**2 Timothy**	
8:7	138	3:20	77n21	1:7–8	15
8:8	138	6:9–11	135	3:5	16
8:9–11	137	9:8	77n22	3:14–17	15
8:12–13	138, 138n106	9:10	77n22	3:16	15, 97n73
8:12–17	141	9:21	106		
8:13	138	10:6	14n4	**Hebrews**	
8:14	138, 138n106	11:1	140	1:1–2	79
8:14–17	139	14:34	77n22	7:15–25	62
8:15	134n89, 138, 138n105, 139, 139n110, 142	15:3–5	80	9:24	14n4
		15:49	105	11:1	60
				11:4	41n13
8:17	139	**2 Corinthians**		11:4–38	60
8:23	136n100, 139, 139n110, 142	3:6–7	16	11:10	65n40
		6:2	77n22	11:26	61
8:29	139, 141	9:9	77n21	11:27	60
8:36	77n21	16–18	77n22	12:24	41n13
9:15	77n22				
9:17	77n22	**Galatians**		**1 Peter**	
9:25	77n22	2:9	105	3:21	14n4, 133
10:6	77n22	4:5–6	134n89		
10:8	77n22	4:24	14n4	**2 Peter**	
10:11	77n22	4:30	77n22	1:20–21	18
10:16	77n22				
10:19	77n22	**Ephesians**		**1 John**	
10:20	77n22	4:7	77n22	2:15	65
10:21	77n22	5:14	77n22		
11:2	77n22			**Revelation**	
11:4	77n22	**Philippians**		1:8	16
11:9	77, 77n21	2:5–8	140	3:12	105
12:2	106			13:5	76n16
12:19	77n22	**1 Thessalonians**		21:6	16
14:11	77n22	1:6	140	22:13	16
15:2–3	141			22:18–19	16–17

Other Books in This Series

Worthy Lamb: An Exegetical-Spiritual Commentary on John's Apocalypse, Andreas Hoeck (2024)

The Word of Truth, Sealed by the Spirit: Perspectives on the Inspiration and Truth of Sacred Scripture, ed. Matthew C. Genung and Kevin Zilverberg (2022)

Augustine's Confessions *and Contemporary Concerns,* ed. David Vincent Meconi, SJ (2022)

In the School of the Word: Biblical Interpretation from the New to the Old Testament, Carlos Granados and Luis Sánchez-Navarro (2021)

Piercing the Clouds: Lectio Divina *and Preparation for Ministry,* ed. Kevin Zilverberg and Scott Carl (2021)

The Revelation of Your Words: The New Evangelization and the Role of the Seminary Professor of Sacred Scripture, ed. Kevin Zilverberg and Scott Carl (2021)

On Earth as It Is in Heaven: Cultivating a Contemporary Theology of Creation, ed. David Vincent Meconi, SJ (2016: repr., 2021)

Verbum Domini *and the Complementarity of Exegesis and Theology,* ed. Scott Carl (2015: repr., 2021)